P9-DNE-495

WRITE GREAT FICTION

Characters, Emotion & Viewpoint

WRITE GREAT FICTION

Characters, Emotion & Viewpoint

[TECHNIQUES AND EXERCISES FOR
CRAFTING DYNAMIC CHARACTERS AND
EFFECTIVE VIEWPOINTS]

BY NANCY KRESS

Writer's Digest Books
Cincinnati, Ohio
www.writersdigest.com

WRITER'S
DIGEST
BOOKS

[COPYRIGHT]

Write Great Fiction: Characters, Emotion & Viewpoint. Copyright © 2005 by Nancy Kress. Manufactured in the United States of America. All rights reserved. No part of this book may be reproduced in any form or by any electronic or mechanical means including information storage and retrieval systems without permission in writing from the publisher, except by a reviewer, who may quote brief passages in a review. Published by Writer's Digest Books, an imprint of F+W Publications, Inc., 4700 East Galbraith Road, Cincinnati, Ohio 45236. (800) 289-0963. First edition.

Visit our Web site at www.writersdigest.com for information on more resources for writers.

To receive a free weekly e-mail newsletter delivering tips and updates about writing and about Writer's Digest products, register directly at our Web site at http://newsletters.fwpublications .com.

10 09 08 07 06   6 5 4 3

Library of Congress Cataloging-in-Publication Data

Kress, Nancy
   Write great fiction : characters, emotion & viewpoint / by Nancy Kress.—1st ed.
      p.   cm.
   Includes index.
   ISBN-13: 978-1-58297-316-6 (pbk. : alk. paper)
   ISBN-10: 1-58297-316-4 (pbk. : alk. paper)
      1. Fiction—Technique. 2. Point of view (Literature) 3. Characters and characteristics in literature. 4. Emotions in literature. I. Title.

PN3383.C4K76   2005
808.3—dc22   2004023471
                                                                          CIP

Edited by Michelle Ruberg
Designed by Stanard Design Partners
Interior and cover illustrations by Getty Images
Cover by Nick Gliebe/Design Matters
Production coordinated by Robin Richie

[DEDICATION]

To Jamie, Pat, and all the other authors of the future.

[ABOUT THE AUTHOR]

Nancy Kress is the author of twenty-two books, including sixteen novels. She has won science fiction's most prestigious awards: three Nebulas, a Hugo, and a John W. Campbell Memorial Award. In addition to writing the "Fiction" column for Writer's Digest magazine, she regularly teaches creative writing at various writing festivals around the United States.

table of

contents

introduction

[WHAT DO READERS WANT?]

Have you ever hunted for a book enthusiastically recommended by a friend ("You'll love it!"), bought it, read it . . . and been greatly disappointed? Of course you have. We all have. And the most disappointed person of all, had he known about it, would have been the author of that book.

We writers want readers to love our books. Greedy people that we are, we mean *all* readers. But in our more rational moments, we know that there is no book written that every reader enjoys. This is because people read for different reasons.

Some readers want fast-paced excitement—and will put down a slower-paced book that examines the same reality as their own lives. Others want thoughtful insights into reality—and will put down fantasies of nonstop adventure. Some want to read about people they can identify with, some about characters they will never meet. Some seek clear, straightforward storytelling, and some cherish style: the unexpected phrase in exactly the right place. Some want affirmations of values they already hold, and some hope to be challenged, even disturbed.

It's enough to drive an author to drink (in fact, it sometimes has). But don't hit the bottle before you hit the keyboard. You don't have to win over *all* readers, only those in your particular audience, those with the perception to value what your manuscript can offer. There is a way to do that—and even bring in some of the others who don't yet realize that they would love your story if they gave it a chance.

The magic key is character.

I am not using the word "magic" lightly. Becoming totally absorbed in a story *does* feel like magic: The room around you disappears, time alters shape, and you are transported by the spell of words on a page. We've all had that marvelous reading experience. And almost always, what makes it happen is intense, even passionate, interest in the fate of a character in that story.

Characters are the common denominators of fiction. As many parents and librarians have been delighted to discover, a fascinating character in a fascinating situation (more on that connection later) has led nonreaders to devour J.K. Rowling's Harry Potter books. Compelling characters are responsible for the crossover best-sellers, in which people who don't ordinarily read mysteries will seek out Janet Evanovich's hilarious Stephanie Plum novels. And characters, complex and real, are what keep Jane Austen and F. Scott Fitzgerald in print decade after decade.

In fact, without believable and interesting characters, you don't really have fiction at all. You may have names walking through plot, but without the essential animation of character, a historical novel becomes mostly a history text, a mystery becomes a police report, and science fiction becomes a speculative monograph. Literary fiction simply becomes unread.

Character is key.

AND YET MORE BENEFITS

Reader interest is not the only thing you gain from creating strong characters. Character actually controls many other aspects of the book. We'll be looking at these in greater depth in coming chapters, but for now consider the following:

- Plot depends on character because different people react differently to the same situation. Suppose your story concerns a man whose wife has just disappeared, perhaps deliberately. A timid, introspective man may react to this with anguish that leads eventually to insight about himself and his wife. An adventurous, confident man may assume her defection was not self-chosen and look for her with rescue in mind. A bitter, angry man may look for her with revenge in mind. Different characters, different plots.

- Setting depends on character, in two ways. First, setting shapes character. A twelve-year-old girl growing up in a shack on a Louisiana bayou will have much different perceptions and values than one growing up in a penthouse in New York City. Second, adult characters often seek out settings compatible with their natural personalities; a restless and fearless adventurer is unlikely to stay at a clerical job in a six-by-eight cubicle in an insurance office. What kind of character do you want to write about? Your choice of setting will be affected by your character.

- Style is influenced by character. This is indisputable in first-person narratives but also applies to third person, because the language of description takes on the flavor of the describer. You may write of one man, "John hated fancy parties because there was never no sense to them: no kegs, no plain speaking, no fights to liven things up some." Of another man you would write, "John hated fancy parties; he much preferred substantial conversation to this hypocritical simpering at each other in garments expensive enough to clothe an African village for a year." Different personalities, different writing styles.

If you invest time, effort, and imagination in creating compelling characters, you will automatically gain significant control of your plot, setting, and style.

WRITING AND THE MULTIPLE PERSONALITY

So you're convinced. You want to create memorable, interesting, plausible characters. How?

This book will show you many time-tested techniques. But something else is even more important to your success than are any issues of craft. In fact, it is the *most* important aspect of creating effective characters. You must learn to be three people at once: writer, character, and reader.

What does that mean? Suppose you're writing a scene in which Elizabeth, your point-of-view character, tells her husband, Jerry, that she's leaving him. She's frightened to do this because Jerry has sometimes been verbally and physically abusive. A part of your mind is conscious of choosing which elements to put down in which order: first a line of his dialogue, then a description of his facial reactions, then a line of her dialogue, then a bit of description . . . or a hundred other possibilities. That's you, the writer, making craft choices.

Another part of your mind has become this woman, Elizabeth. You feel what she feels. Even though you may never have been abused, sometime in your life you have been frightened. You're drawing on that fear now, re-experiencing it so that you can know what Elizabeth breathes, what she says, and how she feels. For brief moments, you *are* Elizabeth.

If you're a really good writer and Jerry isn't just a stock villain, at other moments you *are* Jerry. This is true even though he's nothing like you. You become Jerry's rage, his outrage, and his unadmitted fear at losing "his" woman. During these moments, collectively, *you* are the character.

But you also must become a third person: your reader. A part of your mind has stepped back from both the characters *and* the craft choices. This more detached aspect of you is trying to experience both character and writing as would your reader, who is not privy to what's going on inside the rest of your mind. That reader doesn't know that you want to balance dialogue with description. She doesn't care that you need to foreshadow a scene in the next chapter. Nor does she know that to portray Jerry's rage, you are drawing on your own Uncle Nathan, the bastard who terrorized your aunt and scared you halfway to hell when you were nine years old. That memory is powerful and complex and, sitting at your desk, you're re-experiencing all of it, but *the reader doesn't know that*. She only knows what ends up on the page.

And that's why the third part of your mind must become the reader. You must view the actual words on the actual page just as she does, unencumbered by all the other stuff that went on in You the Writer and in You the Character. Unless it's on the page, the reader doesn't get it. So You the Reader must constantly be aware of what that page reads like to someone who is coming to it cold.

All successful writers are thus three people at once.

Does that sound daunting? Let me offer some reassurance. First, the three-way splitting isn't actually simultaneous. Rather, it's a constant jumping in your mind. You write a half-page as the character, stop to think as the writer what else needs to be included in this scene, write another line of dialogue, and then delete it because to the reader it won't really convey just how furious Elizabeth is with Jerry. You substitute another line of dialogue, and as you type it, you slip back into Elizabeth's mind. And so on. The three-way dance is not super-human multiple identities as much as it is sequential mind-sets.

Second—and this is crucial—your ability to inhabit all three mind-sets grows with practice. Experienced writers do this without ever thinking about it. Even beginners do it part of the time. You can learn to do it better and faster through the exercises in this book. And consciously practicing the three-way mind-set as you write will make an enormous improvement in your fiction—far more improvement than you can imagine until you do it.

Why is that? Because by focusing on character, by making craft choices that build character, by becoming that character, and then by ensuring that all your choices and emotion actually have been translated to the page—by doing all that, you give readers what they want. They want to see interesting, compelling people living their individual stories. Readers want to care what happens in the story, and character is how you make them care.

So let's get started on creating characters.

chapter 1

[TYPES OF CHARACTERS — ASSEMBLING YOUR CAST]

Every drama—and fiction is always a kind of drama—requires a cast. The cast may be so huge, as in Leo Tolstoy's *Anna Karenina*, that the author or editor provides a list of characters to keep everybody straight. Or it may be an intimate cast of two. (In "To Build a Fire," Jack London managed with one person and a dog.) Whatever the size of your cast, you have to assemble it from somewhere.

Where do you get these people? And how do you know they'll make good characters?

You have four sources: yourself, real people you know, real people you hear about, and pure imagination.

YOURSELF AS CHARACTER: STRAIGHT FROM THE HORSE'S MOUTH

In one sense, every character you create will be yourself. You've never murdered, but your murderer's rage will be drawn from memories of your own most extreme anger. Your love scenes will use your own past kisses, caresses, and sweet moments. That scene in which your octogenarian feels humiliated will draw on your experience of humiliation in the eighth grade, even though the circumstances are totally different and you're not even consciously thinking about your middle-school years. Our characters' emotions draw on our own emotions. Until telepathy is common, our own emotions are the only ones we've intimately experienced. They're our default setting.

Sometimes, however, you will want to use your life more directly in your fiction, dramatizing actual incidents. This has both strengths and pitfalls.

The strength is that you were *there*. You know the concrete details and can get them right: the way the light slants through a church window at noon, the smell of cooking fat in a diner, the dialogue of cops in the precinct house. These things are invaluable in creating believable fiction.

Even more important, you were there emotionally. You felt whatever exaltation, fear, panic, tenderness, or despair the situation evoked. A well-done biographical incident can therefore have tremendous fictional power. That's why so many successful writers have drawn directly on their own lives for their work.

Charles Dickens used his desperate stint as a child laborer in Victorian England to write *David Copperfield*. John Galsworthy, like his character Jolyon Forsyte of *The Forsyte Saga*, had an affair with and later married the wife of his abusive cousin. Nora Ephron, best-selling author of *Heartburn*, was frank about basing her story of adultery and desertion on her own desertion by husband Carl Bernstein (fiction as public revenge).

Should you create a protagonist based directly on yourself? The problem with this—and it is a very large problem—is that almost no one can view himself objectively on the page. As the writer, you're too close to your own complicated makeup. This makes it very difficult to use that third mind-set (see the introduction) and become the reader, who doesn't know that the character's nastiness in the first scene is actually balanced by your admirable sense of fair play. You know it, and you'll bring it out later in the story . . . but by that time it may be too late. The reader only knows what's on the page, not what's in your mind and heart.

It can thus be easier and more effective to use the situation or incident from your life but make it happen to a character who is *not* you. In fact, that's what the authors cited above have largely done. Rachel Samstat, Nora Ephron's heroine, is sassier and funnier when left by her husband than any real person would be. You can still, of course, incorporate aspects of yourself: your love of Beethoven, your quick temper, your soccer injuries. But by using your own experience with a different protagonist, you can take advantage of your insider knowledge of the situation, and yet gain an objectivity and control that the original intense situation, by definition, did not have.

So where do you get this other protagonist?

PEOPLE YOU KNOW AS CHARACTERS: PARDON ME WHILE I BORROW YOUR SOUL

Many, many famous characters are based, in part, on real people. The key words here are "in part."

?

Question:

If I base a fictional character on the life of my crazy sister, can she sue me?

Answer:

In the United States, anyone can file a lawsuit against anyone else. Whether your sister could win a lawsuit against you for using her in your fiction is another story. Some things to consider:

- Is your sister a public figure? If so, she has little protection. Courts have ruled that public figures may be satirized without penalty. In his novel *Libra*, for instance, Don DeLillo made mincemeat of Richard M. Nixon.
- Is your sister extremely famous? If so, courts may consider that she has "rights of publicity" to her own life, meaning that she, not you, owns the right to gain the publicity from publishing her story. This has been a court ruling mainly in California.
- Have you invaded your sister's privacy? If all you've done is create a character who, like your sister, has three shoplifting convictions and four marriages, these things are matters of public record. She has no case based on invasion of privacy.
- Is what you wrote true? If so, you are safe from defamation and libel. Both must contain untrue allegations to be proved.
- And, finally—how much do you care if your sister never speaks to you again?

Like characters based on yourself, fictional creations based on others seem to be most effective when they're cannibalized. Using people straight can, as in the case of using yourself, limit both imagination and objectivity. So instead of using your Uncle Jerome exactly as he is, consider combining his salient traits with those of other acquaintances or with purely made-up qualities. This has several advantages.

First, you can craft exactly the character you need for your plot. Suppose, for instance, that your actual Uncle Jerome is quick-tempered and cuttingly witty when angered and remorseful later about the terrible (but very funny) things he said while mad. But your character would work better if he were a stranger to remorse, staying angry in a cool, unrepentant way. Combine Uncle Jerome with your friend Don, who can hold a grudge until

7

the heat death of the universe. Combining characters gives you greater flexibility.

This is how Virginia Woolf created Clarissa Dalloway (*Mrs. Dalloway*). Her primary source, according to Woolf's biographer Quentin Bell, was family friend Kitty Maxse. But Woolf also wrote in her diary that she drew on Lady Ottoline Morrell for Clarissa: "I want to bring in the despicableness of people like Ott." Similarly, Emma Bovary (Gustave Flaubert's *Madame Bovary*) and spymaster George Smiley (John le Carré's series) are composites of people their creators knew.

A second, lesser advantage of cannibalizing traits from people, instead of just dumping your friends on the page in their entirety, is that your family and friends are less likely to recognize themselves and become upset with you. It also avoids potential lawsuits.

STRANGERS AS CHARACTERS: ONE SMALL SPARK

In addition to composites of people you know, you can also base characters on people you don't know personally but have only heard or read about. This can work very well because you're not bound by many facts. You're actually making up the character, with the real person providing no more than a stimulus for inspiration.

Say, for example, that you read about a woman whose will leaves six million dollars to a veterinary hospital she visited only once, forty years earlier, with her dying cat. You never met this woman. All you have is the newspaper story and a blurry picture. But something about the situation has caught your attention. What kind of person would do that? You begin to imagine this woman: her personality and history, what that cat must have meant to her, why there were no other people important enough to her to leave them any inheritance.

Before long, you've created a full, interesting, and poignant character, someone you might want to write about. Yes, you started with secondhand information—but now the character is fully yours.

Sometimes the original spark can be very small indeed. I once based a character on a photo of a new bride in the newspaper. I have no idea what the actual woman was like, but her polished, blonde radiance somehow struck my imagination, suggesting a pampered joyfulness that grew in my mind into a complete personality.

As Charlotte Brontë famously remarked, reality should "suggest" rather than "dictate" characters.

CHARACTERS FROM IMAGINATION: FANCY RUNS FREE

Creating purely invented characters is actually very similar to basing characters on strangers. With strangers, a small glimpse into another life sparks the writer's imagination. Made-up characters, too, usually begin with the spark of an idea popping into the writer's mind. The writer then fans the spark into a full-blown person.

William Faulkner, for example, had a sudden mental image of a little girl with muddy drawers up in a tree. That image became Caddy in *The Sound and the Fury*, which Faulkner considered his best novel.

No matter what your initial source—reality or imagination—characters usually present themselves encased in at least the rudiments of a fictional situation. Caddy is up in a tree (why?). The deceased lady has left six million dollars to an animal hospital. You have something here to work with. Your next task is to look hard at this character/situation in order to decide if the character is strong enough to sustain a story. In part, of course, that depends on how well you write about her and whether you *want* to write about this person. Some guidelines exist for making that decision.

STARS, FEATURED PLAYERS, AND FURNITURE

Not all your characters will matter equally to the story. One is the star—your protagonist. (There may be more in a long novel.) This is the person whom the story is mostly about: Anna Karenina in her eponymous novel, Stephanie Plum in Janet Evanovich's mysteries, Harry Potter in J.K. Rowling's fantasies. Your star gets the most attention from both the reader and writer, the most word count expended on him or her, and the climactic scene.

Other characters are necessary to the story and interesting in their own right; these are the featured players of your cast. The rest have bit parts. They aren't well developed and are, essentially, slightly animated furniture in your setting. Who should be which?

Before we answer that, I want to make clear that there are no simple rules for choosing who should become your star and who should remain featured players. Choosing a given character as protagonist will result in one novel; choosing someone else will result in a different novel, which may or may not be better than the first. Our goal here is merely to analyze each important member of your cast in order to identify the character you can become excited about writing.

One aspect of this selection process is to look at each character to decide if she would be better as a *changer* or a *stayer*. The distinction is critical to both characterization and plot.

Changers are characters who alter in significant ways as a result of the events of your story. They learn something or grow into better or worse people, but by the end of the story they are not the same personalities they were in the beginning. Their change, in its various stages, is called the story's *emotional arc*.

Let's look at an example. In John Grisham's *The Street Lawyer*, protagonist Michael Brock starts out as an ambitious, married lawyer, piling up hours and salary raises at a prestigious Washington law firm. By the end of the novel, Brock is separated from his wife, relatively poor, and working happily as a legal advocate for the homeless. These external changes have come about because Brock has changed internally. His world has been widened and his compassion deepened as a result of some very dramatic events: being taken hostage by a desperate homeless man, a shoot-out, and the death of a child. Michael Brock, as protagonist, is a changer. His emotional arc is a large one.

Other equally successful protagonists are stayers. This tends to be especially true in series books. Janet Evanovich's Stephanie Plum is a brash, foul-mouthed, fashion-impaired, hilarious bounty hunter in her first book, *One for the Money*. Nine books later, she hasn't changed. Nor do her readers want her to. Stephanie is too much fun just as she is.

Other characters are stayers because the point of the book is that they come to grief because of their blindness. These books present the idea that people cannot change but instead are locked into destructive patterns, either personal or societal. In such fiction, the protagonists defiantly, destructively go on being as they start out. An example is F. Scott Fitzgerald's *The Great Gatsby*. Jay Gatsby cannot become other than he is: idealistic, unrealistic, and enthralled by love. His obstinacy kills him. Likewise, Daisy and Tom Buchanan are stayers who will, we are explicitly told, go on being "careless," messing up other people's lives and then retreating into the safety of their vast fortune. Only the narrator, Nick Carraway, is a changer—which is one reason he's the narrator. Fitzgerald wanted someone in his novel to change because he had some points he wanted to make about Jazz Age society, and a changer who became disgusted with the entire social scene was the best way to make them.

Does that mean that changers are always better than stayers as protagonists? No. It all depends on the particular story you want to tell. Nick Carraway is right for *The Great Gatsby*; Stephanie Plum is right for *One for the Money*.

AUDITIONING YOUR PLAYERS

Now, the big question: What does all this have to do with *your* protagonist?

It gives you flexibility to make choices before you begin writing. Playing mentally with these choices can help you assemble the right characters for your cast. There are a hundred ways to tell any story, and the more of them you consider before you begin, the greater the odds of finding just the combination that will most fire your imagination and lead to the best fiction you can write.

Start by asking a few preliminary questions. You already have some idea of the situation you want to write about, since characters seldom appear in a vacuum. That old woman isn't just any old woman—she's leaving six million dollars to a veterinary hospital. That man isn't just any man—he's a detective with the NYPD who has a murder to solve, a drinking problem, and his dead sister's kid to raise. You've got a little information you can use as a springboard for evaluating your character. So, to choose your stars, ask yourself:

- Am I genuinely interested in this character? Do I find myself thinking about him in odd moments, imagining his previous life, inventing bits of dialogue? If not, you won't write him very well.
- Is this character or situation fresh and interesting in some new way? We've seen a lot of NYPD cops with murders to solve and drinking problems. Maybe the orphaned nephew will be enough of a new twist. Do you care about the cop? The nephew? Is the murder significant in some way?
- Can I maintain enough objectivity about this character, combined with enough identification, to practice the triple mind-set—becoming author, character, *and* reader as I write?
- Do I want this character to be a stayer or a changer? If she's going to be a changer, does it feel as if she has the capacity to change through the emotional arc I plan for her?

This last one needs some explanation. For an emotional arc to work, we must believe that the character is capable of change. Some people are not. There are alcoholics who are never going to even try to stop drinking. There are believers in a flat Earth who will not be convinced that the planet is round, no matter how many photos taken from space you show them. In fictional terms, there are Tom and Daisy Buchanan.

On the other hand, consider Cuyler Goodwill, a major character in Carol Shields's Pulitzer Prize-winning novel *The Stone Diaries*. Cuyler's life until 1903, when he was twenty-six, was joyless and deadeningly monotonous:

> His family, the Goodwills, seemed left in the wake of the stern, old, untidy century that conceived them, and they gave off, all three of them, father, mother, and child, an aroma of impotence, spindly in spirit and puny of body . . . when Cuyler turned fourteen his father looked up from a plate of fried pork and potatoes and mumbled that the time had come to leave school and begin work in the Stonewall Quarries where he himself was employed. After that Cuyler's wages, too, went into the jam pot. This went on for twelve years.

Then Cuyler meets Mercy Stone, marries her, and is "miraculously changed" by a "tidal motion of sexual longing [that] filled him to the brim." All this is told in flashback; the story proper begins with Mercy's death. But because we have seen that Cuyler is capable of having released in him a strong surge of previously unexplored behavior, we accept his later changes in the book. He has been established as a person who throws himself completely into whatever seizes his heart. Thus, we believe the author when she subsequently shows us a Cuyler completely given over first to religion, then to business, and finally to despair. We know he doesn't do anything by halves.

How about your prospective character? Is he someone you can portray as capable of change? If so, he may be a good candidate to be your star. But don't decide quite yet.

PUTTING IT ALL TOGETHER: AND THE LEAD GOES TO . . .

We've thought about one character who may or may not end up the protagonist of this story. Now let's think about the rest of the actors, plus all the ways you could cast this story taking shape in your mind. Each would lead to a significantly different novel.

Let's say your first character is the old woman who has left six million dollars to the veterinary hospital. Who might be the featured players in this drama? A few possibilities:

- The veterinarian, now elderly, who cured her cat forty years ago. Does he even remember her?
- The woman's son, furious over not inheriting her money.
- The young lawyer handling the will, who is troubled by this situation. If the son can break the will, it won't be good for the lawyer's fledgling career.
- The veterinarian's daughter. The vet will die before the will is probated. In fact (you just thought of this while making your list!), the original will is missing, all the lawyer has is a copy. The vet dies under mysterious circumstances. The daughter is suspicious.
- The old woman's twelve-year-old grandson, witness to all this fighting.
- The old woman's housekeeper, also a cat lover, who wonders why the money was left to that veterinary hospital, which the deceased never patronized again for all her subsequent cats.

Whew! All these actors, and anyone of them could be the star. The rest would, of necessity, end up featured players. What kind of story do you want to write?

If it's a mystery, maybe the veterinarian's daughter is the star. She will be investigating her father's death, which she suspects is traceable to the son. He's very angry about that will . . .

Or the mystery plot might be the son's story. He did not kill the old vet. But there's something weird about his mother's legacy—she was peculiar but not *that* peculiar. Someone influenced or coerced her, and he's going to find out who and how. The son loves cats himself, but this is ridiculous.

Or perhaps you're not writing a mystery at all. You're writing a social drama about how people are corrupted by money. Then maybe the housekeeper is your star. She barely makes a living wage herself, she struggles to raise her own kids, and she observes this greedy family, each member already comfortably off, throwing away every decency and principle for six million dollars. Then she herself faces temptation when she sees a way to make off with some of that money.

Or you want to write a coming-of-age story. Then the grandson might be the star, a definite changer, coming to grips with the weaknesses and foibles of a family he nonetheless loves.

Or maybe the young lawyer is an animal activist, and this is his story because he's enraged that a veterinary hospital devoted to the care of animal species, which are fully as worthy as humans, is going to be cheated out of this inheritance.

You see the point. Any of these could make a good story because everybody is the star of his own life and your characters *all* have lives. You choose your star based on the following considerations:

- what sparks your imagination
- which characters appeal most to you
- whether you want to focus on a changer or a stayer; if a changer, who seems to have the potential for genuine change
- who could progress through an emotional arc you want to portray

Is there a character who fits these criteria? Do the rest seem to fall into roles as supporting members of your protagonist's story? If so, congratulations! You have a basic cast.

You're on your way.

A USEFUL TOOL: THE MINI-BIO

Some writers make extensive notes before and during the writing of a book. Others make none. Nearly everyone, however, keeps a "bible," even if it consists of no more than scribbled jottings on a sheet of notebook paper.

A writing bible is a memory list. It keeps track of what you've named characters, how you've spelled those names (Marcia? Marsha? Marcya?), what age the characters are, what streets they live on, what day of the week different scenes occur—whatever your particular fiction requires. Keeping this in sufficient detail will save you a lot of cursing as you scroll back through a manuscript hunting for your protagonist's brother's wife's first name.

An equally useful tool, which doesn't impinge too heavily on the nonnote-makers' style, is the mini-bio. You keep one of these on each major character, and you begin it before you begin writing. In fact, it's best if begun *way* before writing, because it can help you focus your thinking about a character. The mini-bio is not concerned with personality or character—we'll get to those in later chapters. Right now the aim is to record the basics, both to spark thinking and avoid later confusion.

The form on page sixteen is useful for mini-bios. Photocopy it in quantity. An important note: If you can't fill out this elementary bio for a major character, you're not ready to start writing her.

Mini-bios have one final use. If you're not certain who will be the star of your story and who will be the featured players, or if you're just interested in other possible castings of your repertoire, try filling out a mini-bio for all your characters. Then study them. Did the questions reveal hidden possibilities for someone? Maybe the cat-honoring woman's housekeeper is a more intriguing character than you thought. Can you use her more extensively in your plot?

BECOMING THE READER, REDUX

You've assembled your cast, at least tentatively. You'll add more characters as the story gets written, and you may fire some of the ones you already have. Before you begin writing, do one more thing. Try to detach from everything you've done so far. Instead, look at your cast with the eye of a reader who as yet knows nothing about them.

This is not easy to do. *You* know that the housekeeper is going to reveal, in chapter six, a secret that will knock the socks off everyone who reads this book. But chapter six is a long ways away, and your reader doesn't know it's coming. Look at what he sees *now*. Is this a collection of people he might be interested in? Ask yourself:

- Are there enough differences among the characters to provide variety?
- Is it plausible that these people would know each other or can be brought to know each other through your planned story events?
- Is the entire group so bland or depressed that no one will want to spend four hundred pages with them? (A few bland or depressing ones are fine.)
- Are these the people that might plausibly be found in your setting? You can certainly plunk down an émigré Russian princess in 1910 Harlem if you want to, but you better be prepared to explain how she got there, and there better not be more than one of her in that setting.
- Do you have all the characters that circumstances logically require? For example, if you're writing about a murder, you pretty much have to include professional law enforcement characters eventually, even in an amateur-detective *cozy*. The pros tend to show up when people get killed, even if they aren't integral to your plot. Another example: In Regency London, well-bred upper-class young ladies did not travel without, at a minimum, an abigail or maid. Write her in.

Your characters are waiting in the wings. Now let's see how to get them on stage.

MINI-BIO FOR KEY CHARACTERS

Name _____

Age _____

Birthplace _____

Marital status _____

Children and their ages _____

General appearance (whatever seems useful)

_____

_____

_____

Living arrangements (i.e., lives with wife and three young children; rents
a ramshackle apartment alone; has tent in nomadic tribe with three
concubines)

_____

_____

Occupation, including name of employer (if applicable)

_____

_____

Degree of skill at occupation (beginner, really competent, experienced but
a bumbler, etc.)

_____

_____

Character's feelings about his occupation (loves it, hates it, regards it as
"just a job," has mixed feelings, is actively searching for other employment)

_____

_____

_____

Family background (whatever you think is important: ethnicity, siblings'
names, parents' names, social status, clan affiliation, total repugnance
toward everybody he knew before the age of twelve)

_____

_____

_____

RECAP: ASSEMBLING YOUR CAST

You have four sources from which to draw characters: yourself, people you know, strangers you hear or read about, and pure imagination. For the first three sources, characters are usually more effective when they are modified from their real-life models rather than used *whole*.

Once you have a list of potential characters for your story, the next step is to choose a protagonist, your star; the other characters will then become featured players. Any character can be chosen as your star, although different choices will result in much different stories.

One consideration in choosing your protagonist is whether you want to write about a character who is altered by story events (a changer) or one who remains essentially the same (a stayer). Changers progress through an emotional arc, a logical sequence of character alterations caused by the story's action. Before you start writing, try to examine your assembled cast, both changers and stayers, from the viewpoint of your potential reader. Are they interesting? Sufficiently diverse? Plausibly connected to each other and the situation you want to write about?

Your major characters, especially your protagonist(s), should be people you are genuinely excited about creating. You should know them well. If you can't fill out a mini-bio on each major character in your book, you don't yet know enough about that character to begin writing.

EXERCISE 1

Pick a novel or story you like and know well. Write a few sentences describing the protagonist at the start of the work: his attitudes, beliefs, and behavior. Now write a few sentences describing that character at the end. Do you see any significant differences? Is the character a changer or a stayer? How would you describe his emotional arc?

EXERCISE 2

Read (or reread) today's newspaper, looking specifically for characters you would like to write about. These should be people that spark your individual imagination. If you find one, write down everything you actually know about this person. Now fill out a mini-bio, inventing answers to the other questions. Is this someone you might like to build a story around?

Fill out a mini-bio for your most interesting relative. When it's complete, start changing answers. What if you keep Cousin Ann's job (nurse) but change her attitude toward it (instead of loving it, she hates it)? What would a boisterous, quick-tempered person like Ann do if she hated nursing (besides quit)? What if you change her job to doctor? Presidential advisor? Hairdresser? What if you change her marital status or plunk her down in a much different setting (say, Regency England)? Would Ann, with alterations, make a better character for something you might want to write?

Pick a story or book you know very well and list the major characters. Look at each one in turn and think how different the story would be if *he* were the star.

You might, for instance, choose *Sleeping Beauty*. If Beauty were not the star but instead a featured player (maybe even a bit player who doesn't show up until the end), who might star? Perhaps the prince, with the story becoming his struggle to find a bride. Perhaps one of those poor failed princes who died in the briar hedge before the hundred years were up. Perhaps the bad fairy who put a spell on Beauty—whatever happened to her after that?

In fact, some of these stories have already been written. Same plot, different stars.

This is the most important exercise for this chapter. Make a list of characters you either might want to write about or have begun to write about. Don't worry if the list is not complete; three or four will do. Fill out a mini-bio for each, inventing as you go along.

Now pick up and study each mini-bio. As each is in your hand, imagine that character as the star of your story. He will receive the most attention from you and the readers, the highest word count, the emotional arc (if there is one), and the climactic scene.

How does the story change each time you recast it?

Which version do you like best? Why?

Save this list and these mini-bios. We will use them again.

chapter 2

[INTRODUCING CHARACTERS — FIRST IMPRESSIONS COUNT]

Sociologists tell us that we form impressions of strangers in the first ten seconds after we meet them, and that these impressions are remarkably durable. With fictional characters, it may take longer than ten seconds (there are both, slow readers and slow-paced writers), but that first impression is equally important. Thus, it's a terrific idea for you, the writer, to carefully control the information that is presented during your character's first appearance on the page. By information I mean this fictional person's appearance, mannerisms, first actions, environment, and implied backstory.

But let's start with something even more basic than that—your character's name.

A ROSE BY ANY OTHER NAME

Juliet was sure she would have loved Romeo even "were he not Romeo called," and perhaps she was right. Still, one has to wonder. If at that masked ball she'd met young Skunkwort Montague, would she really have been so eager to trumpet his name to the night from her balcony?

Names affect our initial impressions of people, including fictional people. Thus, you can use the naming of your characters to affect how readers perceive them. In fact, it's surprising how much information a reader may assume from a simple name, including family background, age, personal relationships, and personality traits. Since these automatic assumptions are going to happen anyway, it's in your best interest as the writer to control them.

Ethnicity is the most obvious assumption a reader will make from your character's name. The first sentence of Carol Shields's *The Stone Diaries* is, "My mother's name was Mercy Stone Goodwill." The name immediately suggests an Anglo-Saxon, fundamentalist woman in a stern milieu, and that's exactly what Mercy is. Her name subtly prepares us for what comes next, and

19

the fact that the subsequent story matches the name reinforces our faith in the author. We can trust her. She knows what she's doing.

Similarly, Karim Shera is assumed to be Arab or of Arab extraction; Angelina Magdalani to be Italian; Reuven Goldstein Jewish. That much is easy, a clear flag to identify the fictional territory. But what is the reader to make of Karim Goldstein or Ethan Washington Magdalani III?

Hopefully, something interesting. Immediate questions rise in the mind: Is Karim Goldstein the child of a Jewish-Arab marriage? Are the Magdalanis trying to be more WASP than the Cabots or the Lodges? The answer might be "yes" or "no," but you've definitely aroused interest. Now you can have the pleasure of satisfying it—which, incidentally, you must do. Names follow a general rule in fiction that the farther you stray from reader expectation, the more obligated you are to explain how you got there (more on this later).

Whether you use ethnicity in names for clarity or you play against expectations, remember that in some regional areas, some ethnicities predominate. This gives your fiction plausibility. The New York Police Department is still dominated by Irish, Italians, Hispanics, and African Americans. Creating an entire Manhattan precinct filled with Russian-named cops will simply undermine readers' faith that you know your territory.

In addition to ethnicity, other aspects of family background can be foreshadowed by names. The family that names its son John Addams Carrington IV is making a definite statement: "We're proud of our distinguished lineage." At elementary school with young John are twins, Sunshine and Sweetmeadow Smith. This family is making a very different statement, and readers will expect a hippie or New Age background for the twins—especially if they're boys.

Gender-specific names, too, provide family background clues. In some upper-class circles, female-line family names are preserved by giving them to daughters. Thus McKenzie Wells, a girl born before 1975, comes with a certain amount of family expectation baggage. If you write her story, that baggage might reasonably be a part of it.

In recent decades, some names have migrated much more easily across the gender barrier in that names once exclusively male have been appropriated for girls: Ashley, Sidney, Madison, Taylor. However, few names have gone the other way. As with ethnicity, if your male character has a traditionally female name, you need more verbiage to explain why. Shel Silverstein wrote an entire song on this phenomenon: "A Boy Named Sue," sung by Johnny Cash. The family that calls a boy Sue or Deb or Millicent probably has some interesting dynamics going on—and you've foreshadowed them by the simple use of a name.

Names are obviously not infallible guides to age, but they can give subtle hints. Gladys and Myrtle, for instance, were popular names a century ago, but you'd be hard put to find a female infant now named Myrtle. Similarly, Janet was popular for the generation that came of age during World War II, Linda for their daughters, and Jennifer for their granddaughters. Boys' names show less variation over time; still, a character in a contemporary novel named Tertius either is very old or has constant explanations to make to classmates.

Generation-appropriate names really matter in a historical novel. English Regency belles were simply not named Madison or Linda. Janet was still a diminutive of Jane, not a name in its own right, as was Nancy for Anne. (Boys, however, might well be named Tertius.) Do careful research on whatever era and locale you're writing in. Again, the aim is to create reader confidence in you as a writer, as well as to begin building a mental image of the character in the reader's mind.

The most dangerous use of names is to indicate personality traits. Nineteenth-century writers got away with it. Dickens's Uriah Heep *sounds* oily and unappealing; Brontë's Heathcliff suggests that young man's wild, untamed nature. However, contemporary audiences tend to dismiss this sort of thing as implausibly ridiculous—unless you're writing comedy or children's books.

The Harry Potter books use names as tip-offs to personality. Draco Malfoy, with its echoes of dragons and malevolence, sounds like a villain (junior grade). Neville Longbottom is destined to be the butt of schoolboy jokes, as is Luna Lovegood. If you write juveniles—better yet, funny juveniles—you may wish to exploit names as keys to character. Otherwise, it's best to leave this tactic in past centuries.

WHAT SHOULD I CALL YOU, DEAR?

Not everyone in your story needs to address your character the same way. In fact, variations in address can be a subtle and sure way to indicate variations in relationships. Russian novelists were masters of this, so much so that my English translation of *Anna Karenina* provides a glossary of diminutives for, say, Nikolai. You probably don't want to go that far, but do consider the fictional implications of all your character's possible names.

For instance, a young schoolteacher is named Diane Eugenia Ramsay. Her small pupils call her Ms. Ramsay. Some of their mothers also say Ms. Ramsay, while others insist on Miss Ramsay, even when told she prefers Ms. Her boyfriend calls her Princess Di, which alternately amuses and irritates her. Her mother persists in Didi, a baby name that definitely irritates Diane (the mother, too, has been corrected numerous times). Her girlfriends call her Diane except for those from junior high, when Diane went through a romantic period and was known by her middle name. These buddies still use Eugenia or sometimes Genie. The IRS calls her Diane Eudora Ramsay, having confused her with somebody else, an error that Diane needs to straighten out immediately.

Look how much you've learned about this woman before she performs a single action in your story.

APPEARANCE: WHAT'S THAT YOU'RE WEARING?

A person's appearance consists of two different aspects: those things he's chosen and those he has not. We don't choose our height, age, shoe size, or face shape. If a man is born with a very low forehead and small, squinty eyes, barring major surgery, that's what he's stuck with. This is unfair, because small, squinty eyes are often read as sly and devious, and in fact the man may be a totally honest and open person.

We do choose our clothing, hairstyle, and level of grooming. But even these are not completely free choices, in that they are constrained by such factors as income (many more people would choose to wear Armani than can actually do so), fashion, and custom. This combination of selection with constraining factors is precisely what makes your character's appearance such a strong tool for characterization. All of us, through our appearance, tell discerning others a lot more than we think. And all of us, unfair though it may be, are also judged on the level of attractiveness of things we can't control.

Unless you're the writer—then you can control all of it.

The first step is to decide what overall impression you want your character to make on the reader. Worldly and aloof? Gritty and dangerous? Appealingly unsophisticated? Just plain dumb?

Next, choose a few visual details that project that image. "A few" is not an absolute concept; there is no magic number. It depends on the length of

?

Question:

Is a thesaurus useful in writing descriptions of people and places?

Answer:

A thesaurus is either a great aid or a disastrous deceiver, depending on how you use it.

It has value if it's used to remind you of words you already know but that have temporarily slipped your mind. If, for instance, you want your female protagonist to wear a red suit but "red" isn't exactly right, you might use a thesaurus to remind you of other shades. "Ruby" sounds flashier than plain red; "lobster" is faintly comic for a suit; "copper" seems quieter and more sophisticated; "cherry" sounds youthful. A thesaurus can hand you all these shades (plus, in my Roget's, seventy-three more), letting you find one with exactly the right connotations for your particular character. As Mark Twain put it, "The difference between the right word and the nearly right word is the same as that between lightning and the lightning bug."

On the other hand, a thesaurus used wrongly can utterly wreck your prose. Wrong usage is to search for words that are impressive or different. Unfortunately, these usually end up sounding pretentious, silly, or just plain wrong. Stick to words you are familiar with, and use the thesaurus merely to remind you of what they are.

the work and the importance of the character. More important than the number of details is their ability to add up to a coherent, interesting whole that says what you wish.

Here is where you can take advantage of nature's unfairness. That character with small, squinty eyes is going to be interpreted by your readers as sly and untrustworthy, *despite* the fact that in real life beady eyes do not inevitably point to dishonesty. But since your reader is going to make that assumption, let it work for you. Choose physical details that subtly reinforce whatever impression you want to create, such as:

- thin, lank hair for a woman with a nondescript personality
- fat, sweaty hands for a grasping person
- short stature for a male egoist (the "little Napoleon" syndrome)

However—and this is important—don't overdo reliance on inborn physical characteristics to indicate personality. First, exploiting these stereotypes can seem too mechanical. Second, it can create a sympathetic backlash in your reader, who may think, "But it isn't his fault his hands sweat, poor man!" J.K. Rowling, for instance, has come under fire for her repeated references to the fatness of Harry Potter's unpleasant cousins, the Dursleys.

It's better to use details of appearance that your characters can control. Here, for instance, are two female law enforcement officers, each engaged in a professional investigation on a hot day. The two women even look a bit alike: frizzy dark hair, slim build, and light eyes.

> She knew she looked younger than her age of thirty-four, and she was self-conscious about maintaining an air of authority. What she lacked in height she compensated for with her direct gaze, her squared shoulders. She had learned the art of dominating a scene, if only by sheer intensity. But this heat was sapping her resolve. She had started off dressed in her usual blazer and slacks and with her hair neatly combed. Now the blazer was off, her blouse was wrinkled, and the humidity had frizzed her dark hair into unruly coils. She felt assaulted on all fronts by the smells, the flies, and the piercing sunlight. There was too much to focus on at once. And all those eyes were watching her.
> —(Detective Jane Rizzoli in *The Apprentice*, by Tess Gerritsen)

> I wasn't sure what one wore to the Pit, but slut hair seemed like a good idea, so I did the hot roller and teasing thing. This increased my height from five foot seven inches to five foot ten. I tarted myself up with a lot of makeup, added a short black spandex skirt and four-inch heels, and I felt very kick-ass. I grabbed my leather jacket and took the car keys from the kitchen counter. Hold on. These weren't car keys. They were motorcycle keys. Shit! I'd never get my hair in the helmet.
> —(Bounty hunter Stephanie Plum in *Seven Up*, by Janet Evanovich)

There is no chance of confusing these two characters (one can't imagine that Jane Rizzoli even owns a spandex skirt and hot rollers). Without a single line of dialogue, we get clear impressions of Jane (dedicated, self-conscious, a bit humorless) and Stephanie (sexy, funny, vulgar, not noted for planning ahead). The clothes accomplish this, but so does their attitude toward the clothes. Jane Rizzoli dresses to blend in and takes her appearance seriously. Stephanie Plum dresses to stand out and is as feckless about her wardrobe as about everything else (she will ruin this outfit in a mud-wrestling pit).

Both descriptions succeed because they accomplish three things:

- The description provides a strong visual image.
- The description uses details to imply personality traits and/or personal background.
- The description intrigues us about what will happen next. Will Jane maintain her composure despite the heat, flies, and critical scrutiny? Will Stephanie's outrageous outfit fit in at the Pit so she can successfully go undercover?

These are the tests you want to apply to your own descriptions of a character's appearance.

THROUGH OTHER EYES: DRESSING SECONDARY CHARACTERS

Both Jane and Stephanie are point-of-view (POV) characters (more on this later—much more). With those who are not POV characters, appearance is even more important because readers will not also be privy to the character's thoughts. Everything we know about him must come from the outside. The right choice of clothing can imply a great deal about the character's life circumstances.

Here is the first appearance of DeVon Hardy, a secondary character in John Grisham's best-selling *The Street Lawyer* (it is also the opening of the novel):

> The man with the rubber boots stepped into the elevator behind me, but I didn't see him at first. I smelled him though—the pungent odor of smoke and cheap wine and life on the street without soap. We were alone as we moved upward, and when I finally glanced over I saw the boots, black and dirty and much too large. A frayed and tattered trench coat fell to his knees. Under it, layers of foul clothing bunched around his midsection, so that he appeared stocky, almost fat. But it wasn't from being well fed; in the wintertime in D.C., the street people wear everything they own, or so it seems.
>
> He was black and aging—his beard and hair were half-gray and hadn't been washed or cut in years. He looked straight ahead through thick sunglasses.

From this description, we know things about DeVon Hardy that go beyond the purely visual. He's had a rough life. He gets his clothes used from wherever he can. He's given up on basic amenities like bathing. He drinks too much. And, as we will learn in the next paragraph, he's very out of place in the elevator of this upscale Washington law firm. The description succeeds in meeting our three critical tests: coherent impression, personality/background clues, and reader interest.

However, as with most characters in most novels, there is a complication. We don't get objective descriptions of them; we see people only through the eyes of whoever the POV character is at that moment. In the case of DeVon Hardy, we are given what the POV character, Michael Brock, notices. Brock's description is fairly objective; he notices what most people would notice. But you don't have to write it that way.

You can, instead, let us see secondary characters through the eyes of highly biased POV characters. This can actually be a great asset to a writer, because the POV character can offer a perspective on other characters' appearances that they would never see themselves. The reader thus gets a doubly enriched description: some concrete details, plus an interpretation of those details that reveals truths about *both* characters.

This is easiest to see by example. Consider Clarissa Vaughan in Michael Cunningham's Pulitzer Prize-winning *The Hours*, as seen through the eyes of Willie Bass, a neighbor:

> There she is, thinks Willie Bass, who passes her some mornings just about here. The old beauty, the old hippie, hair still long and defiantly gray, out on her morning rounds in jeans and a man's cotton shirt, some sort of ethnic slippers (India? Central America?) on her feet. She still has a certain sexiness; a certain bohemian, good-witch sort of charm; and yet this morning she makes a tragic sight, standing so straight in her big shirt and exotic shoes, resisting the pull of gravity, a female mammoth already up to its knees in the tar, taking a rest between efforts, standing bulky and proud, almost nonchalant, pretending to contemplate the tender grasses waiting on the far bank when it is beginning to know for certain that it will remain here, trapped and alone, after dark, when the jackals come out. She waits patiently for the light.

What objective facts have we learned about Clarissa Vaughan? That she has long gray hair, is wearing jeans with a man's cotton shirt and soft slippers, and is waiting to cross the street. However, the description gives a much stronger impression than these police-blotter details. It's an interesting description not because of the concrete images but because of the highly colored, dramatic way that Willie Bass interprets these details. We see not just an older, still pretty woman at a street corner but also a gallant resister to the debilitating effects of age and time.

However, we only see this because Willie Bass does. It's a sure bet that Clarissa is not standing there thinking of herself as a good witch or a trapped mammoth. The richness of description comes from our receiving it through other eyes.

We also, you note, learn about Willie Bass. His own mode of description characterizes him: He is romantic, dramatic in thinking, and a bit condescending. Another man might have seen Clarissa Vaughan far differently, perhaps as a grandmotherly sort. A third type of man might not have noticed her at all.

This is a basic technique in using appearance to characterize. It's especially effective in a multi-viewpoint book because we can see a character from many perspectives. Let us return for a moment to that old woman in chapter one who left six million dollars to a veterinary hospital. Other characters remember her, recalling the same details but with far different interpretations:

- The old veterinarian: "Lydia had always been generous. It was there in her face: the wide mouth made for smiling, the soft eyes. In later years she'd often worn white lace at her throat, so feminine."
- The disinherited son: "She'd been coerced into that will, he knew. Gullible old bat! He could see her flabby lips and wishy-washy eyes above that stupid lace she wore to disguise the wattles in her neck. Vain, gullible, weak-minded."
- The patient housekeeper: "Miss Lydia loved cats. Her tired old eyes, they'd just light up when a cat climbed up on her. She'd even let them pull at those lacy scarf things she wore to keep the chill off her throat."

Which of these is "true"? Maybe, in part, all of them. Collectively, they add up to a multidimensional character.

You can easily use this technique in your fiction. Whenever a new character enters your story, consider whose eyes are describing him. Then choose a mix of details that give readers both some concrete images and a coherent interpretation of those images by this particular observer.

HOW RICH IS SHE? APPEARANCE IN THE SOCIAL CONTEXT

A person's appearance does more than indicate personal choices in hairstyle and clothing. It also can provide clues to where she stands in the larger socioeconomic context of society as a whole.

Imagine this: You are standing in the grocery store. Three middle-aged women pass, pushing shopping carts. One has graying hair parted in the middle and held back with two bobby pins; she is wearing polyester, pull-on slacks and a loose, flowered rayon top. One has her hair cut in a geometric bob; she wears a taupe, silk shirt and Donna Karan slacks. One has a curly mane; she wears jeans and a cotton T-shirt.

Who belongs to the country club? Who works for a housecleaning firm? Who is Mrs. Middle America in shopping mode?

The answers, of course, are, respectively, b, a, and c.

In the United States, we don't often discuss class; in fact, we usually try to pretend it doesn't exist. But the fact is that some people—and hence some of your characters—have more money and education than others. Some have the education without the money and some the money without the education. Some jobs are considered more prestigious than others. Different socioeconomic groups have different preferences in clothing, vacation spots, sports, and even—according to some sociologists—in pets and liquor. For your characters to be convincing, you need to get the socioeconomic details right.

You do that, primarily, through careful observation. Henry James once wrote, "Try to be a person on whom nothing is lost." It's still good advice. Look for the revealing physical detail that suggests where people fit in their societies. Then use it in character description.

This brings us to a specific type of detail: the brand name. Note that I described one of our grocery-store women as wearing "Donna Karan slacks." There are two schools of thought about this. One says that brand names are a quick, valid way of creating verisimilitude in fiction as well as telling shorthand for class and region. The woman in Manolo Blahnik shoes, ordering the arugula and goat cheese salad at a bistro on Fifth Avenue, is clearly not the same person as the woman wearing Target sneakers and ordering chicken-fried steak at a diner in Memphis. Why not use their chosen products to portray that? Certainly many successful writers, among them Stephen King, use brand names extensively.

The other line of thought says that brand names are a lazy shortcut, they date fiction too rapidly, and they're stereotypical, sometimes misleadingly so. It's possible that the lady in the Donna Karan slacks saved up for those pants, owns only one pair, and is on her way to a very important meeting with her husband's new boss. In this case, the pants don't mean she's rich at all.

You'll have to decide for yourself how much use you want to make of Kmart, Giorgio Armani, Gap, and Porsche. But either way, don't neglect other socioeconomic markers. They add considerable realism to fiction.

HOME DECOR: A MAN'S HOME IS HIS CASTLE, EVEN IN THE DUNGEON

Your home, as the shelter magazines constantly proclaim, is an extension of your personality. Where you live and how it looks says a lot about you.

This is absolutely true, for fictional people as well as the rest of us. As with appearance, some of the information trumpeted by our dwellings is chosen and some is not. Consider the teenager who lives in his parents' house. He did not choose its décor, but he has been formed by that environment, even if he did not form it. For this reason, you should give some thought to your character's home. It can convey a surprising amount of background information.

In the following paragraphs, the character's actions remain the same. But notice what a different impression you get of her based on her surroundings:

> Jane was almost ready for her party. The burgers were stacked by the grill, beer chilled in the refrigerator, and Captain, who had an unfortunate tendency to nip at strangers' ankles, was penned in the laundry room. Jane put some Stones on the CD player. Moving a pile of *Newsweek* off the coffee table, she set out chips and dip. The doorbell rang.

> Jane was almost ready for her party. The *poulet aux chanterelles* was ready to slide into the broiler, a nice Chardonnay chilled in the refrigerator, and Machiavelli, who had an unfortunate tendency to nip at strangers' ankles, was penned in her study. Jane put a flute solo on the CD player. Moving a pile of *Vogue* off the coffee table, she set out caponata and tea eggs. The doorbell rang.

> Jane was almost ready for her party. The pizza sat by the microwave, Pepsi chilled in the refrigerator, and Teensy, who had an unfortunate tendency to nip at strangers' ankles, was penned in her bedroom. Jane put Britney Spears on the CD player. Moving a pile of Daddy's stuff off the coffee table, she set out a bag of M&Ms and a plate of Oreos. The doorbell rang.

The above descriptions are all adequate, but they could do more. Just as important as the actual décor is your character's reaction to it. Environment is like clothing: a chance to characterize twice. This is true whether the character is reacting to her own environment or to someone else's. What can you learn about Lydia Blessing, in Anna Quindlen's *Blessings*, from her reactions to the town of Mount Mason?

> So many of her landmarks had gone, the old limestone bank building chopped up into a travel agency, a beauty parlor, and a used-book store; the boxy red brick hardware store refaced with some horrid imitation stone and made over

into a place that sold records. She had had to drive around the circle in the center of town twice, unsure of which way to turn for the commercial strip, and a carful of teenagers had honked at her and driven far too close to her back bumper. And then there had been the horrid noisy glare of the store, and the insistence of the other shoppers on pushing past her and screaming at their dirty children. But she had found light bulbs cheaper than the ones Nadine had found at the ShopRite, and paper towels, too, in a bargain twelve-pack.

Everything about this description is colored by Lydia's perceptions. Are *all* those children really dirty? Probably not. Were the teenagers *really* driving too close to Lydia's car? We can't tell. What we can tell is that Lydia is old and shaky in traffic. She's convinced that the past was better in every way than the present. She's out of touch with the modern world she despises; the year is 2002 and it's very doubtful there are any *records* in that music store. Lydia is also self-righteous, snobbish (those "dirty children"), and either poor or thrifty (the latter). A description of place has also become a portrait of the person viewing it.

This technique is just one example of a larger rule in fiction: Make everything serve more than one purpose. Choose your character's outfits to convey her taste, social status, or personality. Give us someone's reactions to those outfits as you describe them. Do the same with environment.

Let's revisit one of the descriptions of Jane's party to see how much richer it is with Jane's reactions included:

Jane was almost ready for her party. The pizza sat by the microwave—did she get the right kind? Hannah would snicker if the pizza was the wrong kind. At least the Pepsi chilling in the refrigerator was okay; Emily had had Pepsi at her party last week. Teensy, who had an unfortunate tendency to nip at strangers' ankles, was penned in her bedroom, but if the girls wanted to see him, Jane was going to let him out, no matter *what* Daddy said about legal liabilities. Jane put Britney Spears on the CD player. Moving a pile of Daddy's stuff off the coffee table—why did her parents have to be such dorks?—she set out a bag of M&Ms and a plate of Oreos. The doorbell rang. Her stomach clenched.

Now the description not only introduces setting—it introduces Jane. This poor child is socially anxious, feels inferior to Emily and the snickering Hannah, and distrusts her own judgment only a shade less than she distrusts her parents'.

What does your character own, decorate with, drive, and read? Each detail can help your readers not only see him but get to know him, all before he does anything significant or utters one line of dialogue.

FOREIGN TRAVEL: WRITING
THE STRANGER

Sometimes you may want to write about a major character who is a member of a group not your own: different gender, different ethnic group, different nationality, or different historical period. This character may or may not be a POV character.

The pitfall is reaching for secondhand stereotypes instead of the difficult, more complex truths of accurate portrayal. You want a Catholic priest, so you look to either ancient Bing Crosby movies or lurid descriptions of clergymen who end up in the newspapers. You want an Arab, so you make him a fanatic Islamic who always wears a white burnoose. You, a fifty-year-old male writer, want a twentysomething contemporary female, so you borrow one of the girls from *Sex and the City*.

The dangers here are multiple. You will probably get the details wrong. You will possibly end up insulting whatever group your character belongs to. And you will almost certainly weaken your fiction because the character will feel trite and stale.

This does not, however, mean that you can't write characters, even POV characters, who are radically different from yourself. You can—but you must take extra care.

That care might take the form of formal research. For historical novels, of course, this is essential; you don't want to put a late fifteenth-century English lady into a hoop skirt instead of a farthingale. Research into beliefs and attitudes is equally important, and not only for historicals. Is your Arab a Tunisian, Egyptian, or Iraqi? (It makes an enormous difference!) What do young men of various classes habitually wear on the streets of Tunis, Cairo, or Baghdad? What branch of Islam does your character practice—Shiite, Sunni, or something else? How devoutly?

And what about that contemporary twenty-three-year-old woman? Who is she, beyond her age and gender? If she's a sassy, sexy, well-off New Yorker, what sets her apart as an individual from other sassy, sexy, well-off New Yorkers? Once our fifty-year-old male author knows that, he can go on to research the kinds of makeup, clothing, and music she would like—details that will make her seem real, not a clownish stereotype.

Research from books, magazines, and the Internet should be supplemented with firsthand observation. Go to the mall and eavesdrop on shopping twentysomethings. Watch them, listen to them, and note the concrete details that can make your character vivid.

Finally, another way to take extra care is to ask someone who belongs to your character's group to read your manuscript and comment. I did this with my novel, *Stinger*. One of the major characters is an African-American female scientist from the Centers for Disease Control and Prevention, an ex-seventies-militant. I asked two African-American girlfriends (I am not African American) to read the second draft and critique my character. They both said the same thing: "She's believable, I know women like this, but that's not how one deals with black hair, and lose the sunscreen." I made the suggested changes.

If you're writing about contemporary twelve-year-olds, find a twelve-year-old critic. He'll be glad to set you straight on clothes, music, video games, and sneakers. You will never be twelve again; take advantage of the firsthand knowledge of those who are.

However, there is a major modification to all of this. Again, much depends on through whose eyes we are seeing that twelve-year-old character— or the priest or the Arab or the uptown girl. There is no such thing as pure objectivity; even a police report has chosen which details to include (putting in height, for example, but leaving out length of eyelashes). What you write should be tailored to the POV character's perceptions, biases, and preferences, even if they are inaccurate.

Here is a biased character watching a Catholic priest say Mass:

> He wore a dog collar and a silly-looking scarf around his neck, and he handled the so-called sacred wafers without even using gloves. Every once in a while bells tinkled theatrically. How can people be so superstitious?

When your POV character is someone like this, you don't want accurate or complex details. The observer wouldn't see them.

FINAL CAVEATS: NOT TOO BLAND, NOT TOO WEIRD

When we describe the appearance or home of someone (real or fictional), the immediate temptation is to reach for the obvious details: long brown hair, denim jacket, red plaid sofa. These can be serviceable. They are not, however, very interesting. Can you do better? What's interesting about that long hair? Maybe it shines like glass. Maybe her bangs need a trim, so she's constantly blowing them off her face. Maybe blond roots are showing, or gray streaks. Maybe her hair isn't brown but cinnamon, mink-colored, or purple.

Does her denim jacket have an appliqué? Velvet cuffs? Missing buttons? Laboriously sewn-on tiny mirrors?

Does the red plaid sofa have chocolate stains on both arms? One leg propped up on a soup can? A thick plastic cover to keep it "new"?

Reach past the obvious. Do not, however, go so far past it that every single detail is ornate and bizarre for every single character. That kind of exaggeration quickly becomes implausible and then tiresome. The aim is to choose those details of appearance, possessions, and décor that are strongly visual, genuinely revealing, and fresh enough to register. Unless you're writing satire, don't overdo the description.

And don't make it too long, either. Paragraph after paragraph of character description *will* be skipped by readers. Instead, hit them with a few good sentences of description when you introduce a character, and thereafter tuck the details between lines of dialogue, action, or a character's inner musings. Don't linger too long. Your character's first impressions are important—but not as important as the inner person we'll examine next.

RECAP: FIRST IMPRESSIONS

Names can convey much information before a character utters a single line of dialogue. Exploit the power of names and nicknames to suggest family background, ethnicity, age, and class—or deliberately make names play against reader expectation.

Use all aspects of your character's appearance (clothing, hair, body, personal possessions) to build characterization and intrigue the reader. But remember that description almost always comes through another character's eyes and should reflect the observer's tastes rather than "objective" reality. The same is true of how a character furnishes and decorates his home. Décor may characterize, but it may also tell us about economic limitations. For this reason, how a character *feels* about his appearance and his living space is as important as the tangibles.

Keep these descriptions brief but not so bland they're boring or so bizarre they distract from the story.

Using brand names can add verisimilitude and convey information about characters, but brand names can also seem dated, stereotyped, or misleading. Use with caution.

Also be cautious when writing characters outside your own group (age, class, ethnicity, nationality). Avoid stereotypes by striving to find authentic details. But for biased POV characters, write what they would naturally think.

EXERCISE 1

Pull out the character mini-bios you wrote for the last exercise in chapter one. Look at each name on your list. Does it do the maximum possible to clue the reader about who this person is? What does each name suggest about that character's ethnicity, age, and/or family background? Would a name that plays against reader expectations be more effective for this person? Does the name suggest variations of address that you can exploit in your story? Change any names that aren't as effective as they could be.

EXERCISE 2

Look yet again at the mini-bios. Pick three. For each character, list one outfit typical of what that person might wear. Be as specific as possible: not just "a cheap suit and tie" but "a shiny blue suit worn at the cuffs with a dingy white shirt, red polyester tie, white socks, and brown loafers." Add an appropriate hairstyle for each. Now scrutinize your descriptions. Does each make a coherent impression? Imply personality traits and/or socioeconomic status? Intrigue readers? If not, dress your people again.

EXERCISE 3

Pick one of your three characters from above and write two brief descriptions of him or her *as seen by the other two characters*. (Note: This exercise is most fun if at least one of the two observers dislikes the observed character.)

EXERCISE 4

Pick one of your three mini-bios and write out answers to each of the following questions:

- What does this person's bedroom look like? Describe it in a paragraph.
- What vehicle does he drive?
- What was the last book or magazine she read?
- What is his favorite possession?

chapter 3

[THE GENUINE SELF—
WHAT IS SHE REALLY LIKE?]

All of us wear social masks. Have you ever stood smiling at a party when you were actually (pick one) bored, angry, sad, or exhausted to tears? Have you ever congratulated someone warmly when you really thought her good fortune wasn't deserved? Spoken cruelly to someone you actually love and admire? Pretended confidence when you were trembling inside with anxiety? Of course you have. We all have.

Your fictional people should, too.

Other times, people feel an emotion very strongly but can't seem to express it. The older, inarticulate man who cannot say "I love you" is a staple in family dramas (maybe because there are so many of them in real life). The young girl who feels strong sexual desire but is afraid to show it ("nice girls don't") turns up over and over again in Victorian novels.

Your fictional people can suppress feelings, too.

There are times when all of us say exactly what we mean and behave exactly as we feel—even when the consequences indicate that we probably shouldn't have.

Your fictional people can do that, too.

It can greatly aid plausibility when we see that a character is acting out of genuine emotion, hiding genuine emotion, or paralyzed by genuine emotion. Unfortunately, it can also greatly aid confusion if done ineptly. So how does a writer portray a character's inner self? How do you show that the inner and outer selves are in conflict? There are no more important questions in fiction, since emotion drives behavior and behavior drives story. And emotion itself? It derives from two other critical concepts: motivation and backstory. What your character feels is a product of both what he wants right now *and* his entire background.

So let's start at the beginning.

BACKSTORY: HOW SHE GOT TO BE LIKE THAT

Your protagonist, like the rest of us, is a product of everything that ever happened to her (the backstory). Obviously, however, you cannot show us everything that ever happened to her, and even if you could, we'd be bored senseless (". . . and then on the first day of third-grade math class . . ."). A character's past, like everything else in fiction, is a matter of selection. You choose the parts you think we need to know in order to understand who this person is today.

How much is that? It depends on the kind of story you're writing. For a short story, or some action-based novels, we may learn virtually nothing of a character's life before the story starts. (If James Bond had trouble in third-grade math, we'll never know it.) In other books, we may learn nothing of people's early lives, but we will learn about events immediately preceding the story line. In still other books, particularly literary novels about young people who aren't far from their childhoods, backstory may take up half the word count through flashbacks, reminiscences, and conversations about personal history. For such works, coming to grips with the past is the whole point, and thus the past is fully portrayed. Other works fall in the middle of the backstory spectrum.

In all cases, however, what matters is that you, the author, know the backstory. *You* must have a sense of your character's past. Only then can you decide how much of that past should go into your story now. The basis for your decision will be motivation. Motivation and backstory are thus intimately connected. Let's see how.

MOTIVATION: YOU WANT *WHAT*?

Motivation is the key to your entire story. I'm going to say that again, because it's so important: Motivation is the key to fiction. You can create fascinating characters, with vivid backstories, appearances described in perfect verbal pitch, and settings so real we can smell them, but all of them will remain sketches, vignettes, or travelogues unless your characters do something. And they won't do anything without motivation.

Motivation means that someone wants something. The character wants to stop an international enemy (James Bond), live with her true love (Anna Karenina), find the guy who skipped bail (Stephanie Plum), or give a successful party (Clarissa Vaughan). Sometimes they don't know exactly what they want, but *you* do. Sometimes all they want is to be left alone. But it is an absolute rule (and fiction has very few of them) that someone must want something, or you don't have a story.

So start by listing what your characters want. Make an actual, brief list if that helps. For some genres, the basics are obvious:

- NYPD detective: wants to solve the murder
- Murderer: wants to not be caught

This may be enough for a simple story, but almost always there is more going on. The detective may also want to be taken seriously by a skeptical boss, stop drinking, prevent his daughter from becoming a hooker, get revenge for a previous brush with this same criminal, vent a deep and primal rage against the world . . . you get the idea. Expand your list.

The murderer, too, also wants more complicated things. Something led him to kill in the first place: What was it? It might be sheer clumsiness, if the murder occurred inadvertently during a bank robbery. But probably there was deeper motivation. Why did he rob the bank? Yes, he wanted money, but many, many people who want more money don't rob banks. Why did this person do it? Perhaps because he's the sort of person who always believes he can get away with anything, that he's special. How did he get that way?

This is where motivation shades into backstory.

You may not want to put that backstory into your book at all, especially if the killer is not a point-of-view character. But you should know it, because it will affect his outer actions. A robber who believes he cannot be caught will act far differently, and more recklessly, than one who carefully plans for every contingency because he believes he *can* be caught.

For some characters, motivation is much murkier. In Anna Quindlen's *Blessings*, handyman Skip Cuddy, barely out of his teens, finds a box left overnight by the garage. Inside is a newborn baby. He does not, as most people would, call the police. Instead, he hides the baby in his apartment over the garage and tries to take care of her. Why? He doesn't really know. And we learn why only gradually, as we see this love-starved young man, whose own parents abandoned him through death and desertion, identify with this dumped infant.

However, so surely is the novel written, I would bet anything that Anna Quindlen knew from the beginning what Skip's motivation was. The second scene of the second chapter gives us Skip's backstory: his mother's early death, his father's moving away and dumping Skip on relatives, the stupid and impulsive convenience store robbery that got him a year in jail, the drifting around friends' apartments until his current job. More important, we see how Skip hated all that. This is a character in search of roots and family, even if he has to create them himself from random chance.

What does Skip Cuddy want? To belong somewhere, with someone. The backstory makes this desire, however bizarrely acted upon, plausible, and real. Another young man would get rid of this baby as soon as possible, but Skip is not just another young man. He is himself, with his personal backstory, and it both illuminates and supports his motivation. In *Blessings*, backstory and motivation are not separable. Without the backstory, in fact, Skip's actions would seem arbitrary, if not incomprehensible.

READER ASSUMPTIONS: WELL, OF COURSE HE WANTS THAT

When do you need to detail a character's backstory, as with Skip Cuddy, and when don't you, as with James Bond?

The criterion is usually reader assumptions about motivation. If we know that James Bond is in the espionage business, we already know what he wants: to stop the bad guys. No backstory is needed to explain that. Nor do you need one to explain why a detective wants to catch a murderer, a young woman wants the man she likes to like her back, a man wants to protect his children, or a woman wants to do well at law school. All these motivations make intuitive sense in contemporary life.

Note, however, that context matters. If that young woman striving for As is attending Yale Law School in 2005, her motivation seems clear to us. But what if she's trying to get into law school in 1904? Then she's not usual, she doesn't match societal assumptions for young women, and you need a lot more backstory to make her motivation real to us. Even in 2005, if she comes from a dirt-poor family in which no one has ever even graduated from high school, her law-school aspirations will go enough against reader assumption that you will need to tell us more in order to make her believable.

Neither her sisters nor her neighbors want to go on to higher education; what is there about this girl that makes her different? Has she always been an achiever? Is she much more intelligent than the rest of her family? Did a teacher encourage her? Is she motivated by a desire for the expensive things she sees on television? Is she unusually idealistic about the law protecting people like her family, and what did she witness that made her that way?

Again, backstory becomes motivation, with the degree of included backstory set by reader assumptions.

The problem with backstory is that, by definition, it's over. It tells about events in the past, not in the present of story time. Thus, it lacks immediacy. Worse, it interrupts the events of story time, making them lose momentum. Backstory in fiction is like commercials on television: an interruption that marks a good time for the watcher to disengage, go get a sandwich, and possibly lose interest.

To keep this from happening, you will need to exercise cunning about where you plant your backstory. There are four ways to include backstory information:

- the brief detail
- the inserted paragraph
- the flashback
- the expository lump

Each requires a different technique.

THE BRIEF DETAIL: A HINT OF TIME GONE BY

The brief detail is easiest; you just include it in an ongoing scene. That way, it doesn't interrupt the story's momentum or jerk the reader out of story time. You can convey a surprising amount of information this way. Here is Miles Roby, in Richard Russo's Pulitzer Prize-winning novel *Empire Falls*, watching out the window of the diner where he works as a cook:

> What drew Miles Roby's anxious eye down Empire this particular afternoon in early September was not the dark, high-windowed shirt factory where his mother had spent most of her adult working life or, just beyond it, the larger, brooding presence of the textile mill, but rather his hope that he'd catch a glimpse of his daughter, Tick, when she rounded the corner and began her slow, solitary trek up the avenue. Like most of her friends, Tick . . .

The story then goes on about Tick, but we have received a piece of backstory that will be significant later: Miles's mother worked for years at the factory. This detail didn't interrupt the narrative at all.

Similar details that suggest backstory in an effortless way might include:

- a casual reference to a phone call made earlier that day to a mother in prison
- a framed Harvard diploma on the wall
- a faded rocking horse given the place of honor in a childless woman's living room
- a garden choked with weeds described as "once, before the accident, the showplace of the entire neighborhood"

Once you get in the habit of this sort of thing, you will find that these quick hints do four things: supply backstory, foreshadow coming events, characterize in the same ways as clothing or possessions, and tantalize the reader. That's a lot to do with less than a sentence!

THE INSERTED PARAGRAPH: A QUICK GLIMPSE OF THE PAST

More elaborate is the paragraph of backstory inserted into story time. This does interrupt the story, but if you hold it to one or possibly two paragraphs, most readers won't feel jarred out of the story proper. Here is Miles again. He is serving lunch to fellow townsman Horace Weymouth, who has a purple fibroid cyst growing out of his forehead. Miles muses that he hasn't noticed Horace's cyst in a while because when you see people every day, you stop noticing their physical oddities. This story time thought segues effortlessly into one long paragraph of backstory:

> Miles hadn't seen much in the way of physical oddity on Martha's Vineyard, where he and his daughter had vacationed last week. Almost everyone on the island appeared to be rich, slender, and beautiful. When he'd remarked on this, his old friend Peter said that he should come live in L.A. for a while. There, he argued, ugliness was rapidly and systematically being bred out of the species. "He doesn't really mean L.A.," Peter's wife, Dawn, had corrected when Miles appeared dubious. "He means Beverly Hills." "And Bel Air," Peter added. "And Malibu," Dawn added. And then they named a baker's dozen other places where unattractiveness had been eradicated. Peter and Dawn were full of such worldly wisdom which, for the most part, Miles enjoyed. The three had been undergraduates together at a small Catholic college outside of Portland, and he admired that they were barely recognizable as the students he'd known. Peter and Dawn had become other people entirely, and Miles concluded that this was what was supposed to happen, although it hadn't happened to him. If disappointed by

their old friend's lack of evolution, they concealed that disappointment well, even going so far as to claim that he restored their faith in humanity by remaining the same old Miles. Since they apparently meant this as a compliment, Miles tried hard to take it that way. They did seem genuinely glad to see him every August, and even though each year he half expected his old friends not to renew the invitation for the following summer, he was always wrong.

Then back to story time and Horace Weymouth's lunch.

What does author Russo gain from this interruption to his story? All four things also gained by briefer bits of backstory:

- **Reader knowledge of previous events:** We have learned that Miles went to college and that he just vacationed on upscale Martha's Vineyard, as he does every summer.
- **Foreshadowing:** Peter, Dawn, and their vacation home will become important near the end of the novel.
- **Characterization:** We now know that Miles has not "evolved," never left Empire Falls, is nonetheless interesting enough to retain sophisticated friends, does not seem to envy them their advantages, and has so little self-confidence that he always expects Peter and Dawn to not invite him again.
- **Reader interest:** A question has now been raised in our minds. Why does a college-educated man, who could leave dying Empire Falls, nonetheless remain there as a fry cook?

Gaining all that is well worth Russo's 261-word interruption of his tale to insert some backstory.

THE FLASHBACK: BACKSTORY DRAMATIZED

A flashback gives us a scene from the past with the full dramatization of story time—dialogue, action, thoughts, everything to make us feel we are present as the characters interact. However, a flashback is *not* story time; it occurred before the story began and thus lacks the visceral immediacy of story time events. However, it is useful for filling in backstory—if a few guidelines are carefully observed.

First, you must earn the right to a flashback. This means that enough interesting things have already happened in the story to anchor us firmly in its present before you carry us off to its past. For this reason, flashbacks should never be your first scene. Nor should they follow a skimpy and action-less "present" like this opening:

> Jan gazed out the window at the winter garden. Snow was falling faster now. She could hardly see the oaks Manny had planted, let alone the lake behind them. The drifting snow carried her back to that other winter afternoon, barely two years ago, when everything had changed. Manny had just come in from the garage . . .

This flat out does not work. We aren't ready to return to the winter afternoon two years ago when we know virtually nothing about *this* winter afternoon. Who are Jan and Manny? How do they relate to each other now? Where are we? Why should we care?

That last question is crucial. You must make us care about Jan and Manny's present before we can be expected to care about their past. Therefore, position flashbacks as at least second scenes—and then only if you've written a compelling first scene, one that gives us a strong sense of your characters and their current situation.

In addition, flashbacks should not tell most of the story. Readers want to experience events firsthand, as they happen. If you keep having to flashback in every single chapter to fill us in on critical backstory, you may have started your fiction in the wrong place. Begin earlier.

Finally, the transition from story time into a flashback is important. If it seems arbitrary or contrived, the entire flashback will also lose conviction. The action or character needs a narrative *reason* for this past event to be recounted at just this time.

In Anne Tyler's *Back When We Were Grownups*, the transition into a flashback comes after Rebecca Davitch, the middle-aged protagonist, has been telling her grandchildren how she met their grandfather. She tells them, in story time, how a baked ham had been dropped on her shoes during a party at his house. The segue into dramatizing that meeting is seamless:

> "Meanwhile," Rebecca said, "your grandpa was going back and forth with hot water and cloths, cleaning up the dining room. And finally he squatted down on the floor and started wiping my shoes off, right while I was standing there helping Biddy toss the salad."
>
> The most memorable of the five senses, she often felt, was the sense of touch. After all these years she could still feel the heat of that cloth soaking

through to her damp toes, and Joe's strong, sure dabbing motion that had reminded her of a mother cat industriously bathing her kittens. And she remembered how, once he'd finished, he rose and clasped her arm to lead her away,
his warm fingers firmly pressing the bare skin above her elbow. "Where are you
taking her?" Mother Davitch had cried in alarm . . .

The backstory of this meeting is necessary to understanding Rebecca's choices
in story time. It deserves the full dramatization of a flashback.

If you choose flashbacks to fill in backstory, make sure they are important
enough, placed well, and provided with smooth transitions.

EXPOSITION: BACKSTORY UNDISGUISED

Finally, you can give backstory by simply stopping story time dead and just
telling us what went on before the book began. The drawback of this method
is obvious, implied in the phrase "stopping story time dead"; sometimes the
dead cannot be revived. A large chunk of exposition jerks your reader out of
story time, and you risk his not wanting to return.

So why do it? Two reasons. First, you may not have much choice. There
are some character histories so intricate and complicated that the only way
they can be conveyed is through an unbroken stretch of explanation. Worse,
such histories are usually necessary to understand anything else that's going
on, so they must be placed near the story's beginning. If you do this, at least
make the backstory exposition the second scene, giving us action first even
if it seems a bit murky. Backstory seldom makes a good hook.

The second reason you might want to stop the story for a chunk of
expository backstory is if the backstory itself is tremendously interesting.
Readers will not get restless if they are fascinated, nor will they desert you if
they are highly amused. Go right ahead and write a lengthy passage of backstory as long as you can make it:

- hilariously funny
- full of events that in themselves make the reader gasp (although in that
  case, why aren't you writing a different novel with this wonderful
  material?)
- written in such a shimmering prose that your readers, who are probably
  literary readers, don't mind that you've left the story to wander in its
  archives

If, on the other hand, you cannot do any of these things in this particular story, try to give us your backstory through casual references, discreetly placed paragraphs, and flashbacks.

PORTRAYING STRAIGHTFORWARD EMOTION

We now have the basic pedigree of emotion down. It looks like this:

backstory ➔ personality/character traits ➔ wanting something (motivation) ➔ emotion

In other words, who your character is, as formed by his backstory, leads him to want something, and that wanting is accompanied by feelings. Desire creates emotion.

Back at the start of this chapter, we talked about two cases of emotion: one in which the character is acting in accordance with what he feels and one in which his outer self and inner self are at odds. The basic techniques for writing both are the same, but the second case adds some bells and whistles. Let's deal first with those straightforward situations in which the character's basic personality, temporary desires, and emotion are all congruent—the person who is not attempting to hide anything.

Here, in W. Somerset Maugham's classic *Of Human Bondage*, Philip Carey is in the grip of strong emotion. Philip was born with a clubfoot:

> But at night when they went up to bed and were undressing, the boy called Singer came out of his cubicle and put his head in Philip's.
> "I say, let's look at your foot," he said.
> "No," answered Philip. He jumped into bed quickly.
> "Don't say no to me," said Singer. "Come on, Mason."
> The boy in the next cubicle was looking round the corner, and at the words he slipped in. They made for Philip and tried to tear the bedclothes off him, but he held them tightly.
> "Why can't you leave me alone?" he cried.
> Singer seized a brush and with the back of it beat Philip's hands clenched on the blanket. Philip cried out.
> "Why don't you show us your foot quietly?"
> "I won't."
> Philip clenched his fist and hit the boy who tormented him, but he was at a disadvantage, and the boy seized his arm. He began to turn it.

"Oh, don't, don't!" said Philip. "You'll break my arm."

"Stop still then and put out your foot."

Philip gave a sob and a gasp. The boy gave the arm another wrench. The pain was unendurable.

"All right. I'll do it," said Philip.

Philip's feelings are clear: shame and anger. These feelings need no elaborate explanation; they are just what we would expect from a boy being so cruelly tormented. The emotions come from a clear desire to be left alone and not have his deformity exposed. How does Maugham succeed in making Philip's emotions so vivid?

Not, you will notice, from naming them for us. The abstract words "shame," "anger," or "fear" don't appear. In fact, naming emotions is usually a poor way to portray them. Even when authors say something like "Fear gripped him," the abstract naming is supplemented by other, more visceral techniques. This is because the aim is not to *label* emotion; it is to make the reader *experience* the same emotion that the character does.

Look at the passage again. Maugham uses all of the following to make us feel what Philip does:

- **Actions.** Philip "jumped into the bed quickly," "held them [the bed-clothes] tightly," and "hit the boy who tormented him." Actions are the clearest expression of feeling. If you can make your character do something that accurately expresses his feelings, readers will make the leap to the emotion driving him to those actions.
- **Dialogue.** Philip doesn't talk about his feelings (fiction is not psycho-therapy). Instead, he says things that a person with those feelings would naturally say. "Why can't you leave me alone?" does far more to create the feeling of anguish in the reader than would an abstract "Philip wanted them to stop." This is because the desperate cry lets us witness for ourselves, and hence enter into, through identification, Philip's anguish. Similarly, "Oh, don't, don't! You'll break my arm" is far more vivid than, "He felt afraid."
- **Bodily sensations.** Emotions originate in the limbic system, a very old part of the human brain. They predate words, as anyone knows who's ever seen a baby express fury. Thus we experience our emotions in our bodies. Philip's clenched hands on the blanket, and his sob and gasp, are all preverbal and vivid. Similarly, characters might feel cold seep

up their spines (fear), hollowness in their chests (anxiety), or the quick swoop of vertigo (shock).

These are the basic methods for rendering emotion, plus one more: a character's thoughts. Maugham doesn't give us Philip's thoughts because Maugham maintains a considerable authorial distance (more on this in chapter twelve), but another author might. Again, a character feeling emotional should not think directly about the emotion itself—"I was angry"—unsupplemented by anything else. It's too weak. Instead, a character would naturally think about what's making him angry and/or his response to it:

- I wanted to tear her head off.
- To have worked so hard for this bitch, and now she goes and . . .
- He stood there, smiling blandly, as if nothing had happened, none of it, and I had to turn away before I said something I would regret later.

In what proportion do you mix these four modes of conveying emotion: action, dialogue, bodily sensations, and character's thoughts? That depends entirely on the author. It's one of the things that define individual style. The important thing is that you rely on these methods of dramatizing your characters' feelings rather than on simply naming them for us.

DECEPTIVE EMOTION: THE SOCIAL MASK

That last statement is true even when your character's actual emotion and behavior are not congruent. The only difference is that some of the emotional indicators will derive from what she's really feeling and some will derive from the feeling she's trying to project.

Let us imagine a different boy in Philip's situation. Schoolmates are trying to force him to show them his foot. This time, however, the foot is not deformed but newly tattooed. The boy is pretending to resist but is secretly delighted with all the attention.

"Let's look at your foot," Singer said.

"No," answered Philip. He jumped into bed quickly.

"Don't say no to me," said Singer. "Come on, Mason."

The boy in the next cubicle was looking round the corner, and at the words he slipped in. They made for Philip and tried to tear the bedclothes off him, but he held them tightly. His grin flashed in the gloomy room.

"Why can't you leave me alone?"

Singer seized a brush and with the back of it beat Philip's hands clenched on the blanket. Philip's nerves thrilled; they were so eager!

"Why don't you show us your foot quietly?"

"I won't."

Philip pushed Singer away, but he was at a disadvantage, and the boy seized his arm. He began to turn it.

Philip laughed. "Oh, don't be stupid—I'm much stronger than you are!"

"Stop still then and put out your foot."

"All right. I'll do it."

Do you see how this is done? The emotional indicators that point toward reluctance on Philip's part are:

- **Actions:** jumping into bed quickly, holding tight to the bedclothes, pushing Singer away
- **Dialogue:** "No," "Why can't you leave me alone," and "I won't."

But, at the same time, other indicators show that Philip is enjoying this game:

- **More Dialogue:** the amiable contempt and lack of fear in "Oh, don't be stupid—I'm much stronger than you are!"
- **Bodily reactions:** the thrill along his nerves, his laughter
- **Thoughts:** that telltale, pleased "they were so eager!"

Note that bodily reactions and inner thoughts trump actions and dialogue. The body doesn't lie. This passage portrays an outer reluctance and inner pleasure about what's going on—but we clearly understand that the latter is real and the former sham.

So we need to amend our diagram a bit. It should now look like this:

backstory → personality/character traits → wanting something (motivation) → emotion (felt inside) + emotion (displayed outwardly)

What are your characters feeling? Once you know their backstory and current desires, this becomes easy to identify. Then you portray it using appropriate dialogue, actions, bodily sensations, and thoughts.

But what if they're feeling such a jumble of different things at once that the diagram won't suffice? We'll take up that situation in the next chapter.

Liar, Liar!

"The body doesn't lie"—but sometimes people do. How can you convey to the reader that a non-POV character is lying?

The easiest way is for the POV character to realize the other person is lying. The POV character can then acknowledge this in dialogue ("You're lying to me") or thoughts ("Carol looked again at Keith. He had that look in his eyes, the one that always made her chest tighten. He was lying to her again.").

However, your POV character may not realize that the other character is lying. In that case, the only way you have to signal the reader is through the liar's behavior. The danger is that an unsophisticated reader might not recognize the physical signs of prevarication. She will usually, however, pick up that something strange is going on, so when the lying becomes clearer later in the plot, you'll at least have foreshadowed it. The signs of lying are:

- Refusing to meet someone's eyes (A right-handed person will often look off to the right if she is lying but off to the left if she is merely trying to recollect something. The opposite is true for lefties.)
- A tightness in the voice or slight rise in pitch
- Slight sweating
- Checking a wristwatch or moving jewelry around
- Inability to remain seated
- Reddening of face
- Anger or defensiveness

Of course, all these behaviors can also stem from other causes than lying (moist skin can come from exercise, fear, or lust). You will need to combine such bodily indicators with dialogue and description to make it clear that your character is lying.

RECAP: A CHARACTER'S INNER LIFE

Different kinds of books include different amounts of backstory; however, no matter how much backstory is included, you should always have strong sense of your characters' pasts. From that past grows present motivations. The more unusual that motivation is, the more backstory we need to see to make the motivation credible.

Backstory can be included through brief details, paragraphs inserted into story time, flashbacks, or exposition. However, neither a flashback nor a long expository passage should be your opening. Ground us firmly in your story's present before we visit its past.

Backstory creates personality/character, which in turn creates motivation, which causes your characters' emotions. Convey those emotions to your reader not through abstract labeling but dramatizing your characters' bodily responses, actions, thoughts, and dialogue.

When a character is feeling one emotion but wishes to project another, make some of his emotional indicators reflect his real feelings and some his pretended ones. However, thoughts and bodily reactions should always describe genuine emotion. The body doesn't lie.

EXERCISE 1

Pick a favorite story that you know very well. List the major characters. Next to each, jot down briefly what he wants.

Now pick one of the characters. Go through a chapter of the novel (or the entire short story) and underline everything that seems to be backstory. Did the author rely mainly on brief details, isolated paragraphs of exposition, long expository stretches, or flashbacks?

EXERCISE 2

Pick three of your mini-bios. Jot down what each character wants. Do you see any plot ideas here?

EXERCISE 3

For one of the characters in exercise 2, imagine a backstory. How does her past relate to what she wants now?

EXERCISE 4

Write a scene of an argument between two people, using only dialogue and descriptions of setting. Print it out, triple-spaced. Now, by hand, insert between the lines of dialogue bits of bodily reactions, gestures, actions, and the POV character's thoughts. Are each character's emotions clearer?

Write a brief scene between a man applying for a job and an interviewer from the POV of the job applicant. Concentrate on showing us both the man's inner nervousness and his outer professional "cool."

chapter 4

[THE MOTIVATIONALLY COMPLICATED CHARACTER— BUT I'M A MESS INSIDE!]

So far we've spoken about motivation as if it were fixed and monolithic: I want this one thing, I have always wanted this one thing, I will always want this one thing. In fiction, as in life, this is, of course, completely untrue. People can want conflicting things, feel conflicting things, and change what they want or feel over time. Nobody is a monolith—although some people are considerably more complicated than others.

As a writer, you want to create complex characters because they feel more real to readers. Readers know that they themselves aren't simple inside and tend to dismiss or distrust one-dimensional characters. Of course, this depends on the genre you are writing. In some genres, such as adventure stories, the simple, all-conquering hero is fine. Nobody wants James Bond to have an oedipal fixation, and if he does, we don't want to hear about it.

Most fiction, however, will feature at least one complicated character. He may be complicated from conflicting desires, from confused basic drives, or from changes that the story forces on him. We'll consider each type of complication separately—although a character may, of course, have more than one source of complication. Even the sources of "being a mess inside" may be a mess.

VALUES, DESIRES, AND INNER TURMOIL

People often want more than one thing because people hold more than one value. What makes life—and fiction—interesting is when those values collide. You might, for instance, value being slim. You also value the pleasurable taste of sweet food. If you're trying to lose weight, these values will collide—as every dieter knows.

Conflicting values are at the heart of ethical dilemmas, and often of political ones, too. For instance, freedom of speech is an important American value. So is public safety. The courts have ruled that news reporters are not required to reveal their sources, even if those sources are criminal, because in this case, freedom of speech trumps the public safety of tracking down criminals. On the other hand, no one may yell "Fire!" in a fireless theater, because in that situation, public safety trumps freedom of speech.

Some of the most interesting stories involve conflicting values, which in turn cause conflicting motivations within a single person. Creating characters with this in mind can greatly enhance your fiction. Let's see how.

GIVING YOUR CHARACTERS TWO DESIRES

You can build more plausible, complex characters if they want not just one thing but two that are in conflict. This not only feels "real" to the reader because it echoes life but also gives you a chance to further characterize by showing us which value the character chooses.

For example, here is sixteen-year-old Rudy Jordache in Irwin Shaw's modern classic, *Rich Man, Poor Man*. Rudy has a crush on his high-school French teacher, Miss Lenaut. In the privacy of his bedroom, Rudy has just written a love letter, first in English and then translated into very bad French, to Miss Lenaut:

> He read the French version again with satisfaction. There was no doubt about it. If you wanted to be elegant, French was the language for it. He liked the way Miss Lenaut pronounced his name, correctly, Jordahsh, making it soft and musical, not Jawdake, as some people said it, or Jordash.
>
> Then, regretfully, he tore both letters into small pieces. He knew he was never going to send Miss Lenaut any letters. He had already written her six letters and torn them up because she would think he was crazy and tell the principal. And he certainly didn't want his father or mother or Gretchen or Tom to find any love letters in any language in his room.
>
> Still, the satisfaction was there. Sitting in the bare little room above the bakery, with the Hudson flowing a few hundred yards away, writing the letters was like a promise to himself. One day he would make long voyages, one day he would sail the river and write in new languages to beautiful women of high character, and the letters would actually be mailed.

This little vignette does not aid the plot because Rudy tears up his letter. Had he actually sent it, there might have been plot developments resulting from his action: Miss Lenaut's reaction, the principal summoning him and his parents, Rudy dropping French class, teasing from his brother and sister, etc. But none of this happened.

So why did Shaw include the tiny scene in his novel? He included it because he gained an enormous amount of characterization in three paragraphs. We have gained a genuine insight into Rudy's soul at sixteen. Specifically, we learn three things:

- We learn what Rudy values. Here he clearly holds two desires: to actually contact Miss Lenaut and to not make a fool of himself in front of her, the principal, or his family. These desires show us that Rudy is a romantic, but he is also careful of his image. And note that we are *shown* both these things, not told them. Rudy's values have been dramatized.
- We also learn which of the two values is most important to him. Rudy is a romantic, but not so much of one that he doesn't weigh consequences. In this small choice, image counts more with him than risking inappropriate love.
- We learn, through paragraph three, Rudy's emotional attitude toward the choice he has made. He's not bitter about it. Instead, he sees his unmailed letter as a "promise" for the future. Someday he will write love letters, mail them, love wonderful women, and travel. His attitude is one of hope and optimism, confident of future glory.

A great deal of characterization to pack into 182 words!

In addition, Shaw has gained something else by dramatizing Rudy's choice. He has foreshadowed much larger choices to come. Both these values, romanticism and concern for his image, will characterize Rudy throughout the novel. Each value will come in conflict with the other. And for most of his life, Rudy will choose concern for image over emotional risks.

You can use the dramatization of small incidents of conflicting values to build characterization for your actors. First, decide what two values or desires are in conflict for the character. Choose ones that indicate the personality you want readers to see. Then decide which value will "win." Finally, consider what your character's attitude toward his choice will be. Will it be hope of eventually attaining the alternative he didn't pick this time? Anger at having to choose? Resignation? Self-blame?

You may have realized that this structure—in which a character chooses between two alternatives, with a clearly defined attitude toward his choice—isn't confined to small vignettes to build characterization. Entire novels can also be built around the structure. At the heart of Tolstoy's *Anna Karenina,* for instance, is a choice Anna must make: her lover or her child. She values the adulterous romantic love she has with Vronsky; she also values living with her child. In nineteenth-century Russia, she cannot have both, and she chooses Vronsky. Her choice eats away at her and their love until her attitude toward everything has become so bitter that she kills herself.

But for the moment, let's focus on character rather than plot. For your character's choices to build characterization, you can't just tell us about them. You still must dramatize values, choices, and attitudes.

DOING, THINKING, FEELING: DRAMATIZING CHOICE

Essentially, you dramatize your character's choices the same way you dramatize anything else: with actions, thoughts, dialogue, backstory, and emotion.

Look again at the passage about Rudy Jordache's aborted love letter. Shaw has made Rudy's choice vivid by:

- Having him perform two definite actions: writing the love letter and tearing it up. This is more effective than if he had just mooned around about Miss Lenaut, confining his longing to his head. Whenever you can, have your characters *do* something to depict their values and choices.
- Sharing Rudy's thoughts with us. He thinks that French is "elegant," that Miss Lenaut is wonderful, and that someday he will have such romantic correspondence. We are inside Rudy's mind, privy to his inner musings. Notice, too, that the conflict of values is dramatized by having him also think about his other value, self-image: He won't send the letter because "she would think he was crazy and tell the principal." For a character juggling two values, both should feature in his thoughts.
- Showing us Rudy's emotions. He feels "satisfaction." We are first told this then shown it through concrete examples of all the things he's satisfied with: his own letter, the way Miss Lenaut pronounces his name, his daydreams about the future. We're also told he tears up the letter "regretfully" (another character might have torn it up angrily or despairingly).

- Giving a bit of backstory. Rudy wrote six earlier letters like this one to Miss Lenaut. Knowing this dramatizes the intensity of his longing; one letter might have been just the whim of a moment.

"LET ME MAKE THIS PERFECTLY CLEAR": USING DIALOGUE TO DRAMATIZE VALUES

Shaw doesn't use dialogue to depict Rudy's choices, but dialogue can be an effective way to dramatize your character's inner complications. There are two ways to do this: through the character's dialogue or through others' talking about him.

In Kazuo Ishiguro's wonderful novel, *The Remains of the Day*, Stevens has a conflict of values. A butler at a great English country house in the 1930s, he is not much given to analyzing his soul. Nor does he give rein to his emotions. However, he is under great stress: His father, also a servant in the house, has just died upstairs while a great dinner is taking place in the dining room downstairs. Stevens has just been informed of his father's death by the housekeeper, Miss Kenton:

> "Dr. Meredith has not yet arrived." Then for a moment she lowered her head and a sob escaped her. But almost immediately, she resumed her composure and asked in a steady voice, "Will you come up and see him?"
>
> "I'm very busy, just now, Miss Kenton."
>
> "In that case, Mr. Stevens, will you permit me to close his eyes?"
>
> "I would be most grateful if you would, Miss Kenton."
>
> She began to climb the staircase, but I stopped her, saying, "Miss Kenton, please don't think me unduly improper in not ascending to see my father in his deceased condition just at this moment. You see, I know my father would have wished me to carry on just now."
>
> "Of course, Mr. Stevens."
>
> "To do otherwise, I feel, would be to let him down."

Stevens is torn between two values: love and duty toward his father and his duties as butler. Reading this passage, it may not seem that he gives much weight to his father's death. But in the context of the entire book, we know that for Stevens to even *think* of justifying himself, as he does to Miss Kenton, is a sign of enormous inner conflict. Ordinarily, he would consider it far beneath him to explain his actions to her or anyone. His father's death matters to him, and his dialogue reveals that.

The same thing could have been accomplished by dialogue between, say, Miss Kenton and the doctor. She could comment that Stevens wishes he could come upstairs but is in the middle of serving at a great state occasion. She could cite some concrete and unprecedented lapses that Stevens, under great stress, has made. These would show us that the usually impeccable Stevens *is* in internal conflict; it is not only Miss Kenton's opinion. However, it's more effective to have Stevens—and *your* characters—talk directly about their complicated turmoil. If Ishiguro could find a way to have as repressed a man as Stevens do this, however obliquely, then you can, too.

TELLING IT STRAIGHT: USING EXPOSITION FOR COMPLICATED CHARACTERS

The riskiest way to present your characters' values, choices, and conflicting desires is by simply telling us about them. Fiction depends on dramatization, not exposition. Readers want to feel they're witnessing a story, watching it unfold step by step, present as the proverbial "fly on the wall." Exposition, in contrast, can often feel like reading a case history.

Still, there are writers who get away with it. They simply stop the story and tell us what's going on in their characters' complicated souls. How do they succeed at this? Why does it work?

There are two reasons. First, it works mostly when we're ready for it. In other words, if you explicate a character's conflicting values before we've seen those values collide in story time, we're apt to be uninterested. A better approach is to show us what the character has, doesn't have, needs, or does—and *then* explain. Although your exposition will still stop the story dead, and you still run the risk of sounding preachy, we'll be far more interested in what you have to say. Create the desire for explanations before you try to satisfy it.

The second criterion for successful exposition is that it should tell us things that are hard-to-impossible to dramatize.

T.H. White's novel *The Once and Future King* (the basis for the play and movie *Camelot*) succeeds on both counts. Here is a passage of pure exposition about Guinevere, twenty years into her adulterous affair with Lancelot:

> Guinevere's central tragedy was that she was childless. Arthur had two illegiti-
> mate children, and Lancelot had Galahad. But Guinevere—and she was the one
> of the three who most ought to have children, and who would have been best
> with children, and whom God had seemingly made for breeding lovely children—

she was the one who was left an empty vessel, a shore without a sea. This was what broke her when she came to the age at which her sea must finally dry. . . . It may be one of the explanations of her double love—perhaps she loved Arthur as a father, and Lancelot because of the son she could not have.

Before this passage, which occurs three-quarters of the way through the book, we have seen dramatized many of the events White is now theorizing about. We've seen the births of Arthur's children and Lancelot's son. We've seen Guinevere interact with these offspring when they're grown. We've seen how she behaves around Arthur and around Lancelot. Thus we're not listening to White's exposition in a vacuum. We have enough *dramatized* information to both understand and evaluate his ideas: Would Guinevere have been good with children? Does she in part treat Arthur like a father? Lancelot like a son? Is it plausible that childlessness might affect this particular woman, in this particular society, badly enough to "break" her?

Had White put this expository paragraph earlier, we wouldn't have known or cared. But he waited until we had seen a lot of these complicated characters' complicated stories so we could be interested in what it might mean.

In addition, the exposition doesn't simply recap what we could have deduced for ourselves from the book so far. Instead, it offers a fresh perspective on Guinevere and sees her from an angle we probably didn't consider. It's a new idea, not a rehash of previous dramatized scenes.

If you want to use expository sections to help us understand why your character is such a mess inside, be sure that your exposition:

- comes after your character has been sufficiently dramatized
- adds a new perspective to the interpretation of dramatized scenes
- is well written enough to compensate for its telling rather than showing

ANOTHER COMPLICATION: THE DUAL EMOTION

In addition to holding conflicting values, characters can also be complicated because they have conflicting emotional responses toward each other. These contradictory emotions are driven not so much by values as by other things: cultural preferences, previous experiences, or primitive drives.

We are all familiar with this phenomenon. You like your boss as a person, but you are also wary of her because she has a reputation for firing people easily, and a lively sense of self-preservation means you'd like to keep this job. So your feelings toward her are mixed—one part of you enjoys her company and wants to relax around her; another part whispers, *keep on guard*.

You might find you enjoy your boorish brother's crude jokes but also are repelled by them. This could be due to many different reasons: He's saying what you wish you could, you enjoy being the "proper" one and need a foil, or the jokes are actually genuinely funny but it's embarrassing hearing them from your brother. Whatever the cause, the result is a contradictory attraction/repulsion every time he tells another crude joke.

Characters in fiction, too, can feel mixed emotions about another situation. How do you portray that? You have three choices:

- You can show different emotions toward the same stimulus in different scenes.
- You can show conflicting emotion toward the stimulus in the same scene.
- You can use exposition to explain the contradiction.

I LOVED YOU YESTERDAY, I HATE YOU TODAY: ALTERNATING SCENES WITH ALTERNATING EMOTIONS

The first method is easier. In the best-selling 2002 novel *The Nanny Diaries*, by Emma McLaughlin and Nicola Kraus, the protagonist (called Nanny) cares for the four-year-old son of rich New Yorkers "Mr. and Mrs. X." They are horrible people, snobbish, insensitive, and exploitive of everyone, including Nanny. The authors portray incident after incident in which one or both parents neglect their son and abuse Nanny. They set impossible expectations, such as never permitting the child to nap and yet expecting her to prevent him from becoming cranky. They expect her to take on duties that should be theirs, such as caring for him alone for an entire weekend when he has a bad case of the flu. They then reprimand her for not following the rules (no eating in the bedroom, yet a sick child must stay in bed). They keep her too late and pay her less than agreed on.

Nanny, of course, dislikes them both; she stays because she feels sorry for, and attached to, the little boy. But if this was her only feeling toward her employers, it would make for a pretty one-note book: Nanny strives hard, Nanny is abused, Nanny strives hard, Nanny is abused, etc. It would also make for some thin characterization.

So the authors have given Nanny more complex reactions. She genuinely dislikes Mrs. X (and with reason), but she also has learned that Mr. X is having an affair with his very predatory assistant, and Nanny feels sorry for Mrs. X. Nanny's protective feelings are aroused, so much so that she tries to conceal evidence of the adultery, hunting down black lace panties (which the assistant deliberately left in the Xs' apartment) before Mrs. X finds them. Nanny's emotion is made plausible by the fact that although Mrs. X is awful, Mr. X is far worse; women need protection from his utterly ruthless self-centeredness.

Here Nanny helps Mrs. X try on dresses for a glamorous Valentine's Day dinner with her husband:

> "Great. Can you zip me?" she calls out. I put down my wine and go around to zip her into a stunningly sexy red sheath.
>
> "Yes," we both say as soon as she looks in the mirror.
>
> "It's beautiful," I say. And mean it. It's the first one that uses her proportions to advantage, making her look sylphlike, rather than emaciated. Looking at her reflection, I realize that I am rooting for her, rooting for them.

When Mr. X stands up his wife and has dinner with his assistant instead, Nanny tries awkwardly to comfort the heartbroken Mrs. X.

Nanny thus comes across as a person with conflicted feelings toward Mrs. X—and thus as a much more real and effective character. Authors McLaughlin and Kraus achieve this by varying Nanny's feelings by scene: a few scenes of pure dislike, then one of confused protectiveness, then more dislike and indignation resulting from Mrs. X's behavior, then another spark of pity and protectiveness. It works to add depth to what might otherwise have been a monotonous (although sometimes funny) recitation of class abuse. In fact, more than one reviewer wrote that Nanny's protectiveness toward Mrs. X was the most interesting aspect of the novel.

I LOVE YOU AND HATE YOU RIGHT THIS MINUTE: THE SINGLE SCENE WITH MIXED EMOTIONS

The other method to depict mixed emotional responses to another character is to show them occurring at the same time. This is more challenging, since characters need to seem consistent to be believable. If a person is feeling or behaving inconsistently (and we all do at times), it requires great care to make the contradictions feel plausible and not merely sloppy or confusing.

How do you do it well? First, you must make us understand the *reasons* behind the contradictory emotions. One way to do this is to include earlier scenes that portray each emotion separately before you show the character feeling the contradictory emotions occurring together.

For example, in David Marusek's acclaimed science-fiction novella "We Were Out of Our Minds With Joy," protagonist Sam Harger, an artist, is in love with rich and powerful Eleanor Starke. We are given incidents of their pleasure in each other, conversationally and sexually. Then Eleanor uses her personal computer system, an all-encompassing artificial intelligence in this high-tech future, to invade Sam's system. In the name of security, she not only snoops in his system, she alters and partially controls it. When Sam discovers this, he's furious and there's a terrible fight. Sam says, "There is no her and me. I'm dropping her."

But Eleanor besieges him with calls, flowers, and justifications. Now Sam feels conflicting emotions toward Eleanor: desire and profound distrust. In the space of two pages, he experiences all the following:

- When a friend says, "No one has so affected you as Eleanor Starke," Sam thinks, "I knew he was right, or nearly so. The only other woman that had so affected me was my first love, Janice Scholero. . . . Every woman in between was little more than a single wave in a warm sea of feminine companionship."
- Sam is still very angry with Eleanor: "I tried to tell her what was wrong. I recorded a message for her, a whole seething litany of accusation and scorn, but was too cowardly to post it."
- Sam yells at a reporter who says extremely negative things about Eleanor: " 'You don't know what you're talking about,' I yelled at the sim. 'El's not like that at all. You obviously never knew her. She's no saint, but she has a heart, and affection, and . . . and . . . go fuck yourself.' "
- Sam thinks, after refusing to communicate with Eleanor, "And yet, when El sent her farewell message—a glum El sitting in a museum somewhere, a wall-sized early canvas of mine behind her—I knew my life to be ashes and dirt."

In the next scene, they marry.

How does Marusek pull off this mass of messily conflicting emotions? First, by carefully preparing the ground so we understand the forces driving Sam both toward and away from Eleanor. Second, Marusek makes use, in these excerpts or in passages too long to quote, of all the techniques we discussed earlier for showing emotion: bodily responses, emotional actions, thoughts, and heated dialogue. Some of these are driven by Sam's positive feelings for Eleanor and some by his negative ones, adding up to a convincing, human confusion.

THE OVERMIND SPEAKS: EXPOSITION TO DEPICT EMOTIONAL CONFUSION

Finally, you can just drop into exposition to explain why a character feels so contradictorily toward another character. As with any exposition, you run the danger of seeming too detached and slow-paced. Also as with any exposition, the authorial intrusion can work if it has been prepared for with prior dramatization, is well written, and offers a fresh perspective.

To return to *The Once and Future King,* consider T.H. White explaining the growing complexity Lancelot and Guinevere feel toward each other. Like David Marusek's characters, the lovers have just had a quarrel and then made up:

> The Queen dried her tears and then looked at him, smiling like a spring shower. In a minute they were kissing, feeling like the green earth refreshed by rain. They thought that they understood each other once more—but their doubt had been planted. Now, in their love, which was stronger, there were the seeds of hatred and fear and confusion growing at the same time: for love can exist with hatred, each preying on the other, and this is what gives it its greatest fury.

Here we are being told, not shown, what Guinevere and Lancelot experience. It would have been difficult, if not impossible, for White to dramatize in one conciliatory kiss everything he says his characters feel: love, hatred, doubt, fear, and confusion—especially since the lovers themselves don't fully realize how their relationship is changing.

If you use exposition to describe complex emotions, first be clear in your mind what that complexity is. Then state it as lucidly and briefly as you can.

Finally, go over your exposition to slightly "elevate" the writing; that is, make it more complex and dramatic than the rest of the story to compensate for the lack of immediacy inherent in exposition. White, for instance, ends with a poetic metaphor, comparing love and hate to "prey" for each other, their battle rising to "fury." In chapter nine we'll look in greater depth at metaphors for vehicles of emotion. For now, just keep in mind that heightened writing must *not* go overboard on fancy language. Your exposition should be only slightly more formal and figurative than the rest of the story's style. Heighten it too much and you risk, at best, a break in tone or, at worst, parody.

?

Question:

What if my character's desires are not only in conflict but irrational, since he's insane?

Answer:

Literature has a long history of characters who are frankly insane (Mrs. Rochester in *Jane Eyre*) or else judged that way because their values are so different from the surrounding society's (Bernard in *Brave New World*). Plus, myriad characters' sanity is a judgment call, with different supporting characters rendering different verdicts (Captain Queeg in *The Caine Mutiny*).

The guidelines for loony characters with conflicting values are the same as for "sane" ones. Dramatize each value thoroughly, even if it makes no sense. The woman who thinks she's being pursued by space aliens who want to dissect her brain should be depicted with all her genuine terror made as compelling as you can. Her deep belief in interstellar cooperation should also be dramatized, perhaps through her attempts to give them other brains (a mouse's? a cat's? her husband's?) for scientific purposes. Remember, these beliefs are as sincere and passionate for her as are yours for you. So try to "become the character" while writing her, even if she scalps her husband and leaves his brain on a pie tin in the backyard for convenient spaceship pickup.

In summary, whenever a character holds mixed feelings toward another character, here are the steps to take:

- Identify in your own mind what emotions the character is feeling.
- Check to see if you have done the groundwork for these mixed feelings by dramatizing the causes of each. If not, you may need to go back and add one or more earlier scenes.
- Decide if you want to portray the two contradictory feelings in alternate scenes, in the same scene, through exposition, or in some combination of these. You might, for instance, use alternating single-emotion scenes followed by a passage of exposition, as White does.
- Include sufficient emotional indicators for us to share *each* emotion the character feels.

WHEN MESSY IS TOO MESSY: THE IMPLAUSIBLE CONTRADICTION

So far we've spoken as if any contradictory motivations, values, and feelings can be made to sound reasonable if only you approach them correctly. Alas, this is not true. Not even the most careful planning or energetic writing will make us accept character contradictions if they just don't seem to make common sense.

It's not that you can't create a nun who commits first-degree murder. You can. What you cannot do is create a nun whom you depict as sweet, pious, dedicated, and meek for six chapters and *then* have her commit a murder. Character contradictions like this must, even more than ordinarily conflicting human feelings, be carefully prepared for. A lot of verbiage—an extreme amount—is needed. We need to see a backstory: What led her to the sisterhood, and where did she acquire the desire to kill? We need repeated scenes showing she's capable of extreme actions. We need some way to reconcile her sweet mildness with murder. A brain tumor might do it, or a mental illness, or a mind-altering drug, but probably not much else. You'd be better off creating a nonmild, distinctly unsweet, inner-enraged nun in the first place.

In a less dramatic vein, the neglectful mother who "suddenly realizes" the error of her ways and comes through for her kids doesn't convince, either. She needs a reason to "suddenly realize," and that means you've both given her one *and* previously shown us that she's capable of change. Ask yourself: Have I dropped enough hints that she has the capacity to sustain major change? If not, you may need to rethink your characterization from the beginning.

One help in thinking about characters is the emotional mini-bio (seen on page sixty-four), a counterpart to the factual mini-bio you created earlier. Fill out one for each major character in your story, even if you don't need the information for your plot. The point is to gain insights that will help clarify your thinking about this fictional person you are striving to make real.

RECAP: COMPLICATED CHARACTERS

Interesting characters often hold two conflicting values and/or desires; which they choose helps readers to know their personalities and beliefs. Just as important as a character's choice is his attitude toward that choice. Small choices should be consistent with, and sometimes foreshadow, larger choices the character makes later in the story.

EMOTIONAL MINI-BIO

Name _____

What three or four things does this person value most in life? (i.e., success, money, family, God, love, integrity, power, peace and quiet)

_____   _____

_____   _____

What three things does he most fear?

_____   _____

_____

What is this person's basic underlying attitude about life?
(i.e. "Things will usually turn out all right," or "They're all out for themselves," or "It's best to expect nothing because then you won't be disappointed," etc.)

_____

What does she need to know about another person in order to accept that other as "all right" and trustworthy?

_____

_____

What would cause this person more pain than anything else possible?

_____

What would this person consider the most wonderful thing that could ever happen to him?

_____

What three words would she use to describe herself, accurate or not?

_____   _____   _____

How accurate is his self-description? _____

What organization most embodies this person's values? (i.e., Mensa, Daughters of the American Revolution, her church, Aryan Pride, PTA)

_____

Does he belong to this group? _____ If not, why not?

_____

Dramatize a character's choices through his actions, thoughts, bodily emotional indicators, and dialogue. Bits of backstory can also help us understand his choices. Exposition works to explain characters' value conflicts if (1) you've prepared for it through dramatization, and (2) it offers a new perspective that dramatization alone could not show.

When a character feels two emotions at once toward another character or event, it often works to dramatize each in subsequent scenes. You can also show both emotions in the same scene. The latter, more challenging method requires that you have previously dramatized the reasons behind each emotion so neither feels arbitrary. However, characters' inner contradictions must not stretch our credibility so far that we reject the situation.

An emotional bio on each major character can help clarify your thinking about that character's values and beliefs.

EXERCISE 1

Write down the names of three real people you know very well. Next to each list at least four things they value. For each person, try to imagine a dramatic situation, suitable for fiction, in which two of his or her values might come in conflict. For example, if your sister inadvertently witnessed a gang killing, her desire to protect her children might conflict with her desire to do the right thing and testify in court. Which value would each person choose?

EXERCISE 2

Choose a story or novel you know very well. List the two or three main characters. Do any of them seem to have a conflict between two values or desires in the story? If so, locate the scenes in which the character demonstrates each one. Then find and study the scene in which he chooses between the two values. How does the author indicate his inner turmoil?

EXERCISE 3

List five values you believe in. Can you imagine a situation in which any of them might come in conflict with another? Which would you choose? Is there a story here that you might want to write?

Write two brief letters home from soldiers in a war (pick any war you wish). Both soldiers enlisted. One soldier's attitude toward this should be positive; despite hardship, he feels he made the right choice. The other soldier's attitude should be bitter and regretful. How does attitude determine what details each person includes in his letter?

Write an argument between a parent and a difficult teenage child. Strive to show that the parent is experiencing at least two different emotions toward this child. Make use of gestures, bodily reactions, actions, thoughts, and dialogue but no exposition. Let dramatization carry the complexity.

chapter 5

[SHOWING CHANGE IN YOUR CHARACTERS—IF I KNEW THEN WHAT I KNOW NOW]

In addition to having multiple emotions at a given time, some of your characters may alter during the course of your story. In chapter one we referred to characters whose values and feelings alter over time as changers. Other characters may not change significantly in personality or outlook, but their motivations may nonetheless change as the story progresses from situation to situation. Both changers and stayers can have progressive motivations.

Confused? Don't be; it's really not hard. Characters come in four types:

- Characters who never change, neither in personality nor motivation. They are what they are, and they want what they want.
- Characters whose basic personality remains the same; they don't grow or change during the story. But what they want changes as the story progresses ("progressive motivation").
- Characters who change throughout the story, although their motivation does not.
- Characters who change throughout the story *and* their motivation progresses.

Because character and plot are intertwined, we'll refer to these four as "character/plot patterns."

THE POPEYE PERSONALITY: "I YAM WHAT I YAM"

Sometimes a character will have a single overriding motivation for the entire length of a story or novel, plus a strong personality that does not alter much. James Bond is a good example. He's a stayer who starts out resourceful, suave, unflappable, and smart. At the end of each of Ian Fleming's novels, Bond is still resourceful, suave, unflappable, and smart.

Nor does his motivation alter. At the start of the book he receives a mission, and his goal is to pursue this mission until it's over, at which point the book ends. There may be interim temporary goals (not getting eaten by alligators, protecting the girl), but they are all part of the single overriding motivation.

It isn't only adventure fiction to which this applies. In John Steinbeck's classic *Of Mice and Men*, both protagonists, George and Lennie, retain the same motivation throughout. They want to earn enough to buy a small farm of their own. Their personalities, too, remain the same: George the planner and caretaker, dim-witted Lennie the well-meaning bumbler who brings them both to tragedy.

If you are writing this type of book, your job is to present to us the character and the goal clearly and forcefully fairly early on. Then unfold your tale; we'll know who your man is and why he's doing what he's doing. This leaves us (and you the writer!) free to complicate other things besides the hero, such as the plot, the conspiracies, or the hardware.

Please note, though, that an unaltering character with an unaltering goal can still feel more than one emotion *at a given moment*. James Bond might, for instance, feel attraction to one of the "Bond women" at the same time that he distrusts her (often with good cause). If your character feels two conflicting things toward another character, use the techniques in the previous chapter to show this in the scene in which it happens. Then—and this is the important part—*return in the next scene to the main goal*.

This tells us that the basic situation is unchanged. Although Bond, for instance, has just made love with a woman, she hasn't fundamentally changed him. He is not altered in either his personality or motivation as a result of her attractions.

PROGRESSIVE MOTIVATION: THE WORLD AS MOVING TARGET

Another type of story features a character who doesn't change in basic personality or beliefs, but what she wants changes as a result of story events.

These characters are often of two types: heroes or villains. The heroic ones are essentially admirable characters from the beginning of the story. They don't change because the author clearly doesn't feel they need to; they embody virtues he wishes to advocate. Two disparate examples are Charlotte Brontë's Jane Eyre (*Jane Eyre*) and Ayn Rand's Howard Roark (*The Fountainhead*).

Jane is spunky, plain, passionate, and moral, even as a child. She believes in the dignity of all individuals, including those at the bottom of the Victorian power structure. We see this early in the book when she stands up for herself, for school friend Helen Burns, or anyone being abused. At the end of the book, she's still doing it.

However, as Jane grows up, her immediate motivations change. At first, she merely wants to survive the brutalities of her terrible aunt and then of the boarding school that the aunt sends her to. Later, she wants a new teaching position to broaden her horizons. Later still, she falls in love with her employer, Mr. Rochester, and wants him—until she learns the truth about him and wants to escape his home. Still more motivations follow.

Howard Roark, even more resolute and heroic than Jane Eyre, never really changes, either. He just rises, without flinching, above the failures and stupidities of the rest of the world. His initial motivation is to design buildings that suit him, with no outside influences dictating his designs; his next motivation is to blow up those buildings because the builders changed some of his architectural plans. Both actions proceed from an unchanged and unshakable conviction of his own superiority.

The point is that if your character is basically heroic, you may not want him to change. In that case, you construct the story this way:

- Your character is trying to live his life, but the outside world imposes an obstacle.
- The obstacle gives the character a motivation: fight it, flee it, change it, or adapt to it.
- That first motivation is met by a consequence, which in turn supplies another motivation (the consequence of Jane's seeking a new teaching post is meeting Mr. Rochester).
- That motivation encounters obstacles, etc.

You may recognize this pattern; it's sometimes referred to as "the classic plot pattern." (Actually, as we're discussing here, it's only one of four possible character/plot patterns.) Its success, as in the "Popeye" character pattern, depends on a strong, interesting character. Once you have that, you set up initial circumstances for her to cope with and then have her motivation change as consequences flow.

However, as with the first type of character, a basically unchanging personality may nonetheless experience changing or conflicting emotions at any given moment. When Jane Eyre's cousin, St. John Rivers, asks her to marry him in order to accompany him to India on his missionary work, Jane has very mixed reactions:

> Of course (as St. John once said) I must seek another interest in life to replace the one lost: is not the occupation he now offers me truly the most glorious man can adopt or God assign? Is it not, by its noble cares and sublime results, the one best calculated to feel the void left by uptorn affections and demolished hopes? I believe I must say, Yes—and yet I shudder. Alas! If I join St. John, I abandon half myself.

During the rest of this scene, Jane will also feel awe, disdain, humility, dread, rebellion, scorn, and hurt. Mixed emotions indeed! But her basic personality and beliefs do not waiver: She is a person who wants more than a loveless marriage, even if that marriage is dedicated to God's work. Jane wants love.

At the other end of the heroism spectrum, some villains have unchanging personalities but changing motivations. They start out venial, greedy, evil, or destructive, and they end up the same way. This is true whether they win or lose. Along the way, however, their motivations often enlarge: They become greedier for greater things, destructive on a larger scale, or want to succeed at different, grander schemes of evil. Or, as with heroes, their motivations may change as a result of story events.

Thus, your villain may start out wanting to rob an armored car. He succeeds, but in the course of the robbery kills a police officer. Now his goal is to elude capture. While pursuing him, your detective is forced to shoot the villain's nephew and protégé, who has drawn a gun on the cop. Now your villain has an additional motivation: revenge on the detective. The stakes have risen with each story event and its consequence.

CHANGERS WITH A SINGLE MOTIVATION: OREGON OR BUST

In many stories, a major character changes significantly. The character has a single motivation and may expend enormous effort to reach it, like those covered-wagon pioneers who risked everything to trek west. However, during the process of achieving (or not achieving) this overriding goal, the character's basic personality and/or beliefs alter. In fact, this alteration is often the point of the story.

For example, a young woman has as her motivation the desire to get out of prison. She forms this desire as soon as she is incarcerated, in the first chapter. The book ends when she gets out, for whatever reason: Her time has been served, she successfully escapes, or her lawyer wins the appeal. However, this character is a changer, which means that while her goal has stayed constant, her personality/belief structure has not.

For instance, as a result of her interactions with the other inmates, maybe she's changed from a superior, scornful snob to one who feels that she and the other women are basically the same. She's gone from scorn to empathy, from disdain to friendship. All the while that she's been working on getting out of prison, prison has also been working on her.

If you write this type of character, there are a few critical points to remember:

- Her character change must come about in response to story events. Create events that could logically lead the character to change in the ways you want. "Devise incidents," W. Somerset Maugham said when asked the secret of writing. This is what he meant: You must think up those plot events that will affect your characters enough for them to react with genuine change.
- Your character must have emotional responses to these events. We must see the emotional responses through use of all the indicators discussed in chapter three.
- The character change, too, must be dramatized. We can't simply be told, "Abby now sympathized with her cell mate." We must be shown Abby's change of heart through things she does that she didn't do before, such as giving and accepting help from this once-despised cellmate. This is called *validation*, and it is essential for all changing characters.
- You must include a final validation at the end of the story so we know that your character's change is not just temporary, but permanent. Usually this ending validation is on a larger scale than what has gone before. For instance, instead of just helping her cell mates with daily frustrations, your protagonist, now out of jail herself, does everything she can to improve the situations of those still inside.

Readers find this kind of story intrinsically satisfying. The single motivation throughout gives the book unity and comprehensibility, and the changing character satisfies the need for fiction to make a comment on life. In the case of the prison story, that comment is positive: People can grow nicer.

You might, however, also use the same character/plot pattern to make a negative observation about the world. In that case, the character with a single goal would, in the course of failing to achieve it, change from naïve innocence to "sadder but wiser." For example, this is the structure of Edith Wharton's *The House of Mirth*. Protagonist Lily Bart sustains the same motivation throughout the book: to marry for money. She does not succeed. Only at the end, both of the novel and of her life, do events force her to change, and then she realizes that she might have had a better life if she'd paid less attention to luxury and more to love. By then, however, it's too late.

The single-motivation, changing character also works in stories in which the character succeeds in getting what he wants but is disappointed in his success. These are the "be careful what you wish for because you might get it" stories. The change in the character can be one of two types. In one, he realizes that he's paid too high a price for success, at which point he may or may not change his life. Or, he never realizes this (or at least never admits it), but he changes to grow regretful or bitter as a result of getting what he thought he wanted.

CHANGERS WITH PROGRESSIVE MOTIVATIONS: WHO AM I AND WHAT DO I WANT NOW?

This is the most complex fictional pattern. A character's goals change throughout the story, and so does her personality/belief system. This is confusing for the character. Your goal is to keep it from also hopelessly confusing the reader.

Consider, for instance, Ensign Willie Keith from Herman Wouk's Pulitzer Prize-winning novel of World War II, *The Caine Mutiny*. Willie undergoes a lot of personal change during the war. He also changes motivation often. In sequence:

- Willie wants to avoid being drafted, so he joins the Navy.
- Willie wants to avoid difficult duty, so he tries to avoid dangerous ships like minesweepers.
- Willie wants to transfer off the minesweeper *Caine*.
- Willie wants to survive the *Caine*'s tyrannical, irrational Captain Queeg.
- Willie wants to get rid of Queeg and joins a mutiny.
- Willie wants to avoid court-martial and dishonorable discharge.

Plot and Character Change

Many writers have made "comprehensive" lists of the basic plot structures in fiction. In 1945 Georges Polti published *Thirty-Six Dramatic Situations*, which he claimed covered all of literature. Other categorizers have decided there are six basic plots, or twelve, or fifteen. Author Robert A. Heinlein claimed there were only three, because plot arises from character change and there are only three ways people can change:

- The "boy meets girl" plot, in which a person changes because of the influence another person exerts on his life. The influencer may be a lover but could also be a teacher, a friend, a child, or anyone else with whom deep bonds are formed. The prototype is *Beauty and the Beast*, in which the beast changes because Beauty accepts him.
- The "little tailor" plot, in which circumstances force a person to discover within himself strengths he did not know he possessed (the little tailor of the fairy tale slays giants).
- The "man learns better" plot, in which a character changes because he tests his previous ideas about the world against reality. Often he ends up sadder but wiser. King Midas learns too late that he would rather have his daughter than all of the world's gold.

Do any of these motivations for character change spark your imagination? If so, then Heinlein's classifications work for you.

- Willie wants, finally, to become a good naval officer and defend his country as well as he can.

From these changing motivations, you can also see Willie Keith's internal changes. He moves from being self-centered, looking for the easy way out, to an assumption of duty and, even more important, to feeling that duty is worthwhile.

If you have a character with both progressive motivation and internal changes, congratulations. You've got a strong character to carry an ambitious book. To keep all these changes from seeming arbitrary, however, it's important to follow all the guidelines set out above for single-motivation changers. Your character's changes must be dramatized, come about as a result of dramatized events, be accompanied by plausibly rendered emotions, and be validated by subsequent actions on his part.

PORTRAYING MOTIVATIONS

We've talked a great deal about dramatizing emotion. Now let's turn to dramatizing its source, motivation.

For characters with a single, story-long goal and for characters with different consecutive goals, it is *your* job as writer to make sure we always know what those characters' goals *are*. There are several ways to do this:

- The character can think about her goal, as Jane Eyre does:

    I had had no communication or letter with the outer world: school-rules, school-duties, school-habits and notions, and voices, and phrases, and faces, and costumes, and preferences, and antipathies; such was what I knew of existence. And now I felt that it was not enough: I tired of the routine of eight years in one afternoon. I desired liberty.

- The character can have his goal dictated to him by others: "Detective, you're assigned to the Riesling murder case."
- The character can talk about her goal with others, as Lennie and George do in *Of Mice and Men*:

    "I forget some a' the things. Tell about how it's gonna be."
    "Someday we're gonna get the jack together and we're gonna have a little house and a cow and some pigs and—"
    "An live off the fatta the lan'," Lennie shouted.

- Others can talk about the character's goals so we readers can "overhear" them. This works well for characters who are neither introspective nor talkative: "Jack is trying so hard to get his brother's approval, and Cal just ignores him."
- The character can demonstrate his motivation through two or, preferably, three attempts to accomplish something, such as getting Cal's attention. More than one attempt is necessary to establish that this is not just habit, politeness, or rules but instead something the character really wants.

There are no hard-and-fast rules about which of these techniques works best for any particular plot. Try one in your story and, if it seems insufficient to illuminate motivation, add another.

THE KEY TO JUGGLING MOTIVATION
AND CHARACTER CHANGE

All of this can, I know, sound overwhelming. Dramatizing motivation, dramatizing emotion, dramatizing change, creating sharp concrete details that characterize—and doing it all simultaneously—can seem too much to juggle (not to mention also "becoming the reader" to see how it all looks to someone else). But there is a way to keep control of your material. It is, in fact, the key to keeping control of many other elements of fiction as well, such as plot and emotional arc.

The key is this: *Write in scenes.*

You don't have to think about the whole book at once, the entire emotional arc, or the progressive motivations of six different characters. All you have to do right now is write this *one* scene. And the way you do that well is by knowing, before you write, exactly what the scene is supposed to accomplish.

Let us assume that you're writing the novel about the lady who left six million dollars to a veterinary hospital (remember her?). You sit down at your keyboard to write the scene in which the woman's son finds a copy of her will in her desk (the original is with her lawyer). The son reads the will. Before you plunge into the action, take a moment to think about what you want this scene to *do*. If you're a list-making person, write it down. Purposes of this scene could include:

- conveying to the reader the contents of the will (the bequest to the veterinary hospital)
- characterizing the son as greedy, selfish, and furious
- giving the son motivation: he wants to prove that his mother was legally incompetent so he can break the will

Now you know what you need the scene to do. Ask yourself: How can I dramatize these things, not just talk about them? What can this guy do to *show* the reader what's going on inside him?

Ideas start to occur to you. Jot them down:

- He tears the room apart in his eagerness to find the will.
- He finds it and reads it. (Reproduce document in story text.)
- He kicks the cat, throws a chair, and curses.
- He makes himself calm down—takes a walk, has a drink or a cigarette—while searching his mind for a way to break the will. He decides on

incompetence and realizes this is stronger if he sets the legalities in motion before anyone knows he's seen the will.

- He carefully replaces the will and puts the room back together.
- He calls the lawyer to ask "if Mama left a will" and to express concern to her about "the neighbor's reports" of his mother's failing mind.

Now you're ready to write this scene. Just *this* scene, in which you concentrate fully on specific, meaningful actions that will advance the plot, characterize the son, and set the stage for scenes to come.

As you write, ideas might come to you that differ from the ones on your list. If they're better, use them. The list is a guide, not a straightjacket. As a guide, it will keep you focused on motivation, emotion, character, and plot.

Our hypothetical scene involved only one person (plus a phone call). Most scenes, however, feature two or more people—and that means many more ways to develop character. The next chapter explores other possibilities.

RECAP: CHANGING GOALS AND EMOTIONS

Characters may or may not change their basic beliefs and reactions over the course of your story. They also may or may not change motivation, progressing to a new goal when the old one is fulfilled or thwarted. The writer's job is always to present both single and progressive goals clearly so readers know at all times what the character wants. Present these motivations through dialogue, thoughts, action, and/or exposition.

All character changes must come about as plausible consequences of story events. A character who genuinely changes needs a *validation scene*, usually at the end of the story, to dramatize that the change is permanent.

Within a given scene, any character, even one with fixed goals, may feel more than one emotion at a time. Follow such mixed-emotion scenes with a scene dramatizing motivation so readers can tell if the character's motivation has changed.

The key to juggling emotion, motivation, and character changes is to write in scenes. Before writing, decide all the things the scene should accomplish. This will help you include all your aims and feel more in control of the scene.

EXERCISE 1

Pick one of the following: a bank robber, kidnapper, war hero, war deserter, or poor man marrying a rich woman. For your choice, write down three different motivations someone might have for this action. Which looks most interesting to write about?

EXERCISE 2

Pick a second character from the list above. Try to imagine a person committing this action for a single strong reason. Now list three possible, different consequences this action might have. Study the possible consequences. Might any of them lead to a change in motivation? To what?

EXERCISE 3

Think of a person in your life toward whom you have mixed emotions. Write down the feelings you have toward him. Now consider how you express these emotions: what actions you take, what you say to him, what thoughts you have, how your body reacts when you interact. Do you ever express both emotions during the same interaction? Are you sending "mixed messages"? How? (Note: The point of this exercise is not personal therapy; it is to make you more aware of human complexity in order to portray it in fiction.)

EXERCISE 4

Think of someone you know who has genuinely changed in some significant way over the course of your acquaintance. How do you know that person has changed? What validating actions proved it to you?

Now answer the questions for a favorite fictional character.

EXERCISE 5

Think of someone you wish *would* change. What validating action would be enough to convince you that she has?

chapter 6

[PROTAGONISTS IN GENRE FICTION—FROM LOVERS TO STARSHIP CAPTAINS]

Genre fiction, which collectively accounts for most fiction sales, includes mysteries, thrillers, romance, westerns, and science fiction. These categories, which have their own sections in bookstores, are partly marketing inventions. A mystery novel, for example, may include a romance between major characters. A "mainstream literary" novel like Ann Patchett's *Bel Canto*, winner of the PEN/Faulkner Award, is built around the type of hostage situation more typical of a thriller. Science fiction often includes mysteries to be solved. Writers are frequently not as interested in rigid classifications as are publishers.

Thus, characters in genre fiction are, foremost, characters. That means that everything said so far applies to them: Some are changers and some are stayers; some have single motivations and some complex ones; all have backstories and dwelling places and families somewhere. Writing genre fiction in no way excuses you from creating multidimensional, interesting characters.

But it does present you with additional requirements and problems. Editors and readers both bring definite expectations to their favorite genres. The woman picking up a romance wants certain things from the characters in her newly purchased book. Knowing what these expectations are can help you create characters that she—or the mystery reader, or science fiction reader—will want to spend four hundred pages with.

ROMANCE NOVELS: I LOVE YOU IN A PARTICULAR WAY

Romance novels are big business. They account for 55 percent of popular paperback fiction sales, totaling more than one billion dollars per year. A lot of people want to read about love.

Of all genres, romance writers get the most explicit character guidelines from publishers. The romance field, like other genre writing, is divided into subgenres: romantic suspense, contemporary romance, Regency, and sensual romance are only a few. The key to creating a successful romance character is knowing what readers want from their favorite subgenre.

For instance, Regency romances (set in 1811 to 1820, when the future George IV ruled as regent for his mad father) almost never involve actual sex, since at that time respectable young women stayed chaste. (If you wish to write a sexy romance set during the British Regency, it is reclassified as a historical romance.) A Regency romance heroine therefore engages in a lot of repartee; Regencies are the wittiest of the romance subgenres.

In addition to subgenres, publishers create imprints or lines with their own specific character requirements. The Harlequin Presents imprint, for instance, wants "spirited, independent heroines" in a contemporary setting and "breathtakingly attractive, larger-than-life" heroes. This is not the place to try your romance between a sweet, plain, overweight girl and the class nerd.

The best way to find out what character requirements exist for each imprint is to contact the publisher directly for author guidelines. Sometimes these are detailed enough to specify character ages and situations, sometimes not. However, nearly all romance heroines share at least these characteristics:

- They are pretty, or at least piquantly attractive. Romance readers are mostly women, and romance novels work as a combination of fantasy fulfillment and reader identification. Readers want to identify with a physically attractive character.
- They are moral. Romance heroines may make mistakes or bad decisions, but they are fundamentally moral women. The sleazy adventuress may work as the protagonist of a historical romance (such as Kathleen Winsor's *Forever Amber*) but not of a category romance. Create characters who try to do the right thing.
- They are single. Romance readers do not, by and large, approve of adultery.
- They are interested in something besides love. Romance happens to them rather than being an all-consuming initial motivation (which can look predatory). Your heroine should start the book with a definite goal: to run a ranch, become a doctor, campaign for a United States senator, or be the best kindergarten teacher she can be.

- They should be lovable, since they will end up loved by the hero. Genre romance characters always end up with a happy ending, and readers want to know they deserve it.

ROMANCE II: THE INDIVIDUAL IN LOVE

Within these givens, you create a successful romance heroine the same way you do any other character. Start with the basics: her name, appearance, and clothing. That should lead you to where she came from. Dovetail her back-story with what she wants now. For instance, perhaps she grew up on a ranch and wants to run one now. Or she decided very young to become a doctor, was wildly encouraged in this by her upper-middle-class family, and now has doubts about whether medical school is really right for her.

Once you have her basic situation in mind, try to *become* the character. What does she feel about her situation? How does she express her feelings: with fiery passion or in caring tact? Toward whom can she demonstrate these characteristics very soon, preferably in your opening scene?

Next, turn your attention to the hero. Once he was required to be, in a classic phrase, "older, richer, taller" than the heroine. These requirements have eased—but not the requirement that he be someone the female reader would like to fall in love with herself. This means that he must personify the "five Ss":

- single
- sexy
- sweet (although this may not be evident at first)
- smart
- solvent, if not actually rich

To create this desirable male, start with his situation. It must be one that will naturally bring him into involvement, and probably into conflict, with hers. If she wants to buy a ranch, he might be the owner who doesn't want to sell or the owner of an adjoining ranch who would like the land for himself. If she is the long-lost daughter of a rich playboy, as in Judith McNaught's best-seller *Night Whispers*, then the hero can be the playboy's next-door neighbor, who is practically engaged to the heroine's new half-sister.

Your hero's situation will not only determine the plot but also suggest some of his personal characteristics. A working ranch owner will probably be hardy, outdoorsy, casual in dress, and more interested in cattle than ballet (although it might be interesting if he loved ballet). The key here is to create a character that is individual—but not too individual. Millions of women should be able to fall vicariously in love with him. If he's too eccentric, they won't.

In short, romance writers must create primary characters who both are individuals and yet do not stray too far from being ideals. That can present quite a challenge, so give it considerable thought before you begin your novel.

MYSTERIES: THE ECCENTRIC FLOURISHES

The mystery novel, like the romance novel, comprises many subcategories, including police procedurals, courtroom dramas, private eyes, historical mysteries, and "soft" or "village" mysteries in which the detectives are amateurs. The wide range of subgenres naturally gives rise to a wide range of characters; Miss Marple does not, on the surface, bear much resemblance to either the classic *noir* detectives like Sam Spade or George Pelecanos's tough private investigator Derek Strange. But look below the surface and some common characteristics emerge, dictated by the form itself.

All mysteries concern the solving of crimes, and in nearly all of them, the crime is solved and the perpetrator caught. In the exceptions, such as Thomas Perry's Edgar-winning *The Butcher's Boy*, the criminal may never be caught but the detectives at least give it a thorough, resounding try. As successful mystery writer Claudia Bishop (*A Puree of Poison*) says, "People read mysteries for a wide variety of reasons, one of which is because they're usually reassuring. Most reaffirm a moral value: Crime is bad and if you try it, you'll pay. Justice, although not always the law, generally triumphs."

This is what readers expect. There are exceptions, of course: Consider Patricia Highsmith's Tom Ripley (*The Talented Mr. Ripley*), who literally gets away with murder—several times. Still, most mysteries end with the criminal being caught, and this can create problems for writers. Because the boundaries of the genre demand that the good guy win, mysteries can hamper character development, especially if the book is part of a series. We don't want Rex Stout's detective Nero Wolfe to suddenly become slim and courteous, nor Janet Evanovich's Stephanie Plum to learn how to dress tastefully. In fact, we usually don't want series detectives (and most mysteries do exist within the framework of a series) to learn much of anything at all. Then they might change radically, and we want to read about them as they are.

This can limit writers. If their major characters are not going to be significantly altered, then writers must find other ways to keep them interesting.

The temptation for village mysteries is to provide an oddball job and a set of mannerisms, and for "hard" mysteries to reach for an off-the-rack tough detective. The result can be characters close to caricatures.

A good writer, however, goes far beyond that. There is a growing body of mysteries with literate, complex characters. As with romance, the limitations of the form can present a challenge that leads to the creation of memorable protagonists.

A strong example is Andrew Dalziel, Reginald Hill's Yorkshire inspector in such books as *The Wood Beyond* and *On Beulah Height*. Through skillful characterization, Hill creates a protagonist who embodies the contradictions of real people: both brutal and sensitive, a shrewd politician with a rigorous sense of justice. Moreover, both Dalziel and his close relationships evolve over the life of the series. An aspiring mystery writer would do well to read Hill's books to see how he creates this fullness of character within the limitations of a series.

So what about the protagonist of *your* mystery? Here, based on reader expectations of the genre, are the requirements:

Your character must be curious. People with very conventional minds, unwilling to examine their own or anybody else's ideas, do not solve crimes (which is why most street cops never make detective). Your character must be interested enough in situations outside his own affairs to pursue an investigation and flexible enough to take it in new directions. This is especially true if the protagonist is an amateur, or else why doesn't she just turn the whole thing over to the cops and stay out of it?

Your character must be reasonably independent and self-reliant. Dependent, passive people do not see a crime investigation all the way through; they expect others to do that.

If your character is an amateur, he must have convincing motivation to pursue the investigation. What of his is threatened: his livelihood, his family, his premises, his reputation, his life? Does he distrust that local law enforcement could handle this case, and if so, why? Is he arrogant enough to think he can do it better? Does he have specialized knowledge that they do not? Is he naturally a busybody? Does the case just sort of fall in his lap? Mystery readers are pretty forgiving of the implausibility of, say, dog trainers solving six murder cases in a row, but they're not totally credulous. You will need logical motivation for this person to be engaged in this activity.

If your character is a professional, then this requirement falls on you: Know the terrain. Mystery readers tend to read a lot of their favorite genre.

Law Enforcement and the Electronic Age

One of the dangers of writing mysteries and thrillers is datedness. If your models are Sam Spade and very early novels of Ed McBain, your stories will not be convincing because law enforcement procedures have changed since the 1950s, let alone the 1930s. Surveillance, deduction, and interrogation still exist, but increasingly the computer is used for everything from tracing a weapon to locating a murderer. For your professional to be convincing, he must regularly search databases, and you must know which ones are available to him. This means careful preparatory research on your part. A brief sampling:

- The National Crime Information Center (NCIC) includes a huge database maintained by the FBI. It contains information on crimes, fingerprints, outstanding warrants, guns, and stolen property. Searches are available only to law-enforcement personnel and a few other federally mandated organizations.
- Private databases with information on nearly everybody are available to licensed private eyes, attorneys, and collection agencies who pay the fees. These include AutoTrackXP®, QuickInfo, and FlatRateInfo.
- Savvy amateur sleuths in search of a missing person will check such public databases as the Social Security Death Master File and the Federal Bureau of Prisons Inmate Locator, as well as Web sites like Classmates.com and the pay sites that resell telephone information (much more recent than Internet white-page directories).

The point is to find out for sure what your character would do electronically before he so much as leaves his office. This aids plausibility, and may even suggest more plot incidents.

Thus, they know how the FBI is set up, what legal restrictions hem in private investigators, and what jurisdictions state troopers have. They know that it's legal in New York, but not in Maryland, to tap your own phone when you talk to someone who doesn't know it's tapped. They know that NYPD cops don't refer to "the twentieth precinct" but to "the two-oh," and that an FBI agent files a "302" on every interview or surveillance. You must know these details, too. If you don't, and are unwilling to do extensive research on law enforcement, don't try to create a character who is a pro.

MYSTERIES II: *WHAT* DO YOU DO?

The range of jobs for professionals includes municipal police (such as detectives), sheriff, state trooper, private investigator, FBI agent, crime-scene team, bounty hunter (who brings in people in violation of subpoenas), park police. Not all of these, of course, are supposed to investigate murders . . . but if you want yours to do so, they must have good contacts and access to crucial databases. What *you* must have is, again, a good working knowledge of the requirements and limitations of these occupations.

The jobs held by amateur detectives in successful mystery series boggle the mind. Various authors have created sleuths whose day jobs are:

- dry cleaner
- trailer-park manager
- hairdresser
- innkeeper
- chef
- clinical psychologist
- wedding planner
- dancer
- rabbi
- astrologer
- stay-at-home mom
- high-school teacher
- garbage collector
- witch

. . . and practically every other occupation you can think of. This creates three pitfalls for writers. First, you will probably not come up with an occupation that does not already have an amateur detective working the territory. Publishers may not feel there is room for two mystery series starring a dry cleaner. Although much depends, of course, on how well your particular book is written, be aware that in choosing an offbeat, "original" occupation, you may not be as original as you'd hoped.

Second, for amateur detectives, occupation defines terrain. That is, your protagonist needs to learn about these crimes and solve them while still carrying on her usual job. "Means, motive, and opportunity" usually refer to the criminal, but they also apply to amateurs who do not have cases assigned to them by their lieutenant. Will this occupation permit your character to become logically involved in the crime? Will it let her travel around enough to gather or witness clues, or will these come to her? Will her profession somehow contribute to solving the crime? Consider these things before setting your protagonist up in any job.

Finally, and perhaps most important, an interesting or offbeat occupation can serve as an all-too-handy crutch to avoid genuine characterization. Your character is an actor, trophy maker, or jazz clarinetist, but that must not be all he is. Clarinetists differ as much in personality as do any other group of people. Don't reach for the first set of characteristics that come to mind for jazz musicians (flamboyant, unreliable, broke) and assume you've created a character. A good amateur sleuth needs the same attention to characterization as any other protagonist. Simon Brett's actor detective, Charles Paris, is much more than an actor: He's a hilarious, sad, ever-hopeful failure we can both cheer for and become exasperated by.

Your protagonist, of course, is not the only one in your book who needs a job. Since the beginning of the genre, mysteries have often featured a sidekick for the main sleuth: Sherlock Holmes and Dr. Watson (Sir Arthur Conan Doyle), Andrew Dalziel and Peter Pascoe (Reginald Hill), Sarah Quilliam and sister Meg (Claudia Bishop), Derek Strange and Terry Quinn (George Pelecanos). A sidekick gives your protagonist someone to discuss the case with ("Elementary, my dear Watson"). The sidekick can also provide a nice complement to the main character's skills or personality. Peter Pascoe, for instance, is a good foil for the down-and-dirty Dalziel; Pascoe is quiet, mild, and sensitive.

THRILLERS AND WESTERNS: THE GUYS IN THE WHITE HATS

It may seem odd to class thrillers with westerns rather than mysteries, but both genres usually feature the same kind of protagonist: a larger-than-life hero who can do things ordinary people cannot and is thus a match for the villains that customarily populate these books. Examples are Ian Fleming's character James Bond opposing various over-the-top terrorists, Tom Clancy's Jack Ryan opposing Cold War Russians, and various Louis L'Amour western heroes opposing outlaws.

Of course, neither westerns nor thrillers are *required* to have incredibly competent protagonists and incredibly dastardly villains. In fact, some of the best do not. Robert Harris's thriller *Enigma*, made into a successful movie, has as its hero an exhausted mathematician who has had a nervous breakdown from overwork and is a bust with women. Clancy's *The Hunt for Red October* features as antagonists not Russians in a nuclear submarine seeking to blow up the West but Russians in a nuclear sub seeking to defect to the West. And some of Louis L'Amour's most interesting heroes, such as the middle-aged poor rancher of "Caprock Rancher," come across as average men rather than the Gary Cooper stereotype of a western protagonist.

But even in these more complex stories, there are genuine villains in the background: the traitor to the British war effort in *Enigma*, the Russians seeking to destroy their defecting countrymen in *The Hunt for Red October*, the outlaws trying to steal the rancher's money. And most thrillers and westerns do feature a basic good-guys-vs.-bad-guys plot.

Your challenge as a writer is to keep your good guy from being too good or your bad guy too bad. The exception is if you're writing books that are clearly meant to be unbelievable, like those involving the unflappable James Bond and his weird opponents—then no feat of daring is too much and no villain too improbable. But for those of us not writing parody, thrillers, and westerns will be improved by creating protagonists with enough human weaknesses to seem real, thus permitting both greater reader identification and greater suspense. After all, if it's a foregone conclusion that your hero is unbeatable, where does the tension come from? Even Superman could be harmed by kryptonite.

The guidelines for a thriller or western protagonist, of either gender, are:

- The hero must have unusual tenacity. After everyone else has given up on the situation, the thriller/western protagonist keeps going.
- The hero is usually a loner. A western hero may indeed have a partner or sidekick, but usually he will end up having to face the villain alone at some point. Undercover agents, almost by definition, work alone, despite having many people both dictating their moves and backing them up. Frequently, as in John le Carré's classic *The Spy Who Came in From the Cold*, the hero may end up defying his supposed allies.
- The hero is emotionally restrained. This is almost a necessity; highly volatile people are not reliable in dangerous situations. As Ed Tucker says in "Caprock Rancher" about a crisis:

> Times like that a man is best off doing one thing at a time and not worrying around too much. . . . Nothing was growing around but some short grass and knee-high mesquite, but I got Pa's leg set and cut mesquite with my bowie and splinted up best I knew how. All that time he set there a-looking

at me with pain in his eyes and never let out a whimper, but the sweat stood out on both our faces, you can bet.

- The hero is not loquacious. Not only does he not emote, he doesn't talk too much during times of action, not even when in pain from a broken leg.
- The hero is resourceful. He is able to use whatever resources he has, whether that means splinting a leg with mesquite or escaping from alligators by leaping nimbly from one reptile's back to another (James Bond).
- The hero has ideals. This is perhaps the most important requirement of all. The thriller or western protagonist may lie, cheat, steal, even kill—but he does it in the service of his country, his family, his homestead, or his idea of right. Even when a character does not conform to the other guidelines (the protagonist of *Enigma* is an emotional mess), the idealism is indispensable. It's how you distinguish the flawed hero from the flawed villain.

What kind of background and personality produces this behavior? Figuring that out, and stretching the limits of the conventional answers, is part of the challenge of writing a good thriller or western.

THRILLERS AND WESTERNS II: THE VILLAIN PROBLEM

Unless you are writing simple adventure, parody, or comic books, the purely evil villain is even less convincing than the purely noble hero. Real human beings, even villains, have reasons for what they do. If you dramatize these reasons, your villain becomes more plausible. However, once readers understand him, he may also become too sympathetic for your purposes.

This was the problem television had with a 2003 movie biography of Adolf Hitler. The attempt to explain how Hitler became who he was also softened him, in the opinion of some critics, so that the portrayal of him became insufficiently monstrous. You will walk the same line with your villain, and there is no simple answer. As a general rule, however, the more clearly you demonstrate negative childhood forces on your villain, the more understandable he may become—and the less evil.

On the other hand, providing no background or reasons, however irrational, for the villain's behavior may render him either unconvincing or underdeveloped. Everyone has justifications in his own mind for even the most heinous of actions. Showing us an antagonist's reasoning makes him seem much more real.

In *Enigma*, for example, the traitor who nearly betrays Britain's efforts to crack the German submarine code is motivated by revenge. He is a Pole, and he discovered that Russia had slaughtered and buried Polish soldiers, including his father and brother. The British command knew of the massacre but kept it quiet in order not to alienate her Russian ally. So the young Pole, who works at the code-breaking base Bletchley Park, tries to sabotage its operations. This motivation is both understandable and treasonous and helps give the novel its moral complexity.

You will have to decide how much of your villain's warped background and/or reasoning is necessary for your particular story.

SCIENCE FICTION AND FANTASY: TOADS AND GARDENS

Paraphrasing poet Marianne Moore, there are two ways to write good science fiction and fantasy: Put real toads in imaginary gardens or imaginary toads in real gardens.

What this means is that these genres have one of two kinds of protagonists. The first type is as much like contemporary people—complex, solid, believable, even "average"—as the author can make them, who are then put into imagined settings: Mars, Middle-Earth, the bridge of a starship, an alien planet, a magic circus. The second type is an imaginary protagonist—a telepath, a wizard, an alien, a woman from a far future and strange culture— who is put into our world. In that case, the setting, either contemporary or historical, will be a part of "real" human history and probably already familiar to readers.

An example of the first kind of protagonist is Frank Chalmers from Kim Stanley Robinson's *Red Mars*. Chalmers, like the rest of Robinson's varied cast, would be completely recognizable in a contemporary setting. Chalmers is a strong leader driven by a plausible mix of idealism, egotism, and resentment of those with superior natural advantages. His "imaginary garden" is a colonized and settled Mars—but you could just as easily put him in a novel about an American political election. He feels very real and contemporary.

Sometimes the imaginary garden is simply one innovation in our world. Daniel Keyes's much-anthologized short story, "Flowers for Algernon," features as protagonist Charlie Gordon, a sweet-natured and mentally challenged young man. Charlie's world is pretty much ours—factory job, tutoring, room in a boarding house—except for one medical breakthrough. Charlie undergoes an operation to vastly increase his intelligence. That is enough to alter his world vastly and turn the story into science fiction.

In fantasy, Jean Auel's very popular *The Clan of the Cave Bear* and its sequels also feature a "real toad in an imaginary garden." Ayla reacts just as modern American women would to most situations, which makes her both understandable and sympathetic to readers. Her imaginary world is prehistoric Earth, populated by an inventively detailed Neanderthal culture. Here is Ayla, newly pregnant, accommodating a male with a tribal right to have sex with her:

> Ayla was startled. She had forgotten all about Broud. She had more important things to think about, like warm cuddly nursing babies, her own warm cuddly nursing baby. Might as well get it over with, she thought, and patiently assumed the position for Broud to relieve his needs. I hope he hurries, I want to go down to the stream and wash my hair.

From these examples, it should be clear that no guidelines are possible for a "typical" science fiction or fantasy protagonist of the first type. Because these are representatives of our world, even when dwelling far from it, the only requirement is that they seem as real as possible, thereby lending reality to the exotic world around them. Any temperament, character, or qualities will work if the writer can create them skillfully enough.

SCIENCE FICTION AND FANTASY II: THE OUTSIDER

Requirements are more stringent for the second type of speculative literature protagonist. This is the "imaginary toad" put in a real setting: the outsider, the alien, the "other." By definition, such a protagonist must be unlike us in some important way.

Leigh Kennedy's *The Journal of Nicholas the American* is such a protagonist, a paranormal empath who cannot shut out the thoughts of everyone around him, a condition which drives him to the brink of madness. His "garden," in contrast, is solid and real: a seedy section of a modern city. In fantasy, J.R.R. Tolkien's monumental *The Lord of the Rings* gives us many nonhuman characters: wizards, Ents, orcs, dark riders, hobbits—a huge cast of imaginary toads. But the landscape through which they move is very recognizable as early England. Despite its fantastic towers and elf glades, the setting consists mostly of hills, orchards, rivers, mountains, and other solid, familiar locales that ground the fantastic in the real.

Can you put an alien or magical protagonist in an alien or magical environment? Yes, but usually there needs to be a major character from our world as well, someone like us to make sense of the foreign. Thus, Aldous Huxley's classic *Brave New World* depicts a future completely strange to us, as are its bottle-grown and genetically engineered people. But key character John the Savage is from our time and thus anchors us in the story by mirroring our reactions. Without him, the story would have given us nothing at all to recognize and identify with.

If your protagonist is going to be an "imaginary toad," here are some points to keep in mind:

- The protagonist must be fully described. We can visualize a "middle-aged black woman" (although probably not in the way you want unless you supply more details), but not an "alien from Grilmal" or a "genetically altered moon dweller" or a "shape changer from the Kingdom of the Lost." Be specific.

- Show us what your protagonist does, rather than describing his characteristics. Habitual behavior characterizes; it's also more interesting to read than long chunks of exposition.

- Make sure your protagonist is consistent. However much his behavior, desires, and the society that produced him all differ from that of humans, those three things must still be consistent with each other. For example, Ursula K. Le Guin's hermaphrodites in *The Left Hand of Darkness* have elaborate sexual rules to keep their mating behavior from interfering with the day-to-day running of their city.

- If your fantasy protagonist is gifted with magical powers, the magic must be consistent and well thought out. Was he born with these powers, must he be trained to control them, or both? Under what circumstances is magic possible? If he cannot cast a spell on page six, then he also must fail at casting it on page twenty-six unless you explain the discrepancy fully and convincingly.

- If your aliens are truly different from us, they may not be comprehensible at all (as in Terry Carr's classic story "The Dance of the Changer and the Three"). In that case, they should not be the protagonists. Give us a human being as point-of-view character to guide us through your plot.

Science fiction and fantasy can focus on important human truths, not merely on adventure and special effects. The key to doing so is the creation of protagonists that readers can care about. It is through the characters, not the often elaborate plots, that speculative literature succeeds.

RECAP: GENRE CHARACTERS

Genre fiction requires the same attention to characterization as mainstream fiction, but it also presents additional requirements. Since these vary with subgenre, the first step for writers is to be very familiar with the subgenre they wish to write.

Romance novels appeal to a combination of reader identification and wish fulfillment. Thus, heroines usually must be attractive, moral, single, lovable, and interested in something else besides romance. Romance heroes should be single, sexy, smart, solvent, and sweet-natured underneath, even if at first they appear otherwise.

Most mysteries satisfy our need for order and justice. To plausibly see a case through to the end, your protagonist should be curious, reasonably independent, and tenacious. Amateur detectives need a credible reason to become involved in the case. Professionals will only be convincing if the writer knows the procedures, laws, and pitfalls of that law enforcement specialty.

Thrillers and westerns usually require both a hero and a villain. The challenge is to keep the hero from being too good and the villain from being too bad; otherwise, both become unbelievable. Give your hero flaws, but also make sure he's tenacious, resourceful, emotionally controlled, and idealistic. The villain should have reasons for his villainy that make sense to him; pure evil only works in parody.

Science fiction and fantasy require either "real toads in imaginary gardens" (people much like readers in exotic settings) or "imaginary toads in real gardens" (exotic protagonists in concretely familiar settings). For the former, create characters readers can recognize, believe in, and perhaps even identify with. For the latter, create characters that, however strange, are self-consistent, fully visualized, and dramatized rather than merely described. Exotic characters in exotic settings usually require at least one "normal" human to guide the reader through all the unfamiliarity.

Choose a favorite romance novel and fill out a mini-bio on the heroine. How complete is it? How did the author let you know all this information: through exposition, dialogue, description, characters' actions, or thoughts?

Pick an occupation that you have worked at and know well. How might a character in this situation come to suspect how a murder has been committed? What specialized knowledge does she have that might help her notice details overlooked by others? Does her specialized knowledge also suggest plot ideas? Is this a story you might like to write?

List your five favorite mysteries. Which use amateur detectives and which professionals? In how many is the criminal caught?

Find a thriller or western in which the hero is *not* emotionally controlled, fairly silent, and brave (the classic "strong, silent type"). How does his departure from the genre norm affect the plot? Is reader identification with this hero easier or harder? If it's harder, is there another character in the story that readers might more easily identify with?

List five science fiction or fantasy books you like. Which have "real toads in imaginary gardens" and which have "imaginary toads in real gardens"? Does one type appeal to you more than the other? Does this provide any clue about what you should write?

Choose someone, a real person, whom you know well. Now imagine him in your favorite genre: confronted with a crime, falling in love, or magically transported to a fantasy kingdom. How would he behave? Does this make him a possible protagonist for that genre—and why or why not? Then do the same for yourself as a character. Try to be honest about your hypothetical reactions.

chapter 7

[THE HUMOROUS CHARACTER— ALL BETS ARE OFF]

Comedy, most writers agree, is difficult. A serious story that doesn't quite work may still have some successful aspects: a memorable character or an interesting plot twist. A humorous story that doesn't work, however, flops totally.

It's difficult to even talk about writing humor. The inimitable E.B. White wrote that "Humor can be dissected, as a frog can, but the thing dies in the process and the innards are discouraging to the pure scientific mind." Nonetheless, there are a few general rules about creating the humorous character that can be of use to the writer brave enough to try.

TYPES OF HUMOR: YOU FOUND *THAT* FUNNY?

Humor comes in several different varieties, and thus so do humorous characters. At one end of the spectrum is the character that is basically serious but has touches of humor, such as the butler Stevens in Kazuo Ishiguro's *The Remains of the Day*. Throughout most of this novel, Stevens struggles to understand and accept his role both in the politically soiled past of Darlington Hall and in his failed relationship with the Hall's housekeeper. But there are flashes of humor, as when Stevens tries to learn to "banter" with the Hall's new American owner, Mr. Faraday. Americans banter, Stevens decides, and so he must, too:

> It occurs to me, furthermore, that bantering is hardly an unreasonable duty for an employer to expect a professional to perform. I have of course already devoted much time to developing my bantering skills, but it is possible I have never approached the task with the commitment I might have done. Perhaps, then, when I return to Darlington Hall tomorrow—Mr. Faraday will not himself be back for a further week—I will begin practising with renewed effort. I should hope,

then, that by the time of my employer's return, I shall be in a position to pleasantly surprise him.

What makes this funny, of course, is the contrast between Stevens's solemn, even ponderous earnestness and his goal. Bantering should be spontaneous and lighthearted, the opposite of Stevens's approach. For characters like Stevens, in which humor is an ingredient but the not the main personality or plot direction, there are no special characterization guidelines. Everything we've discussed so far about creating good characters applies. Stevens is complex, emotional (in a very repressed British way), motivated, and plausible. He just happens to also occasionally be funny.

But here we come to an important point: Not everyone will find him funny at all. Amusement, more than any other reader reaction, is highly individual. This means that writers will never get everyone to appreciate their particular type of humor, no matter how skillfully written. This should not stop you, however. Write the type of humor you like, and readers who share that taste will laugh at it.

Humor can range from very gentle whimsy to savage satire. The techniques for creating humorous characters, however, remain constant through various types of humor. They are exaggeration, ridicule, and reversal of expectations. A funny character may embody one, two, or all three techniques.

EXAGGERATION: PLAUSIBILITY SUSPENDED

When a comic character is very exaggerated, we are not supposed to believe he could really exist. This is where all previous rules on creating characters simply don't apply. The super-exaggerated character is not supposed to be a human being but merely the essence of some human trait, writ solo and large.

For example, Woody Allen's comic story "A Giant Step for Mankind" consists of a "diary" kept by a scientist working with two others to find a method to counteract choking; they were scooped by the invention of the Heimlich maneuver. The diary, which is very funny (to me, anyway), exaggerates scientific procedure and stereotypes of scientists way past any believability. One colleague, Shulamith Arnolfini, has experimented with recombinant DNA, which "led to the creation of a gerbil that could sing 'Let My People Go.' " The scientists spend long hours in the lab:

Today was a productive one for Shulamith and me. Working around the clock, we induced strangulation in a mouse. This was accomplished by coaxing the rodent to ingest healthy portions of Gouda cheese and then making it laugh . . . Grasping the mouse firmly by the tail, I snapped it like a small whip, and the morsel of cheese came loose. Shulamith and I made voluminous notes on the experiment. If we can transfer the tailsnap procedure to humans, we may have something. Too early to tell.

Clearly, none of this is believable, nor is it meant to be. Many characteristics of actual scientists are exaggerated way past credibility: dedication, willingness to try strange experiments, solemn evaluation of results, caution in judgment ("Too early to tell"). The result is characters that serve their purpose in the story without conforming to any known parameters of successful fictional creations. For stories like this, exaggeration is what matters, not credibility, and the more exaggerated the better.

A lesser degree of exaggeration exists in a comic character like Mr. Collins in Jane Austen's *Pride and Prejudice*. Here the story is meant to be read as "real" in that we can believe it is happening while engrossed in the book. The major characters, such as Elizabeth Bennet, Mr. Darcy, and Lydia, are completely plausible. Only the comic characters like Mr. Collins are exaggerated; he is more egregiously unctuous, stupid, and socially blind than is quite credible.

This is a common technique in many novels: Keep the main characters plausible but exaggerate the comic ones to humorous effect. The writer thus reaps the benefits of both humor and a solid, meaningful story. The technique works across all genres. Consider two examples: In Claudia Bishop's Hemlock Falls mysteries, sisters Sarah and Meg Quilliam are well-rounded and plausible characters, whereas villagers Dookie Shuttleworth and Davey Kiddermeister are exaggerated caricatures. In science fiction, Connie Willis's "At the Rialto," an extremely funny story, features a believable narrator but wildly exaggerated physicists and hotel clerks.

Stevens, in the passage above from *The Remains of the Day*, embodies an even milder form of exaggeration. Here the character is meant to seem as real as the author can make him. Only one characteristic, Stevens's willingness to please his master, is exaggerated. What makes this work so well is that not only is it amusing, it's also sad, because this very desire to please is what led Stevens decades earlier to stick blindly to a master who backed the Nazi Party.

If you wish to use exaggeration to build a comic character, here are some questions to ask yourself:

- How much plausibility do you want this character, and by extension the story, to have? If it's a purely comic piece, then exaggerate without bounds. If you want the story to be meaningful as well as funny, a lesser degree of exaggeration may work better.

- Is this character your protagonist? Generally, readers make closer identification with protagonists than with minor characters, so in a novel you want to seem "real," a lesser degree of exaggeration works better for major characters, with more pronounced exaggeration for minor ones.
- Which qualities should be exaggerated? There are two criteria: What will be funny, and what will be of use to your plot? Good exaggeration should serve both. Mr. Collins, for instance, is funny because he's so absurd, but he's also useful in that his exaggerated unctuousness leads him to carry all gossip to his patroness, including the news of Elizabeth's supposed engagement to Mr. Darcy. This helps lead to the real engagement.
- Will a very exaggerated character undermine the plausibility of your invented world as a whole? Mr. Collins works in *Pride and Prejudice*, but just barely. Had he been as exaggerated as Woody Allen's mad scientists, the novel as a whole might have suffered because the plausibility of its created world would have been called into question. The reasoning goes something like this: If I can't believe this character, why should I believe the rest? So exercise caution with the degree of exaggeration in otherwise serious stories.

RIDICULE: A REFLECTION OF THE AUTHOR'S WORLDVIEW

Closely related to exaggeration is the comic technique of ridicule. This involves exaggerating characters in order to make fun of them and, by extension, of what they represent in the real world. Ridicule can range all the way from gentle whimsy to savage satire. The degree of savagery is often a good reflection of the author's view of life.

For example, P.G. Wodehouse's character Bertie Wooster is a playboy with the wits of a cabbage. He and his upper-class pals get into one absurd scrape after another. Wodehouse satirizes the folly of such twits, but he does so very gently. Bertie is ridiculous, but he is also sweet-natured and likable.

More pointed is Stella Gibbons's 1932 cult classic, *Cold Comfort Farm*, which satirizes her contemporaries' romantic, earthy school of fiction. Personified in the novels of D.H. Lawrence, in which "blood calls to blood," the uncivilized rural man, virile and primitive, is the sexual ideal. In the Gibbons novel, the earthy, primitive farmer wants to be a matinee idol in the movies.

His female counterpart only finds happiness after she learns to dress and behave conventionally. The tormented soul warped by once having "seen something nasty in the woodshed," an embodiment of Freudian childhood trauma, gets straightened out by fashion magazines, an airplane, and the prospect of a pleasant life on the Riviera.

These exaggerated characters all revolve around the one sane person on the farm, Flora Poste, and the book revolves around ridiculing the melodramatic stereotypes found in fashionable fiction of the time. The result is an authorial worldview in favor of common sense, restraint, good manners, and clean curtains.

Other stories have ridiculed characters more ferociously. In the novel *Dodsworth*, Sinclair Lewis (winner of the 1930 Nobel Prize in Literature) based his character Fran Dodsworth on his first wife. Lewis exaggerated (at least, one hopes they are exaggerations, for his sake) the woman's self-centeredness, snobbishness, and deadly propensity to belittle others. The result is a satire of a certain kind of American upper-class woman: expensive, spoiled, idle, and useless. Fran Dodsworth is presented as ridiculous but also lethal.

What differentiates gentle satire from its vicious cousin? It's largely a question of authorial sympathy. When the author likes his character, as Wodehouse seems to like Bertie Wooster, he dramatizes the character's folly but does not give it hurtful consequences. When a portrayal is totally unsympathetic, like Lewis's of Fran Dodsworth, the character's follies are presented without any redeeming qualities and often as harmful to others. Then the authorial worldview seems much harsher: Other people are not just laughable, they're dangerous.

If you are writing satire, your characters should be:

- **Representative of whatever institution you're satirizing.** Bertie Wooster is a privileged Jazz Age twit, and ridiculing him served to ridicule the values of his society. Ditto for Fran Dodsworth. When an author ridicules someone or some type, he reveals his own values as well. Make sure you've got the right target.
- **Made unsympathetic to the degree you wish to draw blood.** Really sharp satire upsets people (take another look at Jonathan Swift's "A Modest Proposal." If you want to really skewer some aspect of society, ridicule its representative without mercy. Give his exaggerated folly negative consequences. You do not have to be fair here—really sharp

satire is not interested in multidimensional portraits. You must only be credible enough for your target to be recognizable.

- **Dramatized.** It's never enough in satire to describe folly; we must see the ridiculed character act it out.

REVERSAL OF EXPECTATIONS: STARTLED INTO LAUGHTER

Another type of humor depends on the confounding of our normal assumptions. Many jokes work this way, which is why the ending is called a "punch line." We anticipate one ending and get a different one: a "punch" to our anticipations.

In fiction, reversal of expectations starts from the assumption that most readers share certain beliefs about the world. When characters then reverse these beliefs, the result can be funny. (It can also be shocking, as when a child, assumed to be an innocent, turns out to be a murderer. But that's a different topic.) The laughter is partly at the characters but partly ourselves for our unfounded dogma.

Richard Bradford is a master of this kind of reversal. In his *Red Sky at Morning*, the students of Helen De Crispin High in 1944 New Mexico are herded into the auditorium for an assembly. Helen De Crispin herself, "a rich Boston lady," wearing face paint and a feather, is giving her Annual Indian Lore Lecture, open to the public:

> "This is my little friend Billy Birdwing," she went on, indicating the boy with the drum. "He's part Arapahoe and part Cheyenne, and he comes from far-off Oklahoma which, as you know, is a journey of many suns from here."
>
> "I can make it in five hours in the pick-up," an Indian behind me said. . . .
>
> Billy spread his arms out to the side and performed the same step, throwing in a few hey-yahs.
>
> "That's a dance that prays for eagles," she said obscurely. "Once the Indians were a proud race, and the arrows in their quivers were many. They trapped the tender rabbit in their snares and hunted the wily buffalo."
>
> "Oh, come on," one of the Indians behind us whispered, "I got a couple of Guernsey cows that are wilier than any goddamn buffalo."

Why is this funny? Because our expectations are that white people are unsympathetic to the Native American past and that Native Americans revere it. Here, however, a pretentious white woman is making a hash of mythologizing that past, while the Native Americans, like Flora Poste in *Cold Comfort Farm*, are firmly rooted in a common-sense present. All our assumptions have been upset.

Note, too, that this brief humorous passage also makes liberal use of the two qualities previously discussed, exaggeration and ridicule. Mrs. De Crispin is a real type, the person who appropriates and romanticizes a culture not her own, but she is an exaggerated version of the type. That exaggeration, plus her total lack of self-awareness about how inappropriate it is for her to wear war paint and feathers, make her ridiculous. Exaggeration, ridicule, and reversal of expectation work together to create humor.

Reversal of expectation can be used with virtually every aspect of characterization. A character's dialogue may belie his appearance. Or her thoughts may contrast markedly with her dialogue, challenging our assumptions about what such a person is thinking at any given moment. Or his actions may upset our expectations. Vivian Vande Velde makes good use of this in her children's book *Once Upon a Test: Three Light Tales of Love*. Gordon, a peasant, is given three tests of bravery before he can win the hand of a beautiful princess. We expect, from all the fairy tales we've been read as children, that he will succeed. Instead, Gordon says, "You're all crazy," goes home, and marries the miller's daughter.

To create a character who makes us laugh by reversing our expectations, consider the following:

- The expectations you seek to reverse should be fairly widespread. A story that expects to garner laughs by reversing assumptions about sixteenth-century Buddhist monks will have a very limited audience since most of us don't know enough about sixteenth-century Buddhist monks to have assumptions about them. Pick familiar expectations to challenge. Fairy tales are widely familiar; Buddhist chants are not.
- Be aware that controversial subjects produce divided expectations. Bernard Malamud's story "Defender of the Faith" is a funny reversal of common beliefs about religion. However, people who do not regard these beliefs as appropriate subjects for satire may not find the story humorous at all (a classroom of freshmen that I taught years ago did not). That shouldn't stop you from writing such reversals, but you should be aware that you may alienate part of your audience.
- Don't belabor your reversal by adding any exposition "explaining" it. Like attempts to explain jokes, this dooms humor. Your characters should simply do, say, or think their reversed-expectation bits of business. Readers will either smile or they won't.

Characters Laughing

In both comic and more serious stories, there may be times when your aim is not to make the reader laugh but rather to have your characters laugh. Other than "he laughed," how do you indicate that?

One choice is onomatopoeia, which is defined as "a word that imitates a natural sound." For laughter, your choices are pretty much "Ha ha," "Heh heh," or "tee hee," all of which have severe drawbacks. "Ha ha" has come to be associated with villains in melodramas ("With a mocking 'Ha ha!' he tied the lovely girl to the railway tracks"). "Tee hee" sounds like a tittering teenage girl, which is fine if your character is a tittering teenage girl but not otherwise. "Heh heh" leads to pronunciation problems: Is it "hay hay," "hee hee," or "huh huh"? None of them simulate laughter very successfully.

Another choice is to use a synonym such as "He chuckled"—or "snickered" or "hooted" or "roared." These work well, indicating specific kinds of laughter, as long as you don't overdo it. Add too many laughing verbs and your story will start to sound like a zoo at feeding time.

Finally, you can use phases like "burst into laughter," "shook with laughter," or "was convulsed with laughter." The danger here is cliché, which all of these are.

Better to stick with "He laughed" and *show* us what was so funny.

- Make sure your character has a genuine role to play in your story's plot. It can be tempting to add a character just because you know you can make him funny, but this weakens the story overall. Find a way to either include the funny character elsewhere in the plot or save him for another book.

HUMOROUS CHARACTERS AND TONE: THE BIG PICTURE

Ultimately, whether or not we find a character humorous is a function of the overall tone of a book. Tone is difficult to define succinctly. It is the attitude of the author toward his material as expressed in every character, phrase, arrangements of incidents, description, and all the other myriad choices that go into writing a piece of fiction. But hard as it is to define, tone is easy to recognize. We know if a story feels heroic, dark, romantic, or humorous—all common tones.

It's important to realize that any material can be presented in any tone, including the humorous. Here, for instance, are passages about three funerals, written in three wildly differing tones:

> The lords bowed their heads, and the men-at-arms raised their weapons. Among them wound the bier of spear shafts on which lay the dead king. The moonlight glinted on his helmet, and his small son stood bowed with rest, the crown already heavy on his unfledged shoulders, so that the ladies wept to see him.

The tone here is heroic, solemnly treating the characters as important and the occasion as tragic. The passage achieves this though the archaic diction ("unfledged shoulders"), the formal sentence structure, and, above all, the respectful attitude that the author seems to have toward her characters. They are presented without exaggeration, satire, or ridicule.

So are the characters at the next funeral, but here the tone is much different:

> My mother died in the spring, after a short illness. We buried her on a Wednesday. It rained. Afterwards, we all went to my brother's house, where my brother's wife had prepared sandwiches and other people brought cakes and pies. No one spoke much. I left as early as I thought I decently could.

This funeral does not seem heroic. Rather, the tone is understated and affectless, as if the author stood a great distance away from his characters, observing them objectively. Not only does the narrator not reveal much emotion, but the author doesn't seem to feel much for the characters, either. This is achieved through the short, factual sentences, lack of names for anyone at the funeral, and sparseness of descriptive details. This narrator is either uninvolved or repressed, and the author has matched the character with the tone of the prose.

Now consider a third funeral:

> "Don't drop him!" Sal panted.
> "I'm not gonna drop him," Vinnie said.
> "You drop him, the boss'll have your head."
> Vinnie knew this was true because the boss already had Big Louie's head. The body in the coffin they carried between them was without capitation. Big

Louie's head was stored in a meat locker in Hoboken, wrapped in white butcher paper and marked "Fatty Chops." After the funeral the boss was going to send the head to Big Louie's brother, by way of warning. Vinnie felt bad for Big Louie because during the two days he laid in the funeral parlor, closed coffin, not even his mother had come to pay no respects. Big Louie's mother was having an affair with the boss's cousin.

This tone is humorous—macabre, but still funny. The author does not seem to be taking this death very seriously so we don't, either. The details are exaggerated (the head labeled "Fatty Chops"), and our expectations answered with reversals (a mother not mourning, in fact not even attending her son's funeral because of her affair with his murderer's cousin). Everything in the passage urges us to regard this funeral not as tragic or even sordid but ridiculous.

Ultimately, then, creating humorous characters is a matter of tone. Whichever techniques you employ, and in what proportions, your characters will mostly seem funny to us because your attitude toward them is humorous, and we pick up on that. The humor may be gentle or vicious, whimsical, or satirical. It may evoke quiet smiles, belly laughs, or gasps of delighted shock. But it will succeed because you think it's funny and have succeeded in making us see why.

RECAP: HUMOROUS CHARACTERS

Humor comes in many forms, from whimsy to savage satire. Because it is so individual, no one can write anything deemed universally funny.

For basically serious characters who are only occasionally humorous, all the techniques previously discussed apply. They should be complex, motivated, and plausible. Humorous characters, however, may be none of these things if their only function is to amuse us.

The basic techniques for creating humorous characters are exaggeration, ridicule, and reversal of expectations. Any of them may be employed in mild, medium, or outrageous form, depending on the degree of plausibility desired. All three should be applied to characters in ways that benefit the story plot as a whole.

Humor, which should not and cannot be explained in accompanying exposition, ultimately comes down to a matter of tone, which in turn depends heavily on how an author views his characters.

Choose a joke you think is funny and analyze it (you don't want a one-liner here but rather a "story joke"). Does it use exaggeration? Ridicule? Reversal of expectations? Something else? Is the character in the joke funny, or the situation, or both?

Then perform the same analysis for a short story you think is very funny.

Try your joke or short story from exercise one on five different people. Do they all think it's funny? Are they able to tell you why or why not?

Type into your computer the first page or so from a serious story, yours or someone else's. Now try to alter that opening to make it humorous. Exaggerate things, ridicule things, try for reversal of expectations. Did it work? Does altering the passage in this way make it funny, or is more needed? What?

Create a comic character from scratch. Give him a profession, goal, and personality. Write a brief scene in which he has an argument with someone. Pick an absurd topic for the two to argue about and exaggerate it. Is this the start of a story you would like to write?

THE HUMOROUS CHARACTER

chapter 8

[TALKING ABOUT EMOTION— DIALOGUE AND THOUGHTS]

"Give sorrow words," the Bard wrote four hundred years ago, and it was good advice not only for Macduff but also for writers everywhere. Give words to sorrow and joy and lust and contentment and despair and anger. Better yet, let your *characters* give words to their feelings—but not without restraint.

Emotional dialogue is among the trickiest to write. There are few dialogue decisions to make for a character who falls off a cliff ("Help!") or is lost in the supermarket ("Where is the dog food, please?"). But feelings are another story. People differ widely in emotional expression due to differences in temperament, ethnicity, region, family background, and circumstances. This means that dialogue is a tremendous aid in building characterization, but it also means you must be careful about when, how, how much, and to whom your characters talk about their feelings.

The same is true about how your characters *think* about their feelings. Thought is a kind of internal dialogue, so some, but not all, of the same guidelines apply to both.

YOU ARE WHAT YOU SAY— OR DON'T SAY

This heading isn't strictly true, of course. All of us have many more aspects to our inner lives than those we express verbally. But in fiction, what a character says, as well as how he says it, makes a strong impression on the reader. It's possible, as we've already seen, to play thoughts against dialogue. A character may feel one emotion (anger) and deliberately try to present another (indifference) for public consumption. But, for the most part, your reader will assume, in the absence of other evidence, that your characters mean the emotions they express.

This provides you with a great opportunity to build characterization. All of the following statements, for instance, are made spontaneously by characters who have just learned that their dogs have been run over by a speeding truck:

- "Oh, my God, no! No! Oh, not Cinnamon—no!"
- "Goddamn $#%@*& driver! I'll kill him!"
- "Where is she? Can I see her? Who picked up the body?"
- "Did she suffer? Oh, please say death was instantaneous!"
- "I just let her out a minute . . . oh, God, I should have put her on the leash . . . oh, it's my fault . . . poor Cinnamon . . ."
- Silence.

It's easy to see how different these six people are. Even before the writer adds emotional indicators (tears, averted face, tone of voice), the dialogue has shown widely differing emotions among the six. They are, respectively, unrestrained grief, anger, calm self-control (although we don't yet know at what cost), concern for the dog's suffering, self-blame, and a stoic silence that needs to be interpreted in light of other facts about this character.

Note that none of the six *named* his emotion; no one said, "I feel sad about my dog's death." Later, perhaps, some of them might say that, which raises an interesting distinction between talking about emotion as it occurs and talking about it after the fact. They are different, but both can contribute to characterization. Here, for instance, is how these six people might talk about Cinnamon's death a month after it occurred:

- "I loved that dog. My daughter says I should get another puppy, but I'm just not ready yet."
- "This bastard just ran over my dog, and the goddamn garbage company never took any responsibility. Nobody cares anymore."
- "When my dog was hit by a truck, my neighbor Ralph wrapped the body in a sheet and kept it in his garage until I got home from work."
- "My vet said Cinnamon died immediately, without any pain. She never knew she'd been hit, even. I'm grateful for that."
- "I let Cinnamon out without a leash and she was hit by a truck. I still feel terrible about it."
- "When my first dog died, I got Captain here."

When you write emotional dialogue, consider whether it's being said at an emotional moment or after the moment has passed. The latter can be more abstract, naming emotions directly ("I loved that dog," "I'm grateful"). Keep the former as direct and visceral as the character's temperament allows.

Because, of course, it *is* temperament that dictates how each person reacts to Cinnamon's death. You know your character best—what would she feel if a beloved pet dies? If he's rejected by a lover or child? If a court judgment goes against her? If he's stuck in traffic for forty-five minutes? If she's disinherited? If he doesn't get invited to his brother's wedding?

Once you know what your character feels, plus how violently she's likely to express that feeling, the next step is to choose her actual words.

YADDA YADDA YADDA: YAMMERING ON IN A NEW YORK MINUTE

Although individual temperament is the largest determinant of what your character says, it's not the only one. In the musical *My Fair Lady*, Professor Henry Higgins boasted that he could place a man within a few London blocks simply by listening to his accent. You don't have the advantage of skilled actors in presenting sentences in different accents, but you can make your characters' dialogue more realistic and interesting by considering several factors affecting how people speak:

- **Ethnicity.** Yes, there are stereotypes here, and you don't want to fall into the trap of presenting trite characters with hackneyed dialogue. Still, there are differences in ethnic heritage that affect what emotional expression is encouraged and what is discouraged. In some Arab subcultures, it's acceptable for both genders to express grief by falling to the ground and pulling at one's hair. An Englishman who did that would meet with disapproval—subdued disapproval. These mores, although muted somewhat in the melting pot of the United States, nonetheless still have some hold on Americans. A man from an old-line Boston family will have grown up with different emotional expressions from a man of the same age who grew up in the Bronx.

  If you don't know what the emotional conventions are for your character's social group, stop writing and find out.
- **Family background.** Within your character's social group lies his individual family. Certainly, families can produce offspring with widely disparate emotional styles (I'm sometimes not sure my brother and I are related at all). Still, there are family codes; different families tolerate

different degrees of anger, sentimentality, profanity, and unrestrained grief. These sanctioned emotional expressions grow out of larger family values, as Pat Conroy portrayed so well in his novel of growing up under a stern Marine Corps father, *The Great Santini*. If your character is deliberately breaking those codes, and if he interacts with the family much, this should create further emotional stress for everybody.

- **Region.** Various fascinating social science studies reveal regional differences in the way people talk, including emotional talk. It will surprise no one to learn that New Yorkers talk faster than Alabamians. In the Midwest it's considered rude to interrupt a speaker, but in New York, it's considered simply enthusiastic. Where does your character live? Has she always lived there? Does the region affect the way she expresses emotion?

- **Gender.** This is controversial but worth paying attention to. Some studies suggest that women's overall conversational style differs from men's: more elliptical, less competitive, and more concerned with establishing common ground, even when the area of discussion concerns something innocuous like vacation plans. Certainly, females in American culture are still given more license to cry publicly than men. Your ear is your best guide here. Do you perceive females in various situations to express emotion differently from males? If so, is your character likely to conform to gender expectations or deliberately flout them?

- **Education.** Higher education is often an inhibitor. That is, college-educated people often express emotion less violently, at least in public. In addition, they are more likely to use correct grammar and wider vocabularies. Here are two characters expressing a deep dissatisfaction with where they live:

> "As for me, the things I had to do for the newspaper were demeaning, they were so trivial. We made a mistake, I told him, and I didn't believe in being party to a double suicide because of it. I gave him one day to think it over after we got the last threatening telephone call. I told him I was going whether he was coming with me or not." (Eleanor Strand, in *Bread Upon the Waters* by Irwin Shaw)

> "I can't no more. I can't no more."
> "Can't what? What can't you?"
> "I can't live here. I don't know where to go or what to do, but I can't live here. Nobody speaks to us. Nobody comes by. Boys don't like me. Girls don't either." (Denver, in *Beloved* by Toni Morrison)

It's easy to see which character is formally educated. Eleanor uses longer sentences, dependent clauses, correct grammar, and three-syllable words. Denver speaks mostly in one-syllable words; her usage is incorrect ("can't no more"); only one sentence is longer than four words. Some of this is due to differences in region and in historical era, but most of it comes from Denver's lack of formal education.

- **Circumstances.** Characters in tense or dangerous circumstances may speak more tersely than usual ("Fire!" is a single-syllable, noncomplex cry). Or they may "break"—which we'll discuss in detail soon.

How, you may reasonably ask, am I suppose to keep all this in mind while writing an emotional scene? You're not. Just try to "become the character" as you're writing, thinking, feeling, and talking from the character's point of view, and most of the right words will fall into place. Then, when you rewrite, "become the reader," judging how the dialogue might strike your future reader, and fine-tune as necessary to better reflect all the above factors.

FICTIONAL DIALOGUE VS. REAL DIALOGUE

As you both write and rewrite, it's important to be aware that emotional dialogue in fiction is not the same as emotional dialogue in real life. Obviously, some expressions are the same, especially short speeches ("No!" or "I love you"). But in real life, longer emotional utterances tend to be more incoherent, extended, mysterious, and repetitive than in fiction. The feelings are the same, but in effective fiction, the dialogue that carries those feelings is shaped in several ways.

One form of shaping is compression. A person whose dog has been run over may go on about it for ten or fifteen minutes, saying the same thing over and over. The distraught owner may need to vent, or it may take that long to really believe what has happened. But fifteen minutes of verbal grieving is about eight pages in manuscript, and no one wants to read eight straight pages of heartbroken and repetitive speech.

So how long should emotional speeches be, with how much repetition? That depends on the character. A verbose, volatile person might get a page. After that, move on. Similarly, that verbose character might repeat, "I just let her out for a moment" three or even four times, but not the sixteen times a real person might say it. For a more taciturn or self-controlled person, one paragraph might be enough to let us share his grief without violating our idea of his personality.

Another way that fictional speech is shaped is by including more specific references than does real speech. One reason FBI agents have such a hard time getting criminals to commit themselves on wire is that people don't specifically name things they both understand. This conversation is mysterious to us but not, presumably, to the two participants.

> "Did you do it?"
>
> "Naw. He wasn't there."
>
> "He wasn't—did Johnny—"
>
> "No. Couldn't."
>
> "Goddamn!"

Who didn't do what? Who wasn't where? What couldn't Johnny do? Are these two men talking about a murder, a robbery, or getting the carpet cleaned?

Actually, if we are completely familiar with the situation and all its players, the above conversation might work in fiction. But in most circumstances, dialogue that better orients us is preferable:

> "Did you get the money?"
>
> "Naw. Dolobi wasn't there."
>
> "He wasn't—did Johnny talk to Louie about doing it next week?"
>
> "No. Couldn't. Louie ain't back from Florida."
>
> "Goddamn!"

This explicitness also helps readers make sense of grief, passion, fear, or joy. Without being pedantic, let us be sure what's being emoted over.

Yet another way that fictional dialogue is shaped is through understatement. Sometimes the most effective way to show that a usually verbose character is laboring under strong emotion is simply to have him shut up. When we expect an outburst from someone, its lack can convince us that the person really is overcome with emotion.

Near the end of Evelyn Waugh's classic *Brideshead Revisited*, protagonist Charles Ryder loses everything that matters to him when his fiancée, Lady Julia Flyte, decides for religious reasons that she cannot marry him. His reaction is simply, "I know." He has two more sentences in the scene, both equally calm:

- "What will you do?"
- "Now we shall both be alone, and I shall have no way of making you understand."

Yet despite this understatement (nobody does understatement better than the British), we are in absolutely no doubt that Ryder's heart is breaking. The absence of his usual sarcasm and eloquent cynicism says it all.

Finally, dialogue can be shaped to create emotion by where it is placed. It's no accident that Ryder's understated sorrow comes at the end of a chapter. Chapter ends, scene ends, and one-line paragraphs all give emphasis to whatever appears there. By placing an understated emotional utterance in one of these positions, you automatically lead readers to see it as significant, thus enhancing its emotional gravity.

ADVERBS AND TONE OF VOICE

Tone of voice is an emotional indicator easily indicated by an adverb: "he said sadly" or "she cried wildly." Yet writers are so often advised not to use these constructions. Why? And should you listen to this advice?

In my opinion, adverbs have gotten a bad rap. It's true that over-using them can look lazy or even silly. There's a writer's game, named "Tom Swifties" after the dated series of boys' books, in which people try to top each other by creating cute sentences in which the adverb comments on the dialogue (" 'She's dead,' he said gravely"). But used well, adverbs can indeed effectively indicate tone of voice. There's nothing wrong with, for example, "He said gently." Adverbs in unexpected pairings with dialogue can add complexity: " 'I love you,' he said angrily."

On the other hand, "He said loudly" might better be replaced with a stronger verb that eliminates the adverb, thereby gaining in both economy and vividness. Consider, for instance, "He shouted." But strong verbs to replace "said" have their pitfalls as well. Stories in which the writer avoids "said" by substituting a long series of "snarled," "hissed," "guffawed," and so forth takes on a comic tone, whether or not the author intended humor.

The bottom line is that adverbs to indicate tone of voice don't have to be avoided entirely but should be used with restraint.

TYPES OF DIALOGUE

Some emotional speech is particularly potent and requires careful handling. These include profanity, interjections, slang, and dialect.

Emotion and Punctuation

Although the semicolon will never replace "I love you" as a means of stirring readers' feelings, punctuation nonetheless has a useful role to play in indicating emotion.

- *Dashes* at the end of a speech of dialogue indicate that someone is being interrupted. Use these for angry or excited exchanges:
  "Really, Jane, you shouldn't—"
  "Don't tell me what I should or shouldn't do!"
- *Dashes* in the middle of a speech or during thoughts indicate that a character is interrupting himself, suggesting stress, surprise, or scatter-brained thinking: "I didn't go because—the date wasn't—are you *sure* we said Tuesday?"
- *Ellipses* indicate that a speech or thought is trailing off and can be used to indicate uncertainty or giving up: "I never know what to say to you . . ."
- *Italics* are good for emphasis.
- *Exclamation points*, of course, also indicate emphasis and should be used only in dialogue or thoughts. In narrative, the excitement should come from the story, not the punctuation.
- *Single quotes within double quotes* indicate that the speaker regards the quoted words as dubious, outrageous, or sarcastic: "John gave me a 'lovely surprise' last night."

Profanity is a natural means of expressing emotion, but there are two strictures: First, don't overuse it. If your characters use the strongest profanity in English in every other sentence (as some soldiers do), it remains a form of characterization but loses its force. For naturally profane characters, you will need to find some other method to convey feelings. For everybody else, save profanity for situations of high emotion.

Second, the profanity you choose should suit the character. Some people never go beyond "hell" or "damn," no matter what the circumstances (some never go even that far). Pick profanity that accurately reflects the character's temperament, background, and age.

The same is true for the broader class of interjections. No contemporary person under thirty says, "Mercy me!" Nor do octogenarians exclaim, "Bite me!"—unless they are trying very hard to be very hip.

Another danger with interjections, as with slang in general, is that it can easily become either stereotypical or dated. Not every African-American Southern Baptist exclaims, "Praise the Lord!" And almost no Irish-American cops say "faith and begorra" anymore (assuming they ever did). Either be very sure your slang is accurate for the character's time and social group or stick to such generic interjections that don't date, such as "Oh no" or "Ouch!"

Dialect is not really an emotional utterance; it's a general way of speaking. However, you can use it to indicate emotion if your character normally speaks in Standard English but reverts to native dialect when strongly affected (or very drunk). This is especially good for comic effect. Just make sure we understand why his speech is changing, and don't overdo the regionalisms.

THE BREAKING POINT: WHEN YOUR CHARACTER GETS EMOTIONAL

Continuous emotion, like continuous profanity, loses its force. Of course, some characters may be continuously emotional because that's their nature. It often works best, however, if these volatile types are secondary characters and your protagonist is someone who is capable of both calm and emotion. This gives the emotional episodes the power of contrast.

One of the most effective uses of contrast is the character who controls his emotions for a long time, perhaps even most of your book, and then lets go in one glorious venting scene. This "breaking point" is dramatic, interesting, and a natural climax, especially if it propels her to action. What that action is, of course, depends on the story. It may be anything from tears to going completely berserk.

Ebenezer Scrooge, in Charles Dickens's beloved *A Christmas Carol*, reaches his breaking point after being shown his past, present, and future by three ghosts. It's the bleak, loveless future that breaks him. When he wakes to discover he's not dead yet, Scrooge breaks out into a glory of emotional praise and thanksgiving, quickly followed by such actions as sending a turkey to the Cratchits and money to the poorhouse.

A quieter breaking point occurs in Jane Austen's *Sense and Sensibility*. Elinor Dashwood has carefully hidden her love for Edward Ferrars and her sorrow that he is engaged to another woman. In fact, so successfully has she controlled her emotional expressions that her sister Marianne repeatedly calls

Elinor "cold." But when Elinor learns that Edward is now free and he proposes to her, she reaches her breaking point:

> Elinor could sit no longer. She almost ran out of the room, and as soon as the door was closed, burst into tears of joy, which at first she thought would never cease.

For repressed Elinor, this is tantamount to hysteria. (The movie version with Emma Thompson, incidentally, does have Elinor hysterical with joy.)

A breaking point may also be negative. A character who endures humiliation after humiliation with quiet suffering may suddenly reach the end of what he can bear, grab his father's gun, and start shooting. Or, like young Paul Winter in Herman Wouk's *Youngblood Hawke*, he may kill himself. Paul leaves a suicide note in which all his unspoken despair finally breaks out.

If you decide to have your character reach a breaking point and gush with hitherto unexpressed emotion, here are a few things to remember:

- The effectiveness of "breaking point" as a literary technique depends on sufficient preparation by you, the writer. You must *dramatize* for us the repeated pressures that have led to this outburst. Dickens shows us Scrooge's horrifying vision from the Ghost of Christmas Yet to Come. Austen dramatizes the many times Elinor felt sorrow over Edward. Wouk gives us instance after instance of Paul's confusion and unhappiness.
- For each instance of pressure, we must see the character controlling his feelings—until he breaks.
- The form of the break must be in keeping with everything else you've shown us about the character. There's no way Elinor Dashwood would commit suicide. Nor would Paul Winter, that secretive boy, create a public scene. From bursting into song to bursting into full-blown delusional paranoia, your character's form of "break" must seem consistent with his overall makeup.

A breaking-point scene can be very effective if planned for from the beginning of the story. Will it fit yours?

TALK TO ME, BABY: WITH WHOM DOES YOUR CHARACTER GET EMOTIONAL?

People also characterize their lives by whom they select to share their emotions. Your detective protagonist might allow himself to show grief or fear only with his wife. On the other hand, if he stays "strong and silent" with his wife but opens up emotionally to his partner, that speaks volumes about both relationships.

Many people allow petty emotions—impatience, annoyance—to surface at home with their families while maintaining courtesy and charm with outsiders. They "take out on" their spouses and children all the frustrations and insecurities they cannot express elsewhere. The negative emotions they vent can range from constant but mild criticism to raging physical abuse. Is this your character's pattern? If so, be sure to show *both* sides of his behavior more than once so we clearly see the pattern.

Other characters may be emotional with everyone. These "drama queens" of both genders, also need to be depicted in several different situations with several different characters so we understand that she is not simply venting to a trusted friend but instead indiscriminately emoting to whatever audience presents itself.

A particular problem is the character who becomes emotional with no one, the secretive loner who has no intimate and doesn't need one. You may not be able to construct emotional dialogue for this person at all but will have to rely on other emotional indicators: body language, actions, or thoughts if it's a point-of-view character. Please don't have him wander around speaking aloud to himself. Unless he's genuinely delusional, this looks artificial and contrived.

Finally, there are some special instances of emotional dialogue that may fit with your plot:

- **Keeping a diary or journal or writing letters.** Although this lacks the immediacy of dramatization, it can be very effective if combined with scenes. Alice Walker's *The Color Purple* contains moving passages from the protagonist's passionate, pathetic, poorly spelt diary.
- **Talking to a pet.** This may work if your character is the kind of person who keeps and cherishes an animal.
- **Talking to a therapist.** This type of emotional conversation can work very well if your character is a person who would naturally go for professional help; Judith Rossner made such a situation the basis for her novel *August*. It can also work if the character is forced to see a psychiatrist. There can be many reasons for this. A desire to help his suicidal sister led Tom Wingo, with spectacular resistance, to talk extensively with Dr. Lowenstein in Pat Conroy's *The Prince of Tides*. A court

may order psychological help for a criminal defendant; a child may be reluctantly brought to a therapist by a parent; a person may be committed to a substance-abuse clinic and become emotional with her psychiatrist. Finally, a person who normally would shun psychological help may be driven to it by an inability to function; this premise underlies television's successful series *The Sopranos*.

- **A priest or clergyman.** If your character is deeply religious, he may allow himself to be open and emotional with a representative of his faith.

With whom does your character get emotional? Under what circumstances? The answers to these questions should suggest powerful scenes for your story.

THOUGHTS: A CHARACTER'S DIALOGUE WITH HIMSELF

Nearly everything we've said about emotional dialogue also applies to thoughts—with a few additions. A character may think excitedly about an emotional moment while it's occurring, as Dr. Joanna Lander does in Connie Willis's novel about near-death experiences, *Passage*:

> Maisie! Joanna thought in horror. I didn't tell Richard, I have to tell him, but could not remember what it was she had wanted to tell him. Something about the *Titanic*. No, not the *Titanic*.

Or the same character may think clearly, even in the tensest of moments, as Joanna does when she's dying:

> He has a knife, she thought calmly, and looked down at her blouse, down at his striking hand, but even though time was moving even more slowly than the security guard, she was too late. She couldn't see the knife.
>
> Because it had already gone in.

Whether depicting calm thoughts or incoherent ones, you can use all the same techniques as for dialogue: interjections, ethnic words, regional phrasing, profanity, understatement, breaking point, and emphasis (note how the last paragraph above gains drama by consisting of a single, short sentence).

In addition, your character can think things he would never say to anyone nor ever act on. Fantasies, desires, and hurts he would never share with another person are "shared" with the reader as we "overhear" his thoughts. Emotional thoughts can therefore comment on the story's action, making it richer than if action stood alone.

What does your character think about a story event? Let us in on her thoughts, expressed in characteristic words that also help us to know who she is.

OH, C'MON NOW! COMMON PITFALLS IN EMOTIONAL DIALOGUE

Speech expressing feeling is prone to perhaps more traps for the writer than any other kind of dialogue. Things to avoid include:

- **Overwriting.** Exaggerated, "purple prose" dialogue sounds not intense but comic. This is fine if you're writing comedy. If you're not, the character who says, "I will love you until the stars fade and die!" has lost his credibility (and yours). It's just too much. Yes, people do feel this intensely, and yes, some people express their intensity in heated speeches. But on paper they look insincere and faintly absurd. So if you want your character's emotion to be taken seriously by the reader, underplay it rather than overplay.

- **Clichés.** Here lies a pernicious dilemma. If "I love you" is a cliché and "I'll love you until the stars fade and die!" is comic, what's left? Is everyone reduced to mute stares to express love? (And if so, they had better not be "starry-eyed gazes.")

  No. Characters can say "I love you," despite its triteness, because it happens to be what most lovers, in fact, do say. As such, it may be a cliché, but it is also acceptable as dialogue due to its brevity and sheer ubiquity. So are "I'm sorry to hear of your mother's death," "Please accept my apology," and "Go to hell." They're hackneyed—but also short, truthful, and unlikely to cause rolling eyeballs.

  The dialogue clichés you want to avoid are secondhand ones taken not from life but from movies, television, and other books. "You'll be sorry you ever tangled with me" and "I'll break you yet" are empty threats, not because the speaker can't carry them out, but because the language has lost all force and menace. So, as a general rule, keep the everyday commonplace phrases, but look for less hackneyed dialogue when the situation becomes more complex.

- **As-you-know-Bob dialogue.** This mode of speech, always bad writing, is fatal in emotional dialogue, robbing it of all intensity and credibility. Emotional speech should not also be expected to fill in backstory. The character who says, "I've loved you ever since I first saw you, which was when we met in the eighth grade the year after my mother died," has just made an ass of himself. And, alas, of you. During emotional moments, characters should concentrate on the moment.

Whether your characters talk about their emotions or only think about them, emotions are the heart of fiction. Pulitzer Prize-winner Edna Ferber went so far as to say, "I think that in order to write really well and convincingly, one must be somewhat poisoned by emotion. Dislike, displeasure, resentment, fault-finding, imagination, passionate remonstrance, a sense of injustice— they all make fine fuel." You may not want to go so far as to be "poisoned" by emotion, but if you can enter into your characters' feelings, their expressions of emotion will gain authenticity and fire. In other words, *become* your character—at least as you write him.

Then read the scene again and become your reader.

RECAP: DIALOGUE AND THOUGHTS

Emotional dialogue—what feelings a character expresses and in what words— is determined not only by basic temperament but also by ethnicity, family training, region, education, gender, and particular circumstances. In addition, people speak differently about an emotional event after it's over. Paying attention to all these differences can both enhance your character's plausibility and also build characterization.

Fictional dialogue differs from real-life dialogue by being shaped through compression, understatement, or emphasis. For maximum effect, you should employ slang, profanity, and dialect sparingly—possibly more sparingly than your character would use them in real life. Avoid overwriting, clichés, and as-you-know-Bob exposition in dialogue; all undermine readers' responses.

Choose carefully to whom your character talks emotionally and when; it indicates personality. So do her thoughts (talking to herself). Characters' emotional thoughts can be used to show sides of her that her actions and dialogue do not, deepening the reader's total perception of her personality.

Exploiting a character's "breaking point," a dramatically effective use of dialogue, requires portraying both the pressures on him and his previous self-control.

Tape-record a short conversation with a friend or relative. (Note: In some states, you must have the other person's permission to do this legally.) Transcribe the results. How would they need to be compressed, emphasized, explained, or otherwise rewritten to work as fictional dialogue? Rewrite the conversation.

EXERCISE 2

Imagine that six people you know are told, each privately, that they have inherited a billion dollars. Write down the *first* thing each person would say, in your opinion. Study the results. Are they in keeping with what you know of each person's broader character? How can you alter the dialogue to better build characterization while still staying true to the original personality?

EXERCISE 3

Write an intense argument between two people, exclusively in dialogue. Now write a diary entry for each participant, giving his or her thoughts on the fight. How do their emotional reactions differ? What words do they use to express them?

EXERCISE 4

Ride a bus, walk through a mall, or hang around a park. Eavesdrop on conversations. (Try not to look like a suspicious character while doing this.) What slang, profanity, or unusual phrases do people use? What emotions do they express through them? Write the phrases down later, not to use directly in fiction (teen slang, especially, changes very fast) but as practice in hearing and creating individual patterns of speech.

EXERCISE 5

Find a play you really like and pick the most emotional scene in it. Analyze the dialogue to see how the playwright, who had nothing *but* dialogue to work with, has his characters express emotion. Are there any techniques here you can use?

chapter 9

[EMOTION SUGGESTED—USING METAPHOR, SYMBOL, AND SENSORY DETAILS TO CONVEY FEELING]

So far we've discussed ways to convey a character's emotion directly through what he says, does, feels, and thinks, plus what you the author tell us about him in exposition. Emotion can be conveyed indirectly and allusively through metaphors and symbols. These allusions can be both powerful and evocative, suggesting more than the emotion of the moment.

This isn't really surprising. Some scientists believe our brains are hardwired to understand the world through stories, which is why every culture known to man has used stories to educate, entertain, worship, unite, control, and move its members. Humans have religious stories, political stories, heroic stories, and love stories. And all stories, true and imaginary, are in one sense metaphors.

The formal definition of a metaphor is "speech containing an implied comparison, in which a word or phrase primarily used of one thing is applied to another." The usual embodiment of this is something like "His glance sliced through her." Here a "glance" is compared to a knife: sharp, slicing, and dangerous. The metaphor makes her reaction—feeling as if she's been sliced or cut—more vivid than would "His glance hurt her."

In what sense are all stories metaphors? They all create self-contained, imaginary worlds that make us feel the real world more vividly. After seeing *Hamlet*, hearing about George Washington and the cherry tree, or reading *Anna Karenina*, our world has been enlarged. We have not only felt things along with the characters (Hamlet's rage, Washington's integrity, Anna's despair), we have received an additional lens through which to evaluate the world around us. This is true even when the stories are, say, a third-rate television sitcom. It's still a metaphor for real life, and the reason we may reject it as "bad" is because we subconsciously decide the metaphor doesn't fit life ("This is dumb! Nobody would really behave that way!").

Knowing that fiction embodies metaphors on several levels can help you choose the right ones to enhance emotional response to *your* story. Let's look at four such levels: simple comparison, extended metaphor, symbol, and displaced reality.

SIMPLE COMPARISONS: MINING CULTURAL ORE

Metaphors and their cousins, similes (a simile uses "like" or "as" to make its comparison), achieve their effect by doubling the impression on the reader of the thing being described. For example, a scene ends with a character feeling joy. The last line of the scene might be, "All around us, roses bloomed in red, in orange, in the gold of the shining sun." We understand from this not only that the character is standing in a garden but that she, too, is blooming and shining. The flowers have been brought into play as a symbol for her emotions. As a result, we readers feel not only whatever has been evoked by the plot and characters but also whatever associations we readers bring to sunshine and roses. This is the power of metaphors: They evoke something beyond what straightforward phrases can do.

That "something beyond" is where metaphors can get tricky, for several reasons. First, different people may have different associations with the comparison image (called the "vehicle") in the metaphor. If, for you, flowers evoke allergies and not pleasure, you will not feel what the writer intended by his metaphor. Other metaphors are specific to a given culture, which is why some literature does not translate well. Christian imagery—crosses, three-day resurrections, and arks full of animals—may mystify, not deepen, meanings for those not raised with a Christian heritage.

Even within a culture, metaphoric vehicles can change their meaning across time. F. Scott Fitzgerald's *The Great Gatsby* includes these words to describe the triple death of Muriel, Gatsby, and Wilson: ". . . and the holocaust was complete." Written in 1925, the sentence then merely evoked an idea of horrible destruction. But since World War II, the word "holocaust" carries other, more specific connotations of genocide, no longer suited to Fitzgerald's use of it. This isn't, of course, his fault—writers aren't expected to be prescient (except perhaps by editors). But you, writing today, would need to exercise care in using "holocaust" in metaphor.

In fact, a great many words carry connotations beyond their literal meaning. You need to be aware of the emotional baggage such terms carry so you can use them to evoke the feeling you want rather than inadvertently dragging in one you don't.

All of the following objects, for instance, bring emotions (for some readers, strong emotions) along with them *before* you've set up any comparison with anything else:

- mother's milk
- flag
- apple pie
- slave-auction block
- wedding ring
- altar
- kittens and puppies
- noose
- cigarettes
- rhinestones

This is why a slave-auction block used as an altar under a dangling noose is a horrific idea to most people, before there's even a wisp of a story around the setting.

Use these built-in connotations to your advantage. Select vehicles for your metaphors that suggest the emotions you want. One caveat, however: These same vehicles, because they evoke familiar feelings, can seem hackneyed and stereotyped if not used in fresh ways. "The child gamboled like a kitten" is trite, even though kittens *do* gambol and play. Better would be "The child tumbled and laughed and gamboled, all but chasing a nonexistent furry tail."

On the other hand, avoid the obviously bizarre. Weird metaphors that call attention to themselves will stop your story dead: "Her feelings about John were mixed, like greens in a chef's salad." Choose emotional metaphors that are apt, feel unforced, and evoke the emotion you want to create.

One final caveat on using metaphors: The mixed metaphor evokes either derision or confusion. It's always a disaster. "He nipped the storm of protest in the bud" will bounce your reader right out of your story, perhaps to never return.

WEATHER REPORT: THE PATHETIC FALLACY

One class of metaphors deserves special mention because it is so ubiquitous, so tempting, and so risky. That is the use of weather to convey characters' moods.

And it *is* tempting. Nearly everyone responds to weather: the pleasure of sunlight, the fresh beginnings of spring, the gloom of a gray winter afternoon. The problem is that weather as metaphor can feel contrived. After all, does the global climate really arrange itself so that rain will fall on Boston just when your character is depressed in Back Bay? Sophisticated readers have rejected simple one-to-one correspondence between the facts of nature and the emotions of man ever since Wordsworth and the other Romantics over-used them. In fact, so widespread and derided was this technique that it earned its own critical designation: the Pathetic Fallacy.

Does this mean you can't use weather in metaphors? No, it just means you need to use a light hand. The trick is not to make the immediate weather in a given scene an exact and detailed parallel to a character's emotions. Instead, use one facet of weather as just one element in a metaphor (such as the roses-and-sunshine above). Or use weather that isn't actually present in the scene at all. Herman Melville did this nicely when he described Ishmael's restless, gray depression as "November in the soul" in *Moby-Dick*.

EXTENDED METAPHORS: HOW YOU DO GO ON

The second level of comparison used to suggest emotion is the extended metaphor. In this technique, you refer to the same metaphor at two, three, or four different points in a single scene; each mention adds another layer of emotional meaning. For instance, in Joyce Grace Lee's story "Dusk," Ann and Richard are on the verge of a bad marital fight. These sentences appear throughout the scene:

- They faced each other across the living room, and their disagreement flowed between them, trivial and noisy as a stream over rocks. (near beginning of scene)
- "I didn't tell you because—" Ann said, and stopped abruptly. The stream widened, growing swifter. (middle of scene)
- "Then go," Ann said coolly and he felt the flood sweep down on him, carrying everything away. (scene end)

If you use the extended metaphor to convey emotion in a scene, the guidelines are the same as for a single metaphor: aptness, moderation, and congruity with setting. In "Dusk," Richard is a white-water raft guide, which makes the metaphor feel natural to his point of view.

When Emotion Goes Terribly Wrong

A pitfall of metaphors and symbols is overwriting—trying to pack so much meaning into a single sentence that the results become not moving but unintentionally hilarious. Every year the English Department at San Jose State University conducts the Bulwer-Lytton Fiction Contest, named for nineteenth-century author Edward George Bulwer-Lytton (*The Last Days of Pompeii*), who was given to purple prose. The contest is aimed at finding that single perfect example of metaphors tortured into parody.

The proud winner for 2004, by Dave Zobel of Manhattan Beach, California:

"She resolved to end the love affair with Ramon tonight . . . summarily, like Martha Stewart ripping the sand vein out of a shrimp's tail . . . though the term 'love affair' now struck her as a ridiculous euphemism . . . not unlike 'sand vein,' which is after all an intestine, not a vein . . . and that tarry substance inside certainly isn't sand . . . and that brought her back to Ramon."

Unless you're writing a Bulwer-Lytton entry, block that metaphor!

SYMBOLS: AN OBJECT WITH TRANSCENDENCE

Symbols are a type of metaphor in which some object or concept is extended for the entire length of a story. Symbols, if well chosen, can carry much emotional power because a good symbol works on more than one level. As the story goes on, the symbol may take on additional layers of meaning.

The symbol often is an actual object, as in Henry James's novel *The Golden Bowl*. This bowl is bought at an antique store as a wedding gift. There is a slight crack in the bowl. As the story goes on, the bowl, once admired, is broken. We gradually come to realize that the antique bowl represents the institutions, including marriage customs, of this society, which is decaying from within. The characters' emotions occur within, and are affected by, this decay.

When an object is used symbolically, it may either already carry its own cultural implications, as with flags and crosses, or the object may be invested with symbolic significance specifically for this particular story, as with James's golden bowl (usually, bowls don't indicate societal decay). If you invest some unexpected object with layers of meaning, you will need to make this clear enough so most readers will "get it." Please note that I say "most readers"—

there are readers you will never reach with symbols, and it's no use trying. These literal folk enjoy a story on a plot level only, which is why your story should be able to function coherently even if nobody ever gets the symbolic significance.

How clear do you have to make it? That varies with the story. Harper Lee's classic *To Kill a Mockingbird* takes no chances. A third of the way through the book, Atticus Finch tells his son Jem:

> "Shoot all the bluejays you want if you can hit 'em, but remember it's a sin to kill a mockingbird."
>
> That was the only time I ever heard Atticus say it was a sin to do something, and I asked Miss Maudie about it.
>
> "Your father's right," she said. "Mockingbirds don't do one thing but make music for us to enjoy. They don't eat up people's gardens, they don't do one thing but sing their hearts out for us. That's why it's a sin to kill a mockingbird."

The mockingbird as a symbol of harmless goodness reappears with complete explicitness at the novel's end. Eight-year-old Scout is instructed to never reveal that the kind, simple-minded Boo Radley was involved in the murder of the villain, Bob Ewell, while Boo was saving Scout's and Jem's lives:

> Atticus sat looking at the floor for a long time. Finally he raised his head. "Scout," he said, "Mr. Ewell fell on his knife. Can you possibly understand?"
>
> Atticus looked like he needed cheering up. I ran to him and hugged him and kissed him with all my might. "Yes, sir, I understand," I reassured him. "Mr. Tate was right."
>
> Atticus disengaged himself and looked at me. "What do you mean?"
>
> "Well, it'd be sort of like shooting a mockingbird, wouldn't it?"

In other stories, the symbol is not so unambiguously explained. Ann Patchett's novel *Bel Canto* is about an opera singer, along with other people of importance, taken hostage by a group of South American revolutionaries trying to overthrow their government. Throughout this wonderful book, opera functions as a symbol of civilization itself: cultured, beautiful, able to transform men's baser impulses. The symbolism is never explicated, but it informs practically every chapter. On the other hand, a reader could enjoy the story on a plot level without ever becoming consciously aware of how much more is being said. Such a reader would still experience the emotional response to both story and characters that the metaphors help convey.

SYMBOLS II: THE NONTANGIBLE CONCEPT

A nontangible concept is something you cannot touch, see, or taste—it is an abstract such as "justice," "faith," or "history." As such, it's already one step removed from the concrete upon which fiction depends. Nonetheless, in skillful hands, an abstract concept can also function as a symbol.

Catherine Ryan Hyde does this beautifully in her story of neighborhood strife, "Bloodlines." The ostensible argument is over the supposed superiority of Frank's purebred, championship-line Doberman to Cacho's mixed-breed mutt. But as the story intensifies, it becomes clear that what's really at dispute is Frank's supposed "American-born" superiority to immigrant Cacho. The purebred dog becomes pregnant by a mutt that dug into her pen, which Cacho warned would happen but Frank ignored. Cacho takes photos of the mating, "proof" of the pups' mixed bloodlines. Class comparisons ensue, then fistfights, as more neighbors get involved and racial epithets are exchanged. Canine bloodlines become a symbol of human bloodlines, plus a means to express anger, competition, and fear.

Some symbols, like Lee's mockingbird, are not really part of the plot, which would be unchanged even if the passages about mockingbirds were cut from the text. In both *Bel Canto* and "Bloodlines," however, the symbol is so deeply woven into the story that it *is* the plot. Without opera, *Bel Canto* would have had no kidnapping, hostage situation, or story. Without fights over bloodlines, canine and human, Frank and Cacho might have gone on coexisting as distantly friendly neighbors.

To build an entire story around a symbol, and thus create more complex and layered emotion, you need to:

- Choose an object or concept that is *both* an integral part of the plot and something the characters can have strong emotions about. The object can be anything; in Louis Auchincloss's story "Second Chance," an ordinary table fork acquires powerful symbolic significance.
- Develop the story's action around the symbol.
- Decide whether characters are aware of the symbol's significance, or whether they will not be aware but the reader will.
- Give dialogue or thoughts about the symbol to characters who *are* aware of the symbol's significance.
- Give unaware characters chances to interact with the symbol in ways that express their emotions. For instance, if two sisters are cleaning out

their mother's apartment after her death, you might have them argue repeatedly about a beloved but financially worthless hat. As they return to the argument again and again, it becomes clear that it's not the hat they're fighting over but their dead mother's love.

• Try to end scenes or even the entire story with the symbol to boost its significance further.

BORROWED EMOTION: PREVIOUS ART

It is also possible to create feelings in the reader through "borrowed emotion": quoting from songs, poetry, movies, or previously written fiction, or referring to instrumental music or works of art such as paintings and sculpture. In one sense, these things are symbols; certainly they stand for more than themselves. The ceiling of the Sistine Chapel represents for many a sublime harnessing of talent in the service of faith. The popular music of one's youth, whether "Smoke Gets in Your Eyes" or "Eve of Destruction," brings in entire vanished eras in American culture. Different cultural baggage comes into play when a character quotes a movie: "Make my day" or "We'll always have Paris."

There are two schools of thought on this. One is that it's an authentic reflection of the way people think and talk, since cultural symbols (whether high or pop) do in fact permeate daily life. Writers who employ them argue that they serve the same function as brand names: a literary shorthand for placing a character in a certain milieu, since the character quoting Dante is probably not the same one quoting Dr. Dre (although it might be interesting if he is). In addition, quotes or references are legitimate ways to evoke the emotion of the original as long as its relevance to the story situation is made clear.

The opposition argues that the use of quotes and references is nothing more than exploiting secondhand emotion. It's the writer's obligation, say such critics, to create feeling by what happens in *his* story, not in Shakespeare's plays or John Lennon's lyrics.

Just to further muddy the waters, there's a third, very large group that settles for middle ground. These writers use quotations from prose, poetry, or songs as heads for chapters, sections, or the book as a whole without attempting to integrate them into the text. As such, the quotes can help set a mood without having to be part of the story proper.

However you use these excerpts or references, there are a few guidelines to keep in mind. First, other artists wrote the material and thus own it. From

Dante, Shakespeare, and other public domain material, of course, you may quote freely. The same is true of public speeches (from, for instance, candidates for office, which may have use in a historical novel). For copyrighted material, you usually need the author's permission to quote it in fiction (although not in "educational" or review works, provided you stay within fair usage word limits). A dead author's estate retains the rights to quote, and some are not generous about this. Get permission in writing.

Quoting from songs is even more difficult. The American Society of Composers, Authors, and Publishers (ASCAP) governs rules about quoting from songs, and the rules are stringent. Be prepared to pay for permissions.

On the other hand, you may refer freely to titles of anything, since titles are not copyrighted. Your characters are allowed to say, "Listen! They're playing our song!" and then name it. They may also freely go to New York's Lincoln Center to see the New York City Ballet dance *Agon*, go to Nashville's Grand Ole Opry to hear Dolly Parton sing "Jolene," or go to their local library and check out *Bel Canto*.

PROUST'S MADELEINES: SENSORY EMOTION

Finally, an often-neglected way of creating emotion in the reader is through senses other than vision or speech, which most writers use naturally in description and dialogue. Smell, taste, and feel, on the other hand, are often neglected. Properly speaking, these are simply part of good description. But, if used skillfully, they can also bring in more emotion than the description itself suggests.

The most famous example of this is Marcel Proust's *Remembrance of Things Past*, in which the smell of a fragrant little cookie, a madeleine, brings the narrator's entire past flowing vividly through his mind (and through seven hundred pages of text). You probably can't depend on simply naming a cookie to have that effect on your reader since, as with taste and feel, smells are highly individual (just ask any dog). Still, some sensory stimuli have strong emotional connotations you can probably count on.

The easiest is revulsion. Evoking the odor, feel, or taste of feces will make most readers recoil. So might blood, viscera, corpses . . . you get the idea. On the other hand, readers' pleasure responses might be brought into play through the mention of the smell of bread baking, the taste of cool water on a hot day, or the feel of a fire after coming in from a blizzard.

Consider the following passage. What emotions does it arouse in you?

> She walked under the tall trees, drawing deep breaths of the cool dry air scented
> with pine. At the top, silhouetted against the sunset, the branches looked black;
> farther down they were green; underfoot the needles were the color of cinnamon.
> On their soft carpet her boots made no sound. Somewhere an owl hooted, low
> and cool as the pines.

Did you feel peaceful? Tranquil? Balanced? And yet we have no idea what story is transpiring under these pines. "She" could be going to a murder, a lovers' meeting, or the latrine. In the absence of further information, the sensory input alone has created feeling.

What emotion do you want your readers to experience during the scene you're writing? Find sensory details that will reinforce that feeling.

Most of the emotion in your story, of course, will come from the characters and their situations. But consider adding to it through metaphor, symbol, and sensory manipulation—and maybe even through quotations as well.

RECAP: METAPHOR, SYMBOL, AND SENSORY DETAILS

Metaphors are implied comparisons in which a word or phrase primarily used for one thing is applied to another. By choosing that word or phrase carefully, you can add its emotion to your initial situation. You can add even more emotion with extended metaphors, which carry the comparison throughout an entire scene.

Metaphors involving words with strong cultural connotations should be used in situations where you want those additional meanings. One class of metaphors needs particular care: one involving nature, which can all too easily devolve into the Pathetic Fallacy.

Symbols may be actual objects or abstract concepts. Chosen to fit the story, they can either be explicated through characters' thoughts and dialogue or left for the discerning reader to interpret. Symbols should always be chosen to fit the plot or setting.

Quotations, song lyrics, poetry, and references to existing art may either enhance your work by adding its own emotion to your story or may detract from it by being "secondhand." This is a judgment call.

Another very effective way to add to the emotion already present in a scene is to include well-chosen sensory details.

EXERCISE 1

Find three different metaphors for housebreaking a puppy. Jot them down. Which makes the task seem never-ending? Which makes it seem funny? Which seems most accurate? Which do you like best? Write a sentence incorporating the metaphor.

Now do this exercise as applied to a more serious situation, such as a gang murder.

EXERCISE 2

Write a brief scene involving taking the puppy outside in the middle of the night. Use one of your comparisons as an extended metaphor, mentioning it in different ways in the beginning of the scene, the middle, and at the end.

As in exercise one, now do this exercise as applied to a more serious situation, such as a gang murder.

EXERCISE 3

What could each of the following be a symbol of: a roll of money, a spray of lilies, the ocean? Try to think of at least two symbolic interpretations for each.

EXERCISE 4

Open a favorite book to any strong scene. How does the author create emotion? Underline any metaphors or similes in red. Underline the use of symbols in blue. Underline sensory details in yellow. Is he stronger on any of these? If you chose a different author, or a different story by the same author, would the results be different?

EXERCISE 5

Open a copy of *Bartlett's Familiar Quotations*, or a similar volume, at random. Read until a quote catches your imagination. Does it suggest a scene, or even a whole story? If so, would you use the quotation as a header for the finished work? Why or why not?

chapter 10

[SPECIAL CASES OF EMOTION— LOVING, FIGHTING, AND DYING]

Few human acts are emotionally neutral. Even taking out the garbage can evoke some faint blip on the radar of feelings: distaste if it smells, annoyance that no one else ever takes it out, or pleasure at being so organized. Some situations, however, require major emotions from characters, with the hope of evoking correspondingly large reactions in readers. Such scenes are usually major in another way: They climax rising tension in the plot. As such, they require special care to write well. This includes love scenes, fight scenes, and death scenes.

I LOVE YOU, MY WAY

The most important thing to remember about love scenes is that they must fit the temperament of your characters. This should, of course, be true of all your characters' actions, but with love scenes it's especially critical because it's so easy to slip into cliché. By the time you write that big romantic scene in your novel, you have read or seen on television and at the movies hundreds of love scenes. The twin temptations are slipping into unthinking repetition and wanting to do something completely new.

If you simply repeat the usual romantic speeches and actions, your scene will be boring. There are, after all, only so many things lovers usually say or do when they declare love; how can you make them fresh? And if you strive too hard to do so, you may stretch the reader's credulity to the breaking point.

The answer, again, is to use the conventional actions but with attention to your characters' individual personalities. They can still use the usual variations on the basic human formula ("I love you," "Will you marry me?"). They can do the usual things (embrace, kiss). But their other words, their gestures, the props in the scene, the setting, and the emotions they feel in addition to simple desire present enormous potential for individualizing the universal.

You the writer have the choice of presenting your love scene exactly as the characters experience it or of adding enough exposition so the reader gains some distance and perspective on what is occurring.

Here is a love scene from Nora Roberts's best-selling romance novel *Temptation*. Eden Carlbough, jilted by one fiancé, has been resisting Chase Elliott's advances for 213 pages when she finally gives in:

> "Chase—"
>
> "Don't say anything yet." He brought her hand to his lips. "Eden, I know you're used to certain things, a certain way of life. If that's what you need, I'll find a way to give it to you. But if you give me a chance, I can make you happy here."
>
> She swallowed, afraid of misunderstanding. "Chase, are you saying you'd move back to Philadelphia if I asked you to?"
>
> "I'm saying I'd move anywhere if it was important enough to you, but I'm not letting you go back alone, Eden. Summers aren't enough."
>
> Her breath came out quietly. "What do you want from me?"
>
> "Everything." He pressed his lips to her hand again, but his eyes were no longer calm. "A lifetime, starting now. Love, arguments, children. Marry me, Eden."

A basic love scene like this works well in romance novels. Both people are in love; the characters voice their emotions in a clear, straightforward way; the bodily actions and reactions are the expected ones for the situation (kissing, choked-up speech, an ardent look in the eyes). And yet there are concerns individual to this particular pair of young lovers, concerns that have grown out of the preceding plot, such as where they will live and in what manner ("a certain way of life"). The scene is basic but not generic; you could not give these exact same words to another couple in another romance novel. Eden and Chase's love scene is the product of their personalities and their respective pasts.

A MORE COMPLICATED LOVE

When characters are more complex, so must their love scenes be. In E.M. Forster's *Howards End*, lovers Henry Wilcox and Margaret Schlegel are complicated people. Henry, a rich middle-aged widower with three children, is the product of a mannered and emotionally repressed Edwardian life. Margaret, close to middle-aged herself, is insightful and idealistic. Henry proposes bumblingly; Margaret defers accepting at all. Yet this is definitely a love scene, even though Henry has brought Margaret up to London ostensibly to inspect a house he might rent to her:

> "Miss Schlegel—" his voice was firm "—I have had you up on false pretences. I want to speak about a much more serious matter than a house."
>
> Margaret almost answered, "I know—"
>
> "Could you be induced to share my—is it probable—"
>
> "Oh, Mr. Wilcox!" she interrupted, holding the piano and averting her eyes. "I see, I see, I will write to you afterwards if I may."
>
> He began to stammer. "Miss Schlegel—Margaret—"
>
> "Oh, yes! Indeed, yes!" said Margaret.
>
> "I am asking you to be my wife."
>
> So deep already was her sympathy that when he said, "I am asking you to be my wife," she made herself give a little start. She must show surprise if he expected it. An immense joy came over her. It was indescribable. It had nothing to do with humanity, and most resembled the all-pervading happiness of fine weather. Fine weather is due to the sun, but Margaret could think of no central radiance here. She stood in his drawing-room happy, and longing to give happiness. On leaving him, she realized that the central radiance had been love.
>
> "You aren't offended, Miss Schlegel?"
>
> "How could I be offended?"
>
> There was a moment's pause. He was anxious to get rid of her, and she knew it. She had too much intuition to look at him as he struggled for possessions that money cannot buy. . . .
>
> They parted without shaking hands: she had kept the interview, for his sake, in tints of quietest grey. Yet she thrilled with happiness ere she reached her own house.

One cannot imagine Eden Carlbough and Chase Elliott behaving like this. How has this love scene been made so individual?

- Because Henry and Margaret are cultured people in a restrained era, they express their emotions with restraint. Neither says, "I love you." Henry has difficulty saying anything at all; Margaret expresses her feelings only on paper.
- They do not touch each other.

- Margaret's love is not simply a desire to be with this man. It's mixed strongly with her desire to give, to be needed—an essential part of her personality. For this reason, she deliberately avoids watching him struggle to propose and also avoids expressing her own feelings, keeping the love scene "in tints of quietest grey."

- Henry struggles because, as Margaret knows, it's hard for him to admit need, ask anybody for anything, or risk rejection. He must always be in control, and here he is not (she might refuse!).

- No one's emotions are pure. Henry both desires Margaret and is "anxious to get rid of her," in order to escape the risk and tension he feels while proposing. Margaret feels radiant love but knows it "had nothing to do with humanity," not even Henry's humanity; it is instead the realization of an opportunity to be necessary and useful.

This love scene is highly expressive of these two people and no one else.

Key to this is the fact that emotions are mixed. Love can come coupled to so many other feelings: frustration ("Why won't you see this my way?"), anger (ditto, in spades), pity ("I'm moved by your troubles"), fear ("What if I lost you?"), sorrow ("I didn't want things to be this way"), protectiveness ("I want to keep you safe and happy"), even hatred ("My longing for you is ruining my life!"). If you can get more than simple desire into your love scene, it will strengthen and deepen it.

It may also help your plot. Those other emotions, whatever they are, can foreshadow events to come. In *Howards End*, Henry's need to control and Margaret's to give will both be pushed so far that they almost break their marriage.

LOVE SEEN FROM THE OUTSIDE: THE EXPOSITORY LOVE SCENE

Another, if riskier, way to individualize love scenes is to add exposition, describing the characters' love in ways they themselves don't or won't see. We already saw some of this in the passage from *The Once and Future King* in chapter four, in which author White gives his opinion about why Guinevere loved two men ("perhaps she loved Arthur as a father, and Lancelot because of the son she could not have"). Such exposition can be used to interpret love in more sophisticated ways than the lover can.

In Pearl S. Buck's classic *The Good Earth*, Chinese peasant Wang Lung has fallen in love with a prostitute, Lotus. Buck describes his love as a "sickness" and a "suffering." She describes in detail Wang Lung's slavish thirst for Lotus, his neglect of his land and family, his humiliations at her hands, and his sleepless nights. The exposition is far more effective than simple scenes between Wang and Lotus would have been because neither ever mentions, or really comprehends, what is going on. It's not really love, or at least not love alone; it's lust mixed with a desire for beauty denied for a lifetime.

You probably don't want to put every scene between your lovers in exposition alone (not even Buck does this). But you might, if your characters are not introspective or if you have some larger point to make about desire, add a few paragraphs of exposition to a love scene to add dimensions that dialogue and action alone cannot carry.

PUTTING IT TOGETHER: AN EFFECTIVE LOVE SCENE

Your lovers need to declare their love; the plot requires it, and anyway, you've been working up to this declaration for several scenes. Here are the steps to take to make a timeworn necessity seem fresh:

- Think about your characters' individual personalities. Are they shy? Blustery? Anxious? Controlling? What might such a person say while feeling passionate?
- What might such a person do? How physical will each person be? Is this in character?
- Choose a setting for the scene that can also individualize it. This doesn't mean being "original" (the underwater scuba-diving declaration of love) so much as it means revealing personality. Nora Roberts has Chase propose in his house, whose décor shows Eden a more cultured side of Chase than she had suspected him of possessing. Henry Wilcox, typically, proposes in a commercial property he owns and controls.
- Think about each person's bodily responses and include them as important indicators of emotion.
- What else do these lovers have on their minds beside love? Vary their expressions of passion by having them talk about it. This second subject should, of course, be reasonable to expect in a loving moment: vacation plans, say, rather than astrophysics.
- Consider what other emotions your characters might also be feeling

along with, or as a result of, love. Try hard to include these; your portrayal will be much more complex.

• Experiment with including a few sentences or paragraphs of exposition to add depth to how readers view this love scene.

SEX SCENES: HOW GRAPHIC HOW SOON?

If love scenes present pitfalls for the writer, sex scenes are looming abysses. The difficulties are the three P's: parallelism, parody, and pornography.

Parallelism refers to the fact that most sex scenes involve pretty much the same actions, since human beings are designed to fit together in pretty much the same ways. Trying to vary this in graphically described physical acts leads you to pornography. Trying to vary it in graphically described emotion often brings you close to parody. Mention "heaving bosom" just once and your scene is dead.

The solution to all three of these problems is the same. Since sex, as itself, is not usually very interesting to read about it, good sex scenes depend on the usual things happening between characters in whom readers have a heightened interest. In other words, it's not what they're doing that makes a sex scene good, it's that they're doing it with each other, and the act means something to them and to us.

How do you get that in your writing? First, by making us care that these two people are having sex. That means that we care about at least one of them, which in turn implies that we've come to know him/her/them. This is why a sex scene should never open a story. Sex must come after we have had enough exposure to understand what it means to the person engaging in it.

In Tolstoy's *Anna Karenina*, for instance, we have seen sexual desire develop between Anna and Vronsky for several chapters. We have also seen Anna's life apart from him. We have felt the rising tension between her desire for him and her full knowledge that an affair could cost her husband, child, and position in society. When sex occurs between them, it is more than just sex; it's a grenade hurled into Anna's life.

However, suppose the point of your sex scene is that it *is* meaningless to the participants. Then we need to feel that, not just be told about it. Again, prior characterization is the only way to make us feel this sexual encounter's emptiness.

This careful preparation is why generations of novelists could make us

Question:

How sexy is too sexy?

Answer:

There is, of course, no simple answer to this question; it depends on place and time.

In 1946, two years after its publication, Kathleen Winsor's *Forever Amber* was banned in Massachusetts for obscenity. The state's attorney general, George Rowell, contended that bookstores that carried the historical novel were liable for criminal prosecution because the book contained, among other offenses, seventy references to sexual intercourse, ten descriptions of women undressing in the presence of men, and thirteen references ridiculing marriage.

The banning helped propel the book to over two million sales.

It is difficult today to imagine criminal prosecution because a book includes descriptions of women undressing. But publishers may still turn down a novel if the sex is of a kind that does not fit in with their literary line. A greater consideration, however, is whether explicit or unusual sex will be accepted by readers.

Many writers find it helpful to imagine the ideal reader for a particular story. Is it a middle-class woman (the largest single class of book buyers)? A teenage boy? A college English professor? Your mailman? Your sister? Think about what level of explicit sex this reader will accept. Your actual readers, of course, will be a much more diverse group—but focusing on a hypothetical idea can help you find the sex scene that will fit both audience and plot.

feel their characters' sexuality without ever detailing so much as a single caress. The emphasis was on the emotions and events leading up to the bedroom, followed by a quick cut to "afterward." Whether you think this technique was dictated by sagacity or prudishness, it worked.

You may, however, prefer to write the actual sex scene, complete with body parts and positions. If so, keep these points in mind:

• Your characters' actions should still reflect their individuality, even when those actions are pretty standard. In other words, a shy character should be shy in bed. A greedy and insensitive man does not become generous or gentle just because he's between the sheets. More important, your scene does not become interesting just because it features sex; it must feature sex between these particular characters.

• Except in the most intense moments, sex is not all that goes on in bed. What else is on these people's minds? What else creeps into their talk? Is she nervous about her weight? Is he afraid his wife might phone? Or his lawyer? Does she keep looking at her watch because daycare closes in forty minutes? Is he resentful that she's so rushed? Is he desperately in love and she just amusing herself? Again, this sex scene should be about individuals, and the best way to do that is to flavor the scene with not only their personalities but the rest of their lives.

• Different genres allow for different degrees of explicit sexual descriptions. In category romance novels, these are often spelled out in writers' guidelines. For everybody else, it's a question of tone. A police procedural, frank about the body in death, may be equally frank about it in sex. A whimsical fantasy will probably be shattered by an overly graphic sex scene. A first-person narrator who shrinks from violence would not describe rape in detail.

• Does this sex scene have a point? Does it deepen our understanding of the characters, complicate their relationships, or advance the plot? Sex scenes are not exempt from the general rule that scenes must be included in the story for a purpose. If yours is doing nothing but titillate, and you're not writing porn, cut the scene entirely.

FIGHT SCENES: FROM ARGUMENTS TO BLOODSHED

Fights, whether fought with words or battle-axes, are basic to plot development because they are, by definition, divisive. Fights separate people, putting them on opposite sides, and two sides of anything, whether it's mutiny or who takes out the garbage, is the essence of conflict. However, fights also have a second, equally important purpose: They're one of the most effective ways to build characterization. This is because fighting, unlike sex, tends to be highly individual. The term "naked aggression" is apt; we don't dissemble when furious. People express deep layers of their personalities in how often they fight, with whom, how fairly, and how intensely.

Some people argue about everything. These are the chip-on-the-shoulder folks looking for a battle, the know-it-alls who correct everyone around them and get mad at any disagreement, or the purely mean. At the other end of the spectrum are those who let nearly any insult go by, unwilling to fight. It takes a lot to provoke these people, who may be either calm by nature or powerless.

Here is T. Ray Owens from the viewpoint of his fourteen-year-old daughter Lily, in Sue Monk Kidd's best-seller *The Secret Life of Bees*:

> Whenever I opened [a book], T. Ray said, "Who do you think you are, Julius Shakespeare?" The man sincerely thought that was Shakespeare's first name, and if you think I should have corrected him, you are ignorant about the art of survival. He also referred to me as Miss-Brown-Nose-in-a-Book and Miss-Emily-Big-Head-Diction. He meant Dickinson, but there are things you let go by.

This one paragraph tells us so much about both characters. T. Ray is a nasty man who is also jealous of his daughter's education. Lily is canny and self-controlled enough to refuse his provocations (until eventually he goes too far). These vivid impressions, which are set out in the first chapter, help set us up for the rest of the novel, in which Lily will continue to be canny and self-controlled and T. Ray will continue to be a nightmare of a father. All beautifully foreshadowed by how often they're willing to battle.

Closely related to when a character is willing to argue is the question of whom he'll argue *with*. Some people, like T. Ray, will fight with anyone over anything. However, the author might have created a different T. Ray by portraying him as abusive to Lily but charming to everybody else. Such people are very common. They regard their family as personal property to be treated as they like but may go to great lengths to impress the rest of the world with their good character.

Other people are usually kind and patient with those they perceive as subordinate (including children) but are touchy and critical of superiors. These are the characters with "authority issues." Is your rich old lady gracious with her heirs, her cleaning woman, and her gardener but argumentative and unpleasant with cops and doctors? If so, I want to read about her—she sounds interesting. Show me whom she argues with and whom she doesn't.

A third important aspect of fighting style is fairness. Some people, like T. Ray, do not argue fairly. They employ name-calling, sarcasm, profanity, threats, ridicule, belittling, lies, evasions, or physical violence. Others keep scrupulously to one issue, argue it logically, listen to each other's viewpoint, and try to stick to the truth. Degree of fairness applies to all kinds of fighting, from marital spats to interstellar war. Fairness alone tells the reader volumes about character.

Finally, people differ in fighting intensity. There are, for instance, married couples who bicker about differences ("You ignored me all evening") and married couples who divorce about differences ("You always ignore me! I'm leaving!"). There are people who shrug off an insult ("That's just the way she is") and people who commit murder over an insult ("I'm avenging my honor!"). Plus, of course, everything in between. Which is your character?

The answer to that, to be believable, should depend on three things. One is individual personality. How hard does your character take events in general? Does she get really excited over good fortune and really depressed over setbacks? Then we'll find it believable that she gets really angry and reacts accordingly.

The second cause of an intense reaction is the nature of the specific fight you're creating on the page. Lily Owens lets most of her father's insults go by ("the art of survival"). But when he starts in on her mother, the topic is too important to Lily to gloss over. Lily's reaction is intense: She runs away. Another type of character might merely have seethed silently. Still another might have fought T. Ray *more* intensely, setting fire to the house with him inside.

Finally, the strength of fights is culturally determined. Where public or even private scenes are disapproved of (upper-class London, old-money Boston, "well-behaved" families), arguments may be muted, even when the subject matters a great deal. In other cultures, volatility is not frowned on, and people may feel free to scream at each other in public. In extreme cases, murder may even be considered a duty, as in avenging a sister's rape. Where is your story taking place? Are your arguers in tune with local or family culture? Maybe not. You can gain some interesting effects by portraying the rebels against the local mores: the meek child born into a battling family, the furious feminist in polite nineteenth-century English society.

Putting these various aspects of fighting style together creates a huge number of possible combinations. Here are only three:

- a man who hates to fight, avoids it when possible, but on a subject of critical importance will fight with deadly intensity and no rules whatsoever
- a woman who bickers constantly with her family but in such a low-key, basically unthreatening way that they tolerate the irritation
- a political aide who is obsequious and agreeable to those in charge but argumentative and dishonest to those below him in the power structure

GETTING PHYSICAL

The most intense form of fighting, of course, is physical, which includes everything from one thrown punch to high-tech firefights. Everything already said about verbal fighting also applies to physical fighting. People differ enormously in willingness and ability to fight physically, as well as in the intensity, fairness, and preferred weapons with which they do it. If your character gets into a fight with his fists (or sword or Uzi), make sure that how and why he does it match the rest of the personality you've given him.

In addition, effective battles meet these criteria:

• **Physical fights should be plausible.** I cannot emphasize this enough. If you yourself have never engaged in a fight in an alley with a switchblade, find someone who has and question her closely. How does an experienced fighter hold a switchblade? What about an inexperienced fighter? What stance does the fighter take? Where does he strike or try to strike? What are the logical countermoves? How does a switchblade feel in the hand? What does it feel like if your strike goes into the belly? If it glances off the arm?

If you don't know anyone who regularly fights with switchblades (and most writers don't), then find the closest equivalent. Research. Read books about fighting, read biographies that describe fights, or steal details from other writers you trust. The same goes for fistfights, duels, boxing, hand-to-hand combat, and all other forms of violence, stylized or not. Get the moves right.

• **Weapons must be correct.** Unless you are a weapons expert, do meticulous research. Guns, swords, missile launchers—each category of weapons includes many, many variations, and if you get it wrong, knowledgeable readers will be bounced out of your story. (They'll also write you endless letters complaining that even an idiot knows a nine-millimeter handgun from a .45.) If Tom Clancy, without a military background, can do it, so can you. Ask weapons experts; most love to talk about their specialty. Read books. Use the Internet (but only sites you trust to be accurate).

• **Bodies must react to being hit, with anything.** Television shows and movies have a lot to answer for here. Heroes get slammed with a two-by-four in the head, belly, and knees and then, two minutes later, are up again and swinging. If you want your fiction to be taken seriously, you must be more realistic than that. Find out (more research) what damage your imaginary blows are likely to inflict and incorporate that realistically into the story, including recovery time from various injuries. I ask my doctor, who is used to questions like, "What would happen to someone if I pushed him off a train going forty miles per hour onto an inclined grassy bank?" If you think your doctor might call the police at such questions, be sure to explain carefully why you want to know.

Finally, physical fights should have interpersonal consequences in keeping with your story's subculture. If a twelve-year-old schoolboy in a rough Irish immigrant neighborhood in 1890 gets into a public fistfight with another boy, the fight may have no effect whatsoever on their friendship. An hour later they could again be fast pals. But a public fistfight between two senators in 1995 should affect not only their relationship but possibly their voting records, re-election chances, and legal reprisals.

Aggression is hardwired into human brains. Use it to the best advantage not only to drive your story but also to illuminate its characters.

DEATH SCENES: THE LAST CHARACTERIZATION

After love scenes, death scenes are the greatest pitfalls in fiction. Attempts to capture the awe and pain of dying can often, alas, come out sounding either bathetic or satiric. Not even great writers are exempt from the problem. Of Little Nell's death in Charles Dickens's *The Old Curiosity Shop*, Oscar Wilde wickedly wrote: "One must have a heart of stone to read the death of Little Nell by Dickens without laughing."

So how do you write death scenes that move readers to sorrow, not laughter or sneers? The best tactic is probably understatement. This doesn't mean you can't describe the agonies of a difficult death; it merely means you must do so in restrained language. The contrast between the objective language and the intense emotion of the moment actually heightens its impact.

Here is one of the most horrifying deaths in literature, Emma Bovary's in Gustave Flaubert's eponymous novel. Emma, in despair over her insoluble debt and impending disgrace, eats arsenic powder, grabbing handfuls of it and stuffing it into her mouth. The death scene is too long to quote in its entirety, but here is a passage from it:

> She soon began vomiting blood. Her lips became drawn. Her limbs were convulsed, her whole body covered with brown spots, and her pulse slipped beneath the fingers like a stretched thread, like a harp-string about to break.
>
> After this she began to scream horribly. She cursed the poison, railed at it,

and implored it to be quick, and thrust away with her stiffened arms everything that Charles, in more agony than herself, tried to make her drink. He stood up, his handkerchief to his lips, moaning, weeping, and choked by sobs that shook his whole body. Félicité was running up and down the room. Homais, motionless, uttered great sighs . . . Emma, her chin sunken upon her breast, had her eyes inordinately wide open, and her poor hands wandered over the sheets with that hideous and gentle movement of the dying, that seems as if they already want to cover themselves with the shroud.

The language here is almost clinical, but the effect on the reader is horror.

You can eliminate the horror by using language even more restrained. When Beth March dies, after a long wasting illness, in Louisa May Alcott's *Little Women*, we are told only:

As Beth had hoped, the "tide went out easily," and in the dark hour before the dawn, on the bosom where she had drawn her first breath, she quietly drew her last, with no farewell but one loving look, one little sigh.

And John Irving, in *The World According to Garp*, goes farther yet in restraint: After a horrendous automobile accident, we hear about everyone else's injuries, recovery, and subsequent life for twenty-five pages before we even learn that one child, Walt, died in the crash. And even then, all we get is the older child, now fitted with a glass eye, saying, "It's the eye I can still see Walt with." To which Garp replies simply, "I know." In context, it is both shocking and moving.

Consider understatement for your death scene, in both its physical details and in the other characters' reactions. Then, for maximum emphasis, put your understated death at the end of a chapter.

DEATH SCENES FROM THE POINT OF VIEW OF THE DYING

Usually death scenes are written from the viewpoint of someone who will still be around to continue the narrative. However, a few successful death scenes are told from the point of view of the dying character. If you do this, there are a few points to keep in mind:

- Keep the language fairly objective and distant so it feels more plausible that we are in a mind that will soon cease to exist. The feeling should be that we are being told about what the dying person feels and thinks, not shown it directly, because who can really know? Here is Garp's death from a gunshot wound:

> Garp looked at Helen; all he could do was move his eyes. Helen, he saw, was trying to smile back at him. With his eyes, Garp tried to reassure her: don't worry—so what if there is no life after death? There is life after Garp, believe me. . . . And never forget, there is memory, Helen, his eyes told her.

- Keep brief the passages written in the POV of the dying person in order to further aid plausibility.
- Place the death at the end of a scene or chapter to facilitate the change in POV.
- If you write the story in first person, the death scene ends it. This is rare, but one example is Joanna Russ's *We Who Are About To . . .* The narrator is the final survivor of a shipwreck who eventually commits suicide. The last line of the novel is "well it's time."

DEATHBED SPEECHES: THE CHATTY CORPSE

Most people in real life die without any deathbed speech at all. Death is too sudden, the person is too weak, or death occurs during sleep. But there are exceptions; the following are all actual deathbed statements:

- "More light!"—writer Johann Wolfgang von Goethe
- "Mildred, why aren't my clothes laid out? I've got a seven o'clock call."—actor Bert Lahr
- "I am . . . I . . . a sea of . . . alone."—director Alfred Hitchcock
- "Oh, God, have pity on my soul, oh, God, have pity on my soul . . ."—Queen Anne Boleyn (beheaded)
- "(garbled words) . . . Morse . . . (garbled words) . . . Indian . . ."—writer Henry David Thoreau
- "I shall hear in heaven."—composer Ludwig van Beethoven

What do you notice about these? All are short, some make no sense, and none are detailed. What you want to avoid are long deathbed confessions, denunciations, revelations, or changes of heart. They simply don't ring true. If you want a final statement from your dying character for plot or characterization purposes, keep it short and punchy. It can even be elliptical, which might further aid plot ("What did he mean by that? *Who* did he want to inherit?").

You don't need to exercise quite the same restraint in the speeches of other characters present. Death turns some people voluble, some taciturn. Just make sure your characters' various expressions of grief are fully in keeping with the personalities you've given them, and not so flowery that we're tempted to join the reviewer of Dickens's Little Nell.

It's possible, of course, that your particular story will have no love scenes, sex scenes, fight scenes, or death scenes. However, as I scanned my shelves, I was unable to identify any novel without at least a heated argument. Since you're going to be writing these intense scenes, do so with full attention to their potential for characterization as well as for plot movement.

RECAP: LOVE, DEATH, SEX, AND BATTLE

The most important thing to remember about love, sex, fight, and death scenes is that the character should perform them in keeping with the personality you've given him so far. For maximum effect, make full use of bodily responses in all emotional scenes.

Conventional responses such as "I love you" work fine in love scenes because they represent what people actually say—but they should then be supplemented by more individual speech. Love scenes are more interesting if the lovers have, in addition to love, other emotions and concerns on their minds.

Except in pornography, sex scenes become interesting only to the extent that we care that these characters are having sex. To make us care, put emphasis on the emotions and interactions leading up to the physical act. The degree of sexual explicitness is a function both of genre and of a particular work's overall tone—but overwriting in sex scenes will always produce parody, not passion.

An excellent way to characterize is by showing us how readily your character fights, how intensely, how fairly, how physically, and with whom. Both physical fights and public arguments are, in part, culturally determined, so take this into account when determining how violent your character becomes. For physical fights, do research to get the moves, weapons, and injuries right. Movies and television shows are terrible models.

The best way to make death scenes effective is to understate them. Deathbed speeches are most plausible when short and nonflowery.

EXERCISE 1

Write a three- or four-paragraph love scene in which the characters do not touch and do not say "I love you" or any variant of that. Don't go into either person's thoughts. Convey their feelings for each other through bodily responses, different dialogue, and small actions. Does this work for you?

EXERCISE 2

Pick three strong fictional characters you know well from books, television, or movies. Imagine how each might express love to a romantic partner. What words might he or she use—tender, joking, terse, or embarrassed? What gestures, tone of voice, or actions? Are the three declarations of love markedly different from each other? (They should be.)

EXERCISE 3

Find a love scene you think works in a novel or short story. Does it mix love with any other emotion or concern? What?

EXERCISE 4

Find a sex scene in a novel or short story that you think is successful. Does the scene combine sex with any other emotion or concern? What?

EXERCISE 5

This one might be tricky—but try it if appropriate. The next time you are in a sexual situation, take a moment to note your *own* bodily responses. Can you put them into words useful for your fiction? (Remember, writers routinely cannibalize their own lives.)

EXERCISE 6

The next time you overhear an argument (public, familial, or among friends), listen closely. Who seems angrier? How can you tell? Are these arguers fighting fairly?

EXERCISE 7

Read Edward Albee's play *Who's Afraid of Virginia Woolf?*, which is one long marital battle of unusual intensity, variety, and complexity. How does Albee vary the tone from scene to scene? Is there anything here you can use?

EXERCISE 8

Go back to the emotional mini-bios you filled out earlier. Pick three. If each of these characters had a chance to make a deathbed speech, what would they say? Keep each one to a maximum of two sentences, and try to make them as plausible as possible.

chapter 11

[FRUSTRATION — THE MOST USEFUL EMOTION IN FICTION]

Quick—what is the most important emotion your fictional characters feel? Love? Hate? Anger? Desire? All of those are critical. Love for a person or desire to attain a goal drives most plots. Hatred or anger drives most of the rest. Anna Karenina loves Vronsky; the wicked queen hates Snow White; Ahab is furious at Moby Dick; Nero Wolfe desires to solve murders. However, despite this impressive list, and despite everything said in previous chapters about motivation and values, the most important emotion in fiction is something else.

Frustration.

I say this because, without frustration, there *is* no plot. Frustration means that someone is not getting what he wants, and that's what makes a story work. Motivation, values, and desires start the character on her fictional journey. Climaxes are often provided in scenes of love, battle, or death. But everything in between, the meat of your story, is driven by frustration.

Consider: If Anna got Vronsky easily and with no frustration to anyone, or if Ahab harpooned that white whale the first time he tried, the novels would both be over. Instead, Anna and Ahab (plus the wicked queen and Nero Wolfe) are frustrated in attaining their goals. Frustration creates story.

It thus behooves you, the writer, to pay considerable attention to frustration. How is frustration tied to character? How can you use your character's frustration to best advantage? How do you portray this important emotion most effectively? As with everything in writing, there are no simple and absolute answers, but there are some time-tested guidelines.

FRUSTRATION AND CHARACTER: SHE DID *WHAT*?

Think about the people you know. I'm sure, even though I've never met your friends and family, that they differ from each other in many significant ways, one of which is how they handle frustration. Some typical ways that people react to being blocked from what they want:

- anger
- tears
- determination to try harder
- blame the closest person
- blame the universe
- blame themselves
- drink
- vent frustration to a trusted friend
- give up
- seek revenge on whatever is frustrating them
- pray
- shrug and pretend stoicism
- slide into depression

Now for the big question: Which of these responses to frustration will your character choose? The answer depends on two things: what kind of person he is and what you want your plot to do.

It's a good idea to think about these questions before you begin writing because how a character reacts to frustration is tied to her characterization as a whole. For instance, a woman who reacts to frustration with no self-control whatsoever, throwing things and screaming, cannot, in the next scene, be cool and calculating. Similarly, a man who blames himself for his troubles will not plausibly go out and murder his frustrator. So what kind of person is your character? This is, of course, the key question we've been asking all along, but consider it now from another angle: your invented person's natural response to frustration, plus how good she is at controlling and modifying that response.

Here, Tom Wingo in Pat Conroy's *The Prince of Tides*, is trying to see his sister Savannah, who has tried to kill herself, and is being frustrated in this attempt by Savannah's psychiatrist:

> "Is the coffee good, Tom?" she asked with complete control.
>
> "Yes, it's fabulous. Now, about Savannah."
>
> "I want you to be patient, Tom. We'll get to the subject of Savannah in a moment," the doctor said in a patronizing voice shaped by far too many advanced degrees. "There are some background questions I need to ask if we're going to

help Savannah. And I'm sure we want to help Savannah, don't we?"

"Not if you continue to talk to me in that unbearably supercilious tone, Doctor, as though I were some gaudy chimp you're trying to teach to type. And not until you tell me where my goddamn sister is."

In this tiny vignette, Tom reacts to frustration with sarcasm ("Yes, it's fabulous"), impatience, and anger. That's pretty much how he reacted as a child and also how he'll react to other problems throughout the book, nearly destroying his family—until life teaches him to behave differently.

Sarcasm and anger are not, of course, the only possible responses to frustration. If Tom had been a different type of person, he might have:

- humbly sought the doctor's help, doing whatever she told him, and been grateful for the direction
- gone to a church, instead of traveling to New York, to pray for Savannah's soul
- written Savannah off as too much trouble and a bad influence on his children, so why should he do anything at all?
- taken Savannah's troubles as just one more sign that the universe is rotten and gone to a local bar to drink away his bitterness

His actual response defines Tom Wingo as a person and as a character in Conroy's novel.

In fact, it *determines* the novel. How?

PLOTTING FROM FRUSTRATION

A different response from Tom Wingo to his frustration would have led to a radically different book. How *your* character handles frustration will determine major elements of your plot. Does she fight back, seeking revenge on whoever is blocking her? Then your plot will feature fights and payback schemes. Does he give up? Then either someone will need to motivate and rescue him, or else he will learn to live without whatever he wants (both respectable plots). Does she try again (and again and again) until she succeeds? Then you will have an upbeat, victory-against-the-odds story.

For example, consider Mario Puzo's best-selling *The Godfather*. When an attempt is made on Don Corleone's life by rival mobsters abetted by a crooked cop, the don's two sons react very differently. Sonny Corleone wants to go roaring off for immediate revenge (he does this later, in response to a different frustration, and that reaction gets him killed). Michael Corleone has a different response to the world's not going the way he wishes. He plans, coolly and rationally, to get even. His plans against everyone who has frustrated his family (dirty cop, rival gangsters, Sonny's killer) provide the plot for the entire rest of this long novel.

So think very carefully about how your character reacts when he doesn't get what he wants. Can his reaction provide you with plot ideas?

FRUSTRATION PLUS: MIXED EMOTIONS

Because frustration is such an important emotion in fiction, how well you portray it can make the difference between characters that seem real and those that seem cardboard.

A common mistake in portraying frustration is to assume that we, your audience, know what your character is feeling. This usually occurs because the author feels exactly what the character does and assumes that we do, too. If the protagonist has not been invited to her sister-in-law's wedding, and such a social slight would make the author feel hurt and depressed, that author may have her character also react with hurt and depression—and expect the reader to automatically know that. After all, both the author and character would feel left out, so wouldn't everybody?

No. As we have seen, people react to frustration with an astonishingly wide spectrum of emotions and actions. (Some people, for instance, would be delighted to be spared a family wedding.) Therefore, you must dramatize this character's frustration, fully enough and convincingly enough for readers to share it *even if* they themselves might react differently. This is a situation in which it is crucial to "become the reader," stepping back from your work to view it as if you were someone else.

Complicating your task is the fact that frustration, like love, is seldom a "pure" emotion. It can come mixed with many others: anger ("How dare they!"), hurt ("Why won't they help me?"), fear ("I'll never get what I want"), self-blame ("I'm not good enough to succeed"), resignation ("Can't win 'em all"), or bitterness ("Life sucks").

The natural response to frustration of Amber St. Clare, the protagonist of Kathleen Winsor's *Forever Amber*, is anger. But notice what happens during a fight with her third husband, who has made her leave a court party early:

> "You made me come away because I was enjoying myself! You can't stand to see anyone happy!"

> "On the contrary, Madame. I do not object at all to happiness. But I do object to watching my wife make a ridiculous display of herself. . . . You know as well as I do what was in the minds of those men tonight."
>
> "Well!" she cried, clenching her fists. "What of it! Isn't the same thing in the mind of all men! It's in yours, too, even if you—" But there she stopped, suddenly, for he gave her a look so swift and so venomous, so threatening that the words caught in her throat and she remained quiet.

Amber's natural anger is modified by fear, and the result is a far more interesting scene than just another fight between her and another of her many men.

To use this technique, ask yourself:

- What is my character's primary response to frustration?
- What else might she be feeling in response to this particular thwarting of her desires?
- Will the secondary emotion also be useful in plotting? (Amber's fear, which grows through several more frustrating clashes with her husband, eventually leads her to murder him before he can murder her.)

VARYING FRUSTRATION: CHANGES IN THE EMOTIONAL WEATHER

Not only do different people experience different mixes of these emotions when frustrated, but the same person may experience different mixes at different times. Mood, health, or that recent fight with the boss all influence how one reacts to a given frustration. Just because your character reacts with anger to one frustration doesn't mean that he need react with anger to all frustrations—although he does need to react in a way that seems plausible and in keeping with what has gone before.

Amber St. Clare, for instance, is a flamboyant character, and anger (with or without fear) is her natural response to being thwarted. But in the following passage, her frustration takes a much different form. Amber and her married lover, Lord Bruce Carleton, are riding in a coach together:

> But, as always, she knew that it had been a mistake to mention his wife. His face closed, the smile faded, and both of them fell silent.
>
> Riding there beside him, jogging around uncomfortably on the hard springless seat, Amber wondered what he was thinking, and all her grievances against him rushed back. But she stole a glance at him from the corners of her eyes, saw

his handsome profile, the nervous flickering of jaw muscles beneath the smooth brown skin, and she longed to reach out and touch him, tell him how deeply, how hopelessly, she loved him.

What does Amber, on this occasion but not on others, respond to frustration with sadness and tenderness instead of anger? Partly because she and Bruce have had so many fights about his wife that she's temporarily weary of them. Partly because she genuinely loves the object of her frustration. Partly just mood; Amber is no more monolithic than anyone else you know. However, this response to frustration does not violate everything else we've learned about her. She is at heart selfish and passionate, and her intense longing for Bruce fits with her overall undisciplined appetite for life. In addition, Amber's somber response is only temporary; two pages later, she's angry again.

So we need to add another question to the previous ones:

- What other responses, besides his primary one, might my character plausibly have to frustration? Under what circumstances?

How do you get all that into fiction? You don't, obviously, get it all in—fiction is a process of selection. But because frustration can evoke such different reactions in characters, and in the same character under different circumstances, it's important to fully dramatize frustration. You do that through bodily reactions, carefully constructed dialogue, and characters' thoughts.

FRUSTRATION 101: THE BODY DOESN'T LIE

An effective technique to dramatize your character's frustration (as with other emotions) is to show us how it affects his body. Emotion occurs in a very old part of the brain, the limbic. We frequently react bodily before we've had a chance to process information rationally. If your natural response to frustration is anger, you don't think, "I should become angry because I'm being denied what's rightfully mine." Instead, anger swoops through your body, affecting hormone levels, gestures, facial reactions, tone of voice, and breathing. Use these to portray your character's frustration in a direct, visceral way.

In Maureen F. McHugh's wonderful science fiction novel *China Mountain Zhang*, Alexei Dormov is visiting Martine Jansch. Alexei's small daughter, Theresa, is playing with Martine's goats:

"Just my luck, my kid's best friend is a goat."

A world of regret in that comment, although he says it lightly enough. When his smile disappears and his face is still for a moment I assume he's thinking of [the resettlement camp]. I almost say, "Kids are resilient," even though it's one of those fallacies like middle-aged women liking children. But that's not what he's thinking at all. "Martine," he says, "they're going to transfer us again, and I don't know what to do."

"What?" I say.

"They're going to transfer me again. Isn't it enough to send us to Mars?" He never raises his voice, it is easy to miss the despair in what he says. . . .

"What makes you think they're going to send you," I say, and realize as I say it that it sounds as if he's some sort of paranoid.

"I *know*. I've been through it four times. I know when they're going to ship us off." He balls his fists and puts them together as it all boils out of him.

Notice that at first even Martine doesn't know what Alexei feels. Then, author McHugh uses Alexei's bodily reactions to help us understand Alexei's frustration. His "face goes still." There is "despair" in his voice, despite its quiet tone. He "balls his fists." Frustration "boils out of him." Later he "looks at [Martine] with hatred" because he's so envious that her position on Mars is secure and his is not. And this is for a basically quiet, non-volatile man. Alexei is no Sonny Corleone, but his body, as observed by Martine, dramatizes his emotion.

For a POV character, you can use bodily reactions even more intimately. Look back at the first quoted passage from *Forever Amber*. Amber clenches her fists, which might be observed from the outside. But she also experiences "words caught in her throat," that awful choking feeling that only the one who feels it can know about.

The best source for such bodily feelings is you. What do *you* feel when you're frustrated? Does your throat close up? Do your eyes tear? Do you get a sick feeling in your stomach? Notice your visceral reactions to frustration and use them to create bodily frustration that your readers can identify with.

DIALOGUE: THE LITERARY VENT

Bodily reactions, however, are often not enough to dramatize a character's frustration. This is true for two reasons. First, the body uses the same reactions for different emotions: Tears might indicate frustration, sadness, or even joy. Balling up fists might be frustration or just free-floating rage against the world.

Second, as we said before, different personality types react differently. What *do* those tears mean for this particular character in this particular situation?

For a non-POV character, supplement those bodily reactions with dialogue that makes his frustration clear. In the above example, the next paragraph begins a long speech by Alexei to Martine, explicating his feelings.

You have to be careful about this, however. You want to avoid As-you-know-Bob dialogue (discussed in chapter eight). Instead, you must set up a situation in which a character would reasonably talk out his frustrations and a listener who might reasonably sit still to hear them. The listener might be a friend, a spouse, a therapist, even a dog. The choice of listener depends on your character's personality and circumstances—as well as where you want the plot to go.

What do I mean by the latter? The listener will have his own responses to the frustration she hears. If it's a dramatic response, it will affect the story. Martine, for example, responds to Alexei's plight by proposing marriage. As her husband, he becomes a landowner and doesn't have to be transferred.

To whom does *your* character express frustration? What is that person's response? Do you want to use that to further complicate plot?

THOUGHTS: CONFUSION VS. PLANNING

For a POV character, you have an additional resource to dramatize frustration: the character's mind. Because we are privy to what goes on in POV characters' minds, we can share their frustrated thoughts directly.

Look again at the brief excerpt from *The Prince of Tides.* Tom Wingo thinks the doctor has "a patronizing voice shaped by far too many advanced degrees." This may or may not be true of the doctor's voice (or her degrees), but the thought is an expression of Tom's frustration with her. Throughout Conroy's novel, Tom is frustrated not only by his crazy sister Savannah but by the psychiatrist, the psychiatrist's husband, Tom's wife, his parents, and his brother. Each time, Conroy lets us see directly into Tom's thoughts, adding depth to the bodily reactions and dialogue that also express his frustration.

Two caveats here. First, if your character is a logical person with a rational response to frustration, don't make her *too* logical. A character who calmly thinks, "Well, Plan A failed, let's move on to Plan B" is usually not convincing. There needs to be some accompanying emotion, and at least a brief period of confusion ("Plan A failed; now what the hell do I do?"). A person is not a machine. Machines don't feel frustration. People do.

Question:

I can handle my characters' frustration fine. But what do I do about mine—I'm halfway through my novel and stuck.

Answer:

Frustration is endemic to writers; if it mounts to high enough levels, it's dignified with the name of "writer's block." Here are some suggestions:

- Lower the productivity bar. Tell yourself it's all right to write less, if you do it steadily. Produce only one hundred words a day for ten days (anyone can do that). It will keep you working just enough to catch fire again.
- Lower the emotional bar. If the problem is that you feel you must produce a masterpiece "or why bother," then give yourself permission to write ten days of dreck at twenty pages a day. It won't be dreck (people can only write as well as they can write), and it will get you going again.
- Find the last place you were interested. If the problem is that you've lost faith in the story, go back to the last scene at which you were still excited. Rethink the plot from that point.
- Change the setting. Try writing in a different place, or at a different time of day (early morning is often good). This sounds simplistic, but a surprising number of pros have found it works. Sometimes, even merely moving your desk can help, or temporarily switching from keyboard to pen.

Second, don't substitute characters' thoughts for action. A frustrated character may think obsessively about his problem, he may plot out every detailed step to overcome what's frustrating him, or he may wallow in despair. Whatever he does, *show* it. Some thoughts are good for clarity and flavor. However, most of your depiction of frustration should be through the character's active and dramatized response—whether that reaction is throwing a fit (Tom Wingo), throwing more harpoons (Ahab), or throwing herself under a train (Anna Karenina).

Frustration is universal. Make it work for you by building characterization, driving plot, and hooking our sympathy on your characters' plights. What frustrates them can greatly benefit your fiction.

RECAP: FRUSTRATION

Frustration, in addition to driving plot, is one of your best chances to build characterization. How your character responds to frustration, plus her ability to modify those responses, should be in keeping with the rest of the personality you've given her so far.

Frustration is often mixed with other emotions. Getting both into the scene adds plausibility and depth to your story. Also, although the same character may react differently to frustration at different times, all his responses should fit together into a believable whole.

Bodily responses are an effective way to convey frustration; pay close attention to your own responses to "borrow" from as needed. Dialogue and thoughts can, if appropriate to your character, clarify causes of frustration. Most characters' frustrated dialogue and thoughts should be slightly incoherent. However, the main expression of your character's frustration should be neither dialogue nor thoughts but action that moves the story forward.

EXERCISE 1

Think back to the last time you felt completely frustrated. Maybe you couldn't get someone else to see your point of view, you couldn't get an appliance to work properly no matter what you did, or you were dealing with a particularly recalcitrant bureaucracy. Sit quietly and remember as much as you can about how you felt, what you thought, and how your body reacted. Jot down the salient points.

EXERCISE 2

List three people you know well and who are different personality types from you. For each, jot down how she might have reacted to the same frustrating circumstances you experienced. What might each have thought? Felt in the body? Said aloud? Done next?

EXERCISE 3

Look at your lists. Are any of these characters interesting to you? If so, imagine giving them something much larger and even more frustrating to react to: repeated harassment from a destructive neighbor. An unfair job firing. Identity theft. Do their reactions lead you to imagine more plot developments for this situation?

If not, put the most intriguing person on your list into a situation that does interest you. What might frustrate him there? How would he react to it?

Find a scene in a favorite book where a character is thwarted in obtaining something he wants. What other emotions, if any, does he feel besides frustration? How has the author made you know that? Is there anything here you can use for your story?

chapter 12

[POINT OF VIEW—WHOSE EMOTIONS ARE WE SHARING?]

Since we lack telepathy, we humans are imprisoned in our own skulls. As Joseph Conrad wrote, "We live, as we dream, alone"—at least alone within our heads. The only thoughts, plans, dreams, and feelings we can directly experience are our own. It's because this one-viewpoint reality is hardwired in us that fiction is so fascinating. It lets us experience the world from inside someone else's head.

This is the definition of point of view: whose eyes we view the action through, whose head we're inside of, whose feelings we experience as that character feels them. As such, your choice of point-of-view character or characters is critical to your story. It will determine what you tell, how you tell it, and, often, what the action means.

In this chapter, we'll survey your choices. In subsequent chapters, we'll take up each possibility in detail.

PROTAGONIST VS. POV CHARACTER: IF I'M NOT THE STAR, WHO IS?

The protagonist of your story is the "star," the person we're most interested in, the one with the interesting action. Usually, but not inevitably, your protagonist will also be a POV character. Thus we see the events of John Grisham's best-selling *The King of Torts* through the eyes of its major character, Clay Carter. Carter is both the star and a POV character.

However, you can obtain some interesting effects by having your POV character be someone other than the protagonist. Two classics that do this are F. Scott Fitzgerald's *The Great Gatsby* and W. Somerset Maugham's *The Moon and Sixpence*. *Gatsby* is told through the eyes of Nick Carraway, who is only peripherally involved in the main action, mostly as a standby friend and go-between. The real protagonists are the illicit lovers, Jay Gatsby and Daisy Buchanan, particularly Gatsby.

Maugham goes farther yet. The protagonist of *The Moon and Sixpence* is Charles Strickland, who abandons his middle-class London existence to travel to the South Seas and become a painter; Strickland is based loosely on Paul Gauguin. The unnamed narrator of the novel, the sole POV character, knows Strickland only slightly, as the friend of a friend. The narrator has several casual encounters with Strickland, first in England and then in Tahiti. At no time does the narrator ever affect Strickland's life or Strickland affect the narrator's. Much of Strickland's later life is told to the narrator by other people, after the artist is dead.

The disadvantages of this convoluted structure are obvious; it lacks immediacy. Everything important that Strickland does, or that is done to him, occurs offstage. The narrator is told about events later, and he tells us about them. Maugham sacrifices a great deal of drama this way. So why did he do it?

Because separating your POV character from your protagonist also confers certain advantages:

- The POV character can continue the story after the protagonist dies, which both Charles Strickland and Jay Gatsby do during their respective novels. Maugham's POV character traces the fates of Strickland's widow, children, and paintings.
- The protagonist can be portrayed as much more secretive if he is not also a POV character. No one learns about Jay Gatsby's real past until he is dead; he has invented for himself a much more glamorous background than his actual one. Had Gatsby been a POV character, we readers would have known that from the beginning, since we would have been "inside his head." Protagonists who are not also POV characters can preserve their mysteries. As Maugham's narrator says, "I felt that Strickland had kept his secrets to the grave."
- The POV character can make observations that would never in a million years occur to the protagonist. Thus Nick Carraway comes to see Daisy Buchanan as a careless lightweight and Jay Gatsby as a touching idealist, views neither character (nor anyone else in the book) would have shared.

The first questions you should ask yourself about your use of POV are: Will my protagonist and POV character(s) be the same? If not, do I have good reason for the split? Will I gain more than I lose?

Once you know whether your protagonist will be a POV character, the next step is to determine who else will occupy that critical role.

CHOOSING POV CHARACTERS: THROUGH YOUR EYES ONLY

It's a good idea, before you write anything at all, to consider all the choices for POV characters. The first choice to come to mind may not be the best pick.

Consider, for instance, Harper Lee's *To Kill a Mockingbird*, which takes place in pre-World War II Alabama. The main plotline concerns the framing of a black man, Tom Robinson, for the beating of a white woman, a crime he did not commit. His lawyer is the respected Atticus Finch, father of two children. Finch forces the identification of the true assailant, the victim's father, who then attempts revenge by attacking Finch's kids. Harper Lee could have told her story from any of these points of view. Instead, she embeds her main plot in a coming-of-age story and makes her first-person narrator one of the children, Finch's eight-year-old daughter Scout. As a result, she ends up with a far different story than if the POV character had been Atticus Finch, Tom Robinson, or the true assailant. A better story? A worse one? No one can say; we didn't see the alternate versions.

But certainly Scout is an effective choice. She meets the general criteria you should consider when choosing your POV character:

- **Who will be hurt by the action?** Someone strongly affected emotionally usually makes the best POV character (although Maugham, as we have seen, chooses to sacrifice emotional immediacy for other goals). Scout is the victim of attempted murder by the disgruntled woman-beater and thus is in danger. Pick for your POV character someone with a strong stake in the outcome, including pain if the outcome will be negative.

  This criteria, incidentally, is why detective novels often work very hard to create a personal connection between the murderer and the detective. It raises the pain possibilities, which in turn increases narrative tension.

- **Who can be present at the climax?** In *To Kill a Mockingbird*, Scout is there. So is Nick Carraway in *The Great Gatsby*. Your POV character should be, too, or else we'll have to be told secondhand about the most important event of your story. This almost never works.

- **Who gets most of the good scenes?** We want to be present at those, too. Scout sneaks into the courtroom to witness her father's defense of Tom Robinson.
- **Who will provide an interesting outlook on the story?** Scout brings to Harper Lee's novel an innocent, fresh view of racism that no adult could. Nick Carraway similarly views the action of *The Great Gatsby* from a more idealistic, simpler vantage point than do its other characters, mostly New York sophisticates. What kind of observations about life do you want to make in your novel? Who is fit to make them? Do you want that character as your "eyes" and "heart"?
- **Whose head are you most interested in inhabiting during this story?** Don't underestimate this criterion; it's key.

DIFFERENT EYES, DIFFERENT STORY

You may think you already know who your POV character will be. Perhaps you're right. But take a few moments to imagine what your story might be like if you chose differently.

Let us suppose, for instance, that you are writing a novel about the abduction of a child. Major characters are the father, the mother, the child, the abductor, a suspicious-but-innocent neighbor, and the lead detective on the case. The child will be recovered, but the family will never be the same again. There are at least six potential novels here, all vastly different.

If the mother or father (or both) is your viewpoint, you will have a novel of anguish (which might be what you want). These are good points of view if the couple will eventually divorce, unable to incorporate the strain into an already fragile marriage. Perhaps one of them has an extramarital affair. Perhaps one mounts an independent investigation. Perhaps one hires someone to murder the neighbor, who turns out to be innocent.

If the child is the POV character, you have a novel of bewilderment, fear, maybe eventual escape. You will, of course, lose all scenes of the investigation and of parental interaction, because the kid won't see them. You'll gain a lot of scenes between the abductor and abducted.

If the neighbor is the POV character, you will have a novel of injustice. This could be quite interesting; stories of people wrongly accused always make for strong reader identification. Everyone loves an innocent underdog.

If the abductor is the POV character, you probably have a novel of either evil or madness. What is his motivation? Do you want to explore that? If so, he's your man.

If the police officer or FBI agent is the POV character, you have a mystery novel. What's his stake in this, beyond professional competence? Do you want to focus on how an investigation looks from the inside?

I want to emphasize that none of these POV choices are inherently better or worse than any other. It all depends on which suits the version of the story you want to tell. But if you don't at least consider points of view other than the one that first occurs to you, you may be cutting yourself off from some very exciting possibilities.

Even existing stories, if they are not protected by copyright, are sometimes retold from another POV. The results can be fascinating. Jean Rhys retold Charlotte Brontë's *Jane Eyre* from the viewpoint of the first Mrs. Rochester, the madwoman imprisoned in the attic, in her novel *Wide Sargasso Sea*. Valerie Martin retold Robert Louis Stevenson's *The Strange Case of Dr. Jekyll and Mr. Hyde* as seen through the eyes of a housemaid in her novel *Mary Reilly*. And Susan Meddaugh produced the delightful *Cinderella's Rat*, which retells the familiar tale from the POV of one with a tail.

Who among your assembled cast might be an interesting POV character, with a more original outlook on the plot than your first choice? If you were not the writer but the reader, who might be the most satisfying POV character?

CAST OF THOUSANDS: HOW MANY POINTS OF VIEW ARE YOU ALLOWED?

There is no one correct answer to this. A general rule of thumb is: Have as few points of view as you can get away with and still tell the story you want to tell.

The reason for this is the aforementioned entrapment in our own skulls. We're used to experiencing reality from one POV. Each time you switch from one fictional viewpoint to another, the reader must make a mental adjustment. If there are too many of these, the story feels increasingly fragmented and unreal.

On the other hand (there is always "another hand" in writing fiction), you may gain more than you lose. If you want to show how a romance feels to both parties, then you need two points of view. If one character simply cannot be present at every important scene you need to present, then you need more than one POV. You may need three, or even more, especially for a complicated or epic plot.

Figure out the least number you can have and still cover all major scenes and internal dialogues that your story requires. The point is to lessen the demands on the reader as much as possible so he can concentrate on the story and its implications, not try to remember what that eighth POV character was doing the last time we saw him, which was two hundred pages ago because it takes a while to cycle through eight points of view and do justice to each. Too many points of view are hard on the reader.

And, I might add, it's not easy on the writer, either.

We'll take this subject up in greater detail in chapter fourteen. For now, limit the number of POV characters as much as you can.

Once you know your POV, the next step is the choice between first person, third person, omniscient, or (rarely) the "novelty" points of view: second, plural first, plural third, and epistolary.

FIRST PERSON: THE GREAT I AM

First person means the story is told as "I." Everything is seen through the eyes of that one person, and we readers exist right there in his head for the duration of the story. Here is an effective example of first person; it is the opening of Michael Frayn's novel *Spies*:

> The third week of June and there it is again: the same almost embarrassingly familiar breath of sweetness that comes every year about this time. I catch it on the warm evening air as I walk past the well-ordered gardens on my quiet street, and for a moment I'm a child again and everything's before me—all the frightening, half-understood promise of life.

This passage illustrates the other advantages of first person, in addition to one-head verisimilitude:

- **Immediacy.** We are inside the character's head, so our experiencing his sensations, such as the scent on the evening air, feels natural and plausible. Such is the power of pronoun that when something happens to a fictional "I," it feels as if it's happening to the reader "I."

- **Language.** This character thinks in fairly formal phrases ("almost embarrassingly familiar breath of sweetness"). This tells us a great deal about him, in terms of class and education, before we have so much as one fact. Contrast this with an opening such as this hypothetical one:
  > I never did get none of that preacher talk. Heaven? Don't make no sense to have a whole other world in the sky when this one's already here.

- **Range.** Frayn's character's thoughts range easily over memory, opinion, and impressions because they're his *thoughts*. We're already inside his head, and these are things that people naturally think about. Introducing thoughts in third person can feel more artificial and even awkward ("His thoughts wandered back to earlier Junes . . .").

These are strong advantages, but first person also has strong disadvantages:

- You cannot include any scene at which your POV character is not present.
- You cannot include any information that your POV character would not naturally have.
- You must include all information the POV character does have; to do otherwise is usually considered cheating. For example, if your POV detective notices a key clue, you cannot withhold it because "it would give the plot away." If he knows it, we know it.
- You are limited to your POV character's view of the world. This is why some writers consider first person "claustrophobic." If your POV character is naturally suspicious, then all the other characters must be described in suspicious terms. You can *show* that another person is actually honorable, but you cannot *tell* us that because no matter what she does, the POV character will interpret it suspiciously. You will have to dramatize her honorableness strongly and repeatedly in order to counteract her viewpoint.
- Perhaps the largest danger of first person is that you already have an "I" in your head—yourself. The temptation, especially for beginning writers, is to assume that because you feel a certain way, so will your fictional "I"—and that this congruence of thought is automatically clear to the reader. It's not. In other words, first-person POV demands, even more than other choices, that the writer be objective enough to "become the reader" in judging what is actually on the page, not merely intended in the author's mind. This stricture is why many writers consider first person the hardest POV to do well.

THIRD PERSON: HE, SHE, OR IT

Third person POV means that the story is told in terms of "he did this" or "she thought this." We can go inside the head of the third person POV character, but we can also see him from the outside. Third person that goes into only one character's head is called limited third person viewpoint. Third person that goes into more than one POV is called multiple third person viewpoint.

Here is a third-person scene opening from Ken Follett's best-selling *Triple*:

> Al Cortone knocked and waited in the hall for a dead man to open the door.
>
> The suspicion that his friend was dead had grown to a conviction in the past three years. First, Cortone had heard that Nat Dickstein had been taken prisoner. Toward the end of the war, stories began to circulate about what was happening to Jews in the Nazi camps. Then, at the end, the grim truth came out.
>
> On the other side of the door, a ghost scraped a chair on the floor and padded across the room.
>
> Cortone felt suddenly nervous. What if Dickstein were disabled, deformed? Suppose he had come unhinged? Cortone had never known how to deal with cripples or crazy men.

This could have been written in first person, in which case it would look like this:

> I knocked and waited in the hall for a dead man to open the door.
>
> The suspicion that my friend was dead had grown to a conviction in the past three years. First, I'd heard that Nat Dickstein had been taken prisoner. Toward the end of the war, stories began to circulate about what was happening to Jews in the Nazi camps. Then, at the end, the grim truth came out.
>
> On the other side of the door, a ghost scraped a chair on the floor and padded across the room.
>
> I felt suddenly nervous. What if Dickstein were disabled, deformed? Suppose he had come unhinged? I'd never known how to deal with cripples or crazy men.

So does that mean that there's no real difference between first person and third person? No. That this particular passage could be transformed so easily only points up that Follett writes in what is called "transparent prose style." This means that he writes plain, straightforward prose more interested in advancing the plot than creating an individual style. Limited sections of transparent prose can often be changed easily from third person to first person, or vice versa—but that doesn't mean the whole story can be, or that all stories can be so transposed. For many, you'd lose too much.

Like what? Let's start with the advantages of third person over first person:

- You can describe the POV characters from the outside, what they're doing and what they look like, which you cannot in first person because people don't think about themselves that way (more on this in the next two chapters).
- You are not limited to the narrator's worldview. You can present objective facts, such as the last two sentences of the second paragraph in the above passage, without filtering them through one person's individual, often quirky, lens on the world. Third person "opens up the story," making it feel less claustrophobic. This point will be taken up in detail in chapter fourteen.
- You can include more than one POV in third person. In fact, much contemporary popular fiction is written in multi-viewpoint third person because it allows the author to roam freely over his plot, including everything major that happens to all POV characters instead of just one character.
- You can withhold crucial information. Simply do not put those characters who possess the information among your POV characters.
- You may gain more objectivity about the characters when you do not write "I," thus more fully imagining them and also becoming more capable of evaluating the results on the page.

The disadvantages of third person are:

- More distance between the character and the reader (although this can be controlled by varying distance, a complex subject we'll take up in chapter fourteen).
- Less distinctive language patterns.
- Greater awkwardness in ranging over memory, flashback, and opinion, unless very skillfully handled.

CHOOSING BETWEEN FIRST PERSON AND THIRD PERSON

So which POV is best for *your* story? Obviously, there's no right answer; it's an individual decision based on how you want to present your material. But there are a few guidelines.

If your story is epic in scope, covering many people in many places (as is *Triple*), you need multiple third person.

If you want the flexibility to pull back from the character and include brief blocks of objective information, you need third person, either limited or multiple.

If you want to describe the character extensively from the outside, as do many romance novels, you definitely want third person.

If you want us to identify strongly with your POV character, seeing the world as she does, you want either first person or limited third person, but first person may end up more vivid.

If your character's thoughts are quirky, far-ranging, and stylistically interesting, you can use either first person or third person, but first person will bring us closer to that quirkiness. On the other hand, if your character is *really* bizarre, first person may not give you enough flexibility to tell us things about him that will help us make sense of his weirdness.

OMNISCIENT POV: I SEE ALL AND KNOW ALL

Omniscient, a POV universal in the nineteenth century and much less so now, has two hallmarks. First, it goes into the mind of any character the author chooses, sometimes repeatedly and sometimes only once. Second, the author himself comments freely on the action, sometimes addressing the reader directly with his comments and interpretations.

Howards End is written in omniscient POV, and at a tense point in the novel E.M. Forster takes full advantage of its flexibility:

> "How do you do, Mr. Bast?" said Margaret, trying to control her voice. "This is an odd business. What view do you take of it?"
>
> "There is Mrs. Bast, too," prompted Helen.
>
> Jacky also shook hands. She, like her husband, was shy, and so bestially stupid that she could not grasp what was happening.

In just fifty-four words, we have dipped into three minds: Margaret's, who is "trying to control her voice;" Jacky Bast's, who "could not grasp what was happening;" and the author's, who tells us that Mrs. Bast is "bestially stupid." Certainly this is neither Jacky's opinion of herself nor Margaret's of Jacky (the two women have just met). Forster is editorializing here, a hallmark of omniscient POV.

Its unlimited flexibility would seem to make omniscient POV the easiest of all viewpoints for the writer. In fact, it is the most difficult. In chapter fifteen we'll discuss how to do it well; for now, just be aware that it's among your options.

NOVELTY POINTS OF VIEW: WHEN YOU WANT TO EXPERIMENT

Finally, there are four rarely used points of view: second person, first person plural, third person plural, and epistolary. If you're in the mood to experiment, these can be interesting to try, although sustaining an entire work in any of them can be difficult, for varying reasons.

Second person means that the protagonist is written as "you." Jay McInerney, amazingly, wrote an entire best-selling novel in second person, *Bright Lights, Big City*. The book begins:

> You are not the kind of guy who would be at a place like this at this time of the morning. But here you are, and you cannot say the terrain is completely unfamiliar, although the details are fuzzy. You are at a nightclub talking to a girl with a shaved head.

The problem with this is obvious; many readers will instantly think, *No, I'm not at a nightclub talking to a girl with a shaved head. The character is, but I'm not.* A large number of readers simply cannot get past this perception. Second person is designed to force an identification with the character (who is "you") but, due to the perversity of human resistance to mucking around with one's identity, it frequently has the opposite effect. Use at your own peril.

First person plural, writing from the viewpoint of "we," and third person plural, writing from the viewpoint of "they," are pretty much limited to experimental science fiction. Both lend themselves to hive minds, telepaths, or ant colonies, but not much else.

Epistolary POV is more common. In fact, the novel form began in epistolary POV, which means the entire story is told through letters from various characters to other characters. The modern epistolary form has been expanded to include diaries, interoffice memos, recorded interviews, e-mails, "excerpts" from imaginary books, and any other form of written communication.

Alice Walker's moving *The Color Purple* is an epistolary novel, consisting mostly of letters between Celie and her sister Nettie, but beginning with Celie's desperate letters to God:

> Dear God,
>
> I am fourteen years old. I am [crossed out] I have always been a good girl. Maybe you can give me a sign letting me know what is happening to me.

The Nonhuman POV

Nonhuman points of view turn up mostly in children's literature and science fiction. In kids' books, of course, animal points of view are a staple, from Beatrix Potter's Peter Rabbit through Kenneth Grahame's Ratty and Mole (*The Wind in the Willows*) to the contemporary media tie-in books for *Barney* and *Sesame Street*. Such animal protagonists inevitably act and talk like humans. This is partly to promote the child's identification with the character, but there is also another reason, which applies as well to most of the aliens in science fiction.

If an animal or alien were to think, act, or talk in ways that are decidedly *not* human, readers wouldn't understand what they were doing, or why. And writers would have an awful time getting into the mind of such creations to use them as POV characters. How can you think like a nonhuman in order to create one?

What both children's writers and science fiction authors thus do is create POV characters that are mostly human but have a few added nonhuman characteristics, such as enhanced smell or strange kinship patterns. This halfway measure works pretty well, as long as readers accept the convention behind it (many people reject science fiction because its aliens are either "too far out" or not strange enough).

Mainstream adult literature uses animal points of view very rarely (although Ernest Hemingway dipped into a lion's POV for one long paragraph in "The Short Happy Life of Francis Macomber"). When an adult book does use animals as POV characters, it tends to be as satire to comment on human behavior, as George Orwell did in *Animal Farm*. If you do this, make sure that your satire is pointed enough to be understood as adult commentary and not as a children's story, and be prepared to be misunderstood or rejected by many readers.

Although letters are, by definition, not immediate because they are written after an event is over, *The Color Purple* retains enormous immediacy and drama. This is because Celie reproduces actual scenes in her letters, albeit as seen through her eyes, but with dialogue, gestures, and action. To sustain epistolary POV through an entire novel, you will need to do the same.

For a short story, however (especially a brief one), we will be willing to infer the scenes from the letters or memos. This format lends itself well to satire.

COMBINING POINTS OF VIEW: THE HYBRID STORY

Can you combine different points of view in one work? Yes, but cautiously.

The easiest to combine is either first or third person with epistolary. For example, Charles Sheffield's disaster novel *Aftermath* concerns the effect of a massive bombardment of cosmic rays, caused by a distant nova, on Earth. All electromagnetic communication is wiped out, including telephone, radio, television, and computers. The novel alternates chapters in multiple third person, fully dramatized, with chapters from the "diary" of a major character. It works well to both give us the big picture of the disaster and to detail its effects on one unusual mind.

Science fiction writer Frederick Pohl combined several viewpoints in his award-winning novel *Gateway*: first person narrative, transcripts of therapy sessions, classified ads, meeting notices, excerpts from "historical documents." Together, they give a fuller picture of a future society than would any one of them alone.

What does not usually work is the beginner mistake of combining first person and third person narrative. This, for instance, is a mess:

> I watched Jane enter the room and close the door. She looked angry and kept clenching one manicured hand. The door closed softly.
>
> Behind it, Jane sighed in relief. Safe! Now all she had to do was try to forget the awful events of the day.

Through whose eyes are we supposed to experience this story: "I" or "Jane"? This switch in POV would be abrupt even if both were third person; from first person to third person, it doesn't work at all.

However, having said that, I must point out that at least one person made it work brilliantly: William Faulkner in *The Sound and the Fury*, which combines first-person narrative with a last section featuring Dilsey, a family servant, written in third person. You really have to be a Faulkner to get away with this, although it does prove yet again that there are no unbreakable rules in writing if a genuine master chooses to break them.

Pick your POV carefully; you'll start using it on page one and be stuck with it for the entire story. And now that you've chosen, let's see how to do each POV well.

RECAP: SURVEY OF POINTS OF VIEW

Point of view means through whose eyes and mind we experience your story. The usual choices are first person, third person limited or multiple, and omniscient. Rarer points of view are second person, epistolary, and first or third person plural.

Your protagonist and POV characters may or may not be identical, since any story can be told from the POV of any of the characters. Imagine your story from different points of view before you commit to one. Use as few POV characters as you can get away with and still tell the story you want to tell.

First person has the advantages of immediacy, individual language, and internal range, but the disadvantages of limited flexibility, claustrophobia, and greater difficulty for the writer in being objective.

Third person has the advantages of greater flexibility, external range, and objectivity, but may be less immediate and individualistic than first person.

Omniscient POV, which goes into many characters' minds at will and includes authorial comments, is hard to do well.

Either first or third person can be combined with epistolary POV—but not with each other.

EXERCISE 1

Pick a story you know well; it may be your own or someone else's. List the five or six major characters. Now try to imagine the story if it were told from the POV of a character the author did *not* choose as a POV character. Does the story feel much different? Are some scenes emphasized more, some less? Does the meaning of the story seem to change?

EXERCISE 2

Consider your favorite novel of all time and choose your favorite character from it. Write a letter from this character to another character in the book, dated after the novel itself is over. What is the character's life like now? How does he feel about it?

Pick a dysfunctional family you know well, either your own or a friend's. Write a page or so of first person thoughts for each member of the family, reflecting that person's view of the family's problems. Try to be fair to each person, even those you disapprove of. Now read the pages over. Is there a story here? Are you interested in writing it?

Pick a novel written in third person and rewrite the first three paragraphs or so in first person. What changes? Do you like the results better or worse? Do you see places to expand by adding more of the character's attitude and thoughts?

Imagine someone as unlike yourself as you can think of: extroverted if you are shy, calm if you are emotional, criminal if you are law abiding. Write one page in first person in which this character has an argument with a grocery clerk. Use dialogue, thoughts, and actions. Is it easier or harder to write in first person if the character is totally different from you?

chapter 13

[FIRST PERSON—I SAW IT WITH MY OWN EYES]

In one sense, first person seems the most natural mode for storytelling because we all use it all the time. We start, "I was barreling along Highway 16 when . . ." and the story follows. It would seem, therefore, that first-person narration would raise no issues for readers or writers. Just tell the story.

In reality, however, it's not that simple.

PROBLEMS INHERENT IN FIRST PERSON

Readers know, of course, that first-person fictional characters are not the ones telling their own stories. That's not Jane Eyre we hear; it's Charlotte Brontë. But we want to believe in the illusion that it's Jane herself, and how well this illusion is sustained is critical to the success of any first-person narrative.

The first problem inherent in first person is that it's not natural. People tell others stories about themselves, yes, but they don't tell four-hundred-page stories with perfectly recalled conversations and detailed descriptions (and if they did, everyone would be asleep before the story finished). The stories that real-life people tell tend to be more like this:

> "I was barreling along Highway 16 when wham! This truck comes out of nowhere and almost sideswiped me. Man, I've never been so scared in my life!"
>
> "Then what happened?" the eager listeners ask.
>
> "Oh, nothing."

Clearly this will not do for fiction. In a novel we want that four-hundred-page, detailed, carefully crafted narrative with rising tension, and if it's in first person, we're willing to accept that, no, people don't really tell stories that way, but this person *is*. Period.

A harder question to resolve is *why* the narrator is telling his story this way. Clearly the whole story is over, since we're holding the entire manuscript in our hand. The narrator knows how the story comes out, yet he's withholding the end from us, building it up and pretending he doesn't know what will happen. It's very artificial.

Many readers, of course, don't care. It's artificial—so what? Just get on with it. For other people, however, the artificiality can jar. It is, in fact, one reason that some authors never write in first person at all.

You can lessen the artificiality of first person with one of two stratagems. First, you can write a frame story with an introduction that frankly acknowledges that the story is over and the narrator is now looking back on it. Daphne du Maurier's classic romantic novel *Rebecca* begins thus:

> Last night I dreamt I went to Manderley again. It seemed to me I stood by the iron gate leading to the drive, and for a while I could not enter for the way was barred to me.

This first chapter goes on to describe a deserted estate destroyed by fire followed by a description of the life that the homeless main characters lead now. Only after we know all that do we start, in chapter three, the actual story to which we've already learned the ending. Obviously, the author loses some tension this way. But she defuses the artificiality of a first-person narrator pretending that she doesn't know what's going to happen.

Michael Frayn also defuses it in *Spies*, quoted in chapter twelve. Here is his passage again:

> The third week of June and there it is again: the same almost embarrassingly familiar breath of sweetness that comes every year about this time. I catch it on the warm evening air as I walk past the well-ordered gardens on my quiet street, and for a moment I'm a child again and everything's before me—all the frightening, half-understood promise of life.

This, too, is an older character frankly admitting, before he recounts his story, that it's over, but unlike du Maurier's novel, *Spies* is not a frame story. The author continues throughout the whole book to interpose comments from his older self among dramatized scenes of his childhood. In this way he not only makes it plausible that he is telling us a story, but he also gains the richness of a dual first-person viewpoint: We see events as they appeared to his child self *and* his adult self.

Of course, Frayn also loses something (everything in writing is a trade-off). He loses the same immediacy that du Maurier does. He cannot surprise himself (since he's already told us he knows the whole story), and this lessens his ability, if the narrator is honest about what he knows, to surprise us as well.

If you are writing a literary novel, you may want to consider these implications of first person. You may even want to take advantage of them by writing the dual-viewpoint first person: younger and older versions of the narrator. If, however, you are writing commercial fiction, I'd advise you to just forget the implied artificiality of first-person narration and write it anyway. Your readers are probably accustomed enough to the convention that the story is happening as it's told (even though the narrator must know the end in order to have written it) that no one will be bounced out of your tale.

FIRST-PERSON DESCRIPTION AND ACTION

A more important aspect of first-person narration is that it determines not only *how* you write things but also *what* you can write.

In first person, you are inside your character's head, and everything must be seen *as he sees it*. This means that certain kinds of description don't work because people don't think that way. Among these are self-descriptions; no one thinks, "I'm six two, a hundred ninety pounds, with short brown hair and light brown eyes, wearing a blue windbreaker and jeans." This is a police-blotter description, and although you can probably use it in a third-person police procedural, in first person it feels false.

So how might this man describe his appearance in first person? Here is one possibility:

> I pull on my jeans and sniff my shirt: a little gamy. Ah, well, it'll have to do; it's the only one that fits since I packed on a few. I might go as much as one-ninety, but I'm not about to get on the scale to check. At least I got a haircut yesterday. Shit—I just realized the shirt is brown and Liz hates me to wear brown. "You're all one color," she'll jeer. "Shirt, hair, eyes—all shit brown." Well, tough. I put on the shirt.

Another character, of course, might see himself much differently. The point is that self-description in first person, in order to seem natural, must occur at a point in the story when the character would naturally be thinking about his own appearance, *and* it must occur in the phrases he would think. You can, in a pinch, have him comb his hair in front of a mirror and note his appearance, although in some writerly circles this is regarded as cheating.

It's not only self-description that you must watch in first person—it's everything. Actions simply look different when you're the person doing them than when you're observing someone else doing them. This includes the action of observation. We see and do things accompanied by *reactions* to them, and it's these reactions that give first person its individual feel.

For example, here is a man observed from the outside unloading his groceries:

> Grunting, Jerry lifted the bag from the car. Halfway to the house he dropped it. Eggs and milk smashed onto the sidewalk, and grapes rolled into the azaleas. Jerry stomped inside and slammed the door.

But if you are inside Jerry's head, you will probably want to include Jerry's reactions. The incident might look like this:

> As I lifted the bag from the car, I felt it slip. Shit! Eggs and milk smashed on the sidewalk, grapes rolling into Linda's azaleas . . . Some days there's no point in even trying. I left the mess and stomped inside.

Or this:

> As I lifted the bag from the car, the flimsy paper those cheapskates use at the market gave way. My groceries smashed onto the pavement, twelve dollars of useless mess. And now I'd have to clean the sidewalk, too. Bastards.

Or this:

> As I lifted the bag from the car, I dropped it. Helplessly I watched egg and milk stain the sidewalk and grapes roll onto the dirt. Linda would kill me.

Each of these includes reactions to the action, telling us much more about the character. One version of Jerry is defeatist; one blames everyone else for his misfortune; and one is passively afraid of his wife. In addition, the individualized reactions add to the illusion that we are inside Jerry's head. Do you have to do this if you write first person? No. You can use the third-person version and simply change "he" to "I." But if you do, you're not taking full advantage of what first person has to offer.

FIRST-PERSON THOUGHTS
AND EXPOSITION

Thoughts present an interesting question in first person because, in one sense, the entire manuscript consists of thoughts. Everything is being "told" inside the head of the narrator, as in this opening passage from Chaim Potok's best-seller, *The Chosen*:

> For the first fifteen years of our lives, Danny and I lived within five blocks of each other and neither of us knew of the other's existence.
>
> Danny's block was heavily populated by the followers of his father, Russian Hasidic Jews in somber garb, whose habits and frame of reference were born on the soil they had abandoned. They drank tea from samovars, slipping it slowly through cubes of sugar held between their teeth; they ate the foods of their homeland, talked loudly, occasionally in Russian, most often in Russian Yiddish, and were fierce in their loyalty to Danny's father.

Again, as with description and action, this is clearly artificial. No one thinks in phrases like "whose habits and frame of reference were born on the soil they had abandoned." It's a rare person who would even have the thought; the language is simply not the natural one occurring inside someone's head.

You have four choices in handling this problem of first-person exposition. First, you can simply ignore it, as Potok does. This is how his first-person narrator, Reuven, is going to tell his story, and you can either accept its artificiality or not. Of course, it helps that Potok's story has so much else going for it: great characters, interesting setting, and compelling questions about life and faith.

Second, you can exploit the first-person POV by limiting exposition to the language and observations natural to that narrator. If Potok had chosen this route, he might have recast the phrase just singled out into something like: "They did everything just the way they'd done it in Russia." This gains naturalness but loses stateliness. Your call.

Third, you can leave out almost all exposition, gaining verisimilitude by confining your prose to what your narrator thinks about what's happening at that second. Raymond Carver does this to great effect in his short stories.

Fourth, you can adopt the dual-first-person POV discussed earlier with an older narrator recalling the story already past. Since it's more natural to ruminate formally on events after they're done than while they're happening, exposition will seem more natural in this format.

First-Person Constructions to Avoid

These constructions (alas, all too common) are redundant, inappropriate, or silly in first person:

- "A smile on my face." A first-person narrator cannot see his own face. Also, where *else* would a smile be? Choose "I smiled."
- "An expression of fear/horror/joy/etc. crossed my face." Same objection as above.
- "I thought to myself." Drop "to myself." Unless your character is a telepath, there is no other possibility. Likewise "I wondered to myself," "I daydreamed to myself," etc.
- "I let my thoughts drift back to . . ." In first person, we're *in* "your" thoughts. Just show us what you're thinking, without announcing that you're thinking.
- "I remembered my son's first birthday." If your character just this moment remembered the occasion, this construction is fine. If not, it's just more announcing. Simply tell us the content of the birthday memory and we'll easily see that it *is* a memory: "On Jim's first birthday, my husband left me."
- "My face grew red" or "I blushed." The first of these is definitely a POV violation; a person cannot see what color his face is turning. "I blushed" also involves a color change but is probably acceptable because it implies facial warmth, which a first-person narrator *can* feel. Better might be "My face grew hot."

However you handle exposition, another aspect of thought should be a part of first person: attitude. People don't just do and say things; they have overall feelings about the life around them. Since we're inside your character's head, we should share these feelings. Is he glad that it's raining? Does she enjoy teaching that class? When the president makes a speech on television, what is her attitude toward this particular Chief Executive?

- President Smith, that puppet, spoke for twenty interminable minutes.
- President Smith made a moving speech, but it was too short, only twenty minutes.

- President Smith spoke throughout the entire time I was giving Susie her bath, bedtime snack, and story.
- In the background, someone talked on the television.

Giving your narrator's attitudes in quick glimpses not only makes first person seem more natural, it's an effective way to build characterization.

FIRST PERSON AND DIALOGUE

First person is most artificial in its presentation of dialogue. No one remembers, thinks about, or recounts ten-minute conversations word for word. In real life, our thoughts are: "I had a big fight with my husband and he said I was impatient. Well, he's the impatient one!" However, if your story treated all dialogue this way, it would be a bore. Readers want to hear exactly what your characters say, firsthand. They want to be that fly on the wall, witnessing that marital fight. Think about it: If you skim a story, what do you skip? Probably passages of description, exposition, and very long speeches. No one skips the short back-and-forth exchanges of dialogue.

So there's no way around it. Put in all the dialogue in your first-person story, artificial or not.

VOICE: THE HEART OF FIRST PERSON

So far we've dwelt on the content of first person. The great advantage of this POV, however, is not what you can say but how you can say it. Because first person is told directly in the narrator's own words, this choice of POV, more than any others, allows us to "hear" the natural voice of the character. And there is no better way to let us know who your character is than by letting us hear his thoughts in his own words.

Words characterize by their diction, cadence, complexity, and attitude. This is true of actions and dialogue as well, but they can be given even greater impact, realism, and emotion by the way the character tells us about them.

Is your character cynical? Then his vocabulary will be cynical as well, faintly mocking. Is she sentimental? Her diction will be, too. Is he simple-minded? His sentences will be short and his knowledge limited. A good example is Benjy in Faulkner's *The Sound and the Fury*. Here Benjy burns his hand:

> I put my hand out to where the fire had been.
> "Catch him," Dilsey said. "Catch him back."

My hand jerked back and I put it in my mouth and Dilsey caught me. I could still hear the clock between my voice. Dilsey reached back and hit Luster on the head. My voice was going loud every time.

This is how the world appears to Benjy: his "voice going" when he screams, with the clock "between" his voice. He makes no connection between the fire, his pain, and his voice. The words reveal more than what he's thinking; they reveal the *way* he thinks.

So, less dramatically, does every first-person narration. Look again at the passage from *The Chosen*. Before narrator Reuven has done or said anything at all, we know that he is intelligent and sharply observant from the careful way he describes the Hasidic Jews. His voice is clear and educated. Had we been given this description in third-person exposition, the Hassids might have been just as vivid, but Reuven wouldn't be.

First person is marvelously flexible in voice. It can reflect region, ethnicity, or historical era as well as character. However, with these variants, a little goes a long way. Suggest them with a few phrases, changed word order, and diction rather than by tortured spelling. "I throwed away all my chances, son," is more effective than "Lookee hyar, boy, Ah done ruint ev'ry chance comin' t'ard me." The latter is hard to read, inaccurate, and condescending. An entire story of it would be intolerable.

DISTANCE AND FIRST PERSON

"Distance" in fiction refers to whether we are seeing the character from the inside or the outside and from how far outside. In first person, we are supposed to be inside the character's head all the time. This means that constructions common in third person don't work in first person because they imply we're viewing the character's very thoughts from outside, and hence the character is, too, which doesn't make sense.

For example, the sentence "I wondered if Jane would call today" is a subtle distancing. We are looking at the narrator wondering. Closer inside his head would be one of the following:

- Would Jane call today?
- Maybe Jane would call today.
- Jane wouldn't call today. She never called when I needed her to.
- Hope fluttered in my belly, unsettling my breakfast: Maybe Jane would call today.

- God, I was pathetic, hoping for a call from that bitch Jane.
- The refrain sounded again and again in my head: Jane. Call. Please.

Not only do these eliminate the distance of "I wondered," but they take advantage of first person's strength: voice that characterizes. The same is true for less-distant versions of "I reminded myself," "I doubted," and "I feared." *Show* us the content of that reminder, doubt, or fear in the words and phrases your first-person character would think about them.

Of course, there are occasions when you might want the greater distancing of "I doubted" or "I hoped." This is true when your first-person character is a distant, reserved, or formal person and you want his diction to reflect that. Once again, this flexibility is the strength of first person.

UNRELIABLE FIRST PERSON: CAN I TRUST YOU?

An interesting variant on first-person narration is the unreliable narrator. Usually, we accept that what a first-person narrator tells us is true: If he says the wall is green, we assume it *is* green. If he says that Jim is a kind man, we assume that Jim is kind. However, you can also employ an unreliable narrator.

With this technique, we start out by assuming that the narrator is telling the truth. As the story unfolds, however, we gradually come to see that things are not the way the narrator has presented them, either because the narrator is deluded or because he's deceitful. This discovery turns the whole story upside down, giving tremendous emphasis to the truth as readers try to figure out just what it is.

A famous example is the barber in Ring Lardner's classic story "Haircut." The garrulous narrator, a barber, talks nonstop to a stranger whose hair he's cutting. He describes the town and its major characters, including a shooting accident that killed Jim Kendall, a beloved local "card." But as the barber innocently relates events, it emerges that Jim was actually a cruel man, and the accident was actually murder. The barber never realizes this, but the reader does, and the barber's ignorance heightens through contrast with the reader's reactions to her discovery.

If you attempt an unreliable narrator, you must set up the story so readers eventually learn he is unreliable. Otherwise, the story simply will not work. This means that your narrator's tale must include enough contradictions, exaggerations, or anomalies so we have grounds for rejecting his credibility.

MULTIPLE FIRST PERSON

First person, by definition, means one narrator (the "first" POV we all know: "I"). Every once in a while, however, a writer will decide to try multiple first person, in which sections or (usually) chapters of a story rotate two or more narrators, each telling their story in "I." One example is Ursula K. Le Guin's wonderful novel *The Left Hand of Darkness*. Alternating chapters are told in first person by two characters from radically different cultures, giving us more intimate looks into these two mindsets than if either character had been the sole narrator. The same is true for the first three-quarters of Faulkner's *The Sound and the Fury*, which are narrated in multiple first person.

On the other hand, jumping from "inside one head" to another, especially repeatedly, may fragment reader identification so much that the story may be ruined. As always, you must weigh the gains and losses to your particular story before you elect this rare POV. It seems to work best where there is a great contrast between the characters and the author wishes to emphasize that wide gulf.

THE AUTHOR AND FIRST PERSON

In any version of first person, the author is invisible. He has merged completely with the narrator and thus has no way of giving us information or interpretations that the narrator does not share. This means that, more completely than in any other choice of viewpoint, you the writer must *become* the character. You must guard constantly against having this person say, think, or feel more than is natural to him just to serve the purposes of plot or theme. If the first-person character doesn't have the wit, or perhaps the opportunity, to see that Uncle Bill is a thief, you'll ruin your story if you force your narrator to realize that. At best, another character can tell him about Uncle Bill's thievery, and he can believe or disbelieve it.

This very limitation of first person can also be its strength. You, the author, are invisible—but you haven't ceased to exist. It's still *you* arranging what the narrator sees, whom he talks to, and what problems are thrust on him. If you choose a very limited narrator, like Benjy in *The Sound and the Fury* or the barber in "Haircut," you gain a strong vehicle for exploring the limitations of human perception in a way that forces the reader to share them. First person is well suited to this kind of story.

It also works well when you want an older-and-wiser character who has learned from life. By telling his own story directly, the more experienced narrator can provide interpretations of events as sophisticated as the author's while recalling the freshness of the character's encounter with the plot when he was younger.

All this, and the character's voice, too. Done well, first person is rich indeed.

RECAP: FIRST-PERSON NARRATION

First person is inherently an artificial POV because no one recounts long, completed, or perfectly edited stories, with full dialogue, as if the narrator does not know what will happen next. You can choose to ignore the artificiality of first person; you can use a double-aged narrator, young and old, to account for it; or you can limit or even leave out exposition.

Description and exposition in first person must be presented as the character sees the information, not the author. This requirement is actually positive in that it aids characterization.

Include all dialogue in first person, even though in actuality no one remembers whole scenes of dialogue word for word.

The strength of first person is the voice of your narrator; make yours reflect his personality not only in what he says but also in how he says it. When creating a voice using any form of dialect or regionalism, use its phrases and wording sparingly. Too much is annoying and may be condescending. Use distancing constructions in first person only when distance and formality are the effects you're aiming for.

Unreliable first-person narrators can create great drama as readers discover the gap between what the narrator says and what story events indicate.

Multiple first person is rare because it's hard to do well, but it can work if the narrators are widely disparate in views or language.

EXERCISE 1

A few days after you've attended some event with at least three other people—a family dinner, an organizational meeting, a walk, anything will do—ask each person, separately, to tell you five things they remember about the event. Make a list for each person. Afterward, compare them. Did they remember (and hence notice) different things? Would their first-person accounts of the event be significantly different?

Pick three of your mini-bio characters and tell a simple event, such as eating breakfast, in first-person narration for each of them. This should not be a diary entry; write each as a short scene, paying particular attention to what each character noticed at breakfast. Are there differences among the accounts? If not, you need to rethink your characters, striving to find the individuality in each.

Choose a famous speech in literature: Hamlet's "to be or not to be" soliloquy, perhaps, or Scarlett O'Hara's "I'll never be hungry again" speech (*Gone With the Wind* by Margaret Mitchell), or Frederick Henry's "life breaks everyone" speech (*A Farewell to Arms* by Ernest Hemingway). Rewrite it according to a radically different person, real or fictional, altering voice but not the essential message. For instance, how might Scarlett's speech have sounded from a rapper? From a John Wayne hero? From Faulkner's Benjy?

Rewrite each of the following to lessen the distance between narrator and author:

- I dreaded Christmas that year.
- I hate the way my boss talks to me.
- I wished for snow on my birthday.

Is the result more vivid?

Write a short argument between two people solely in dialogue. Now go back and add the first-person thoughts of one character between lines of dialogue, then do the same for the other character. Which version is stronger? Why?

Take a few paragraphs of third-person prose, your own or someone else's, and turn them into first person. Don't just transpose pronouns; add attitudes, diction, and commentary from your first-person narrator. You should discover you can't do this without first having a clear idea of who this character is.

chapter 14

[THIRD PERSON— SEE DICK RUN]

Third person is the point of view with which we started our life as readers, as in "Once upon a time there was a beautiful princess." Children's stories are nearly always in third person because it's more natural for small children to visualize that princess than to *become* her (especially for boys). First person, with its insistent "I," demands more reader identification while still maintaining a separate identity, and this can be confusing for children still developing their own sense of self. So Peter Rabbit, Cinderella, Stuart Little, and even Harry Potter are all written in third person.

Adult literature, too, finds third person natural. It is the language of telling stories about other people, whether those people are the neighbors ("So then Wanda Smith went over to her sister's and the sister said—") or Anna Karenina and Count Vronsky. Most commercial novels are written in third person.

This does not mean, however, that third person is itself simplistic or one-dimensional. On the contrary, third person comes in many varieties. Choosing the right one can greatly enhance your story, and choosing the wrong one can unnecessarily limit it.

Third person is either limited third, in which we see the story through the eyes of only one character, or multiple third, in which we enter the heads of two or more characters (sometimes many more). Another important factor that differentiates various flavors of third person is distance. Stories can be written in close third, medium-distance third, or distant third, each with its own advantages and disadvantages.

CLOSE THIRD PERSON: HE'S AN OPEN BOOK TO ME

Close third person is almost as close inside the character's head as is first person. As with first, we know everything the character thinks as soon as he thinks it and experience what he feels as he feels it. When you transpose first person to third person by changing the pronouns, close third is what you get. Thus it has the same advantages as first person: immediacy, character identification, and the chance to use the character's own diction.

Here is Paul D., from Toni Morrison's Pulitzer Prize-winning historical novel *Beloved*:

> The girl Beloved, homeless and without people, beat all, though he couldn't say exactly why, considering the colored people he had run into during the last twenty years. During, before, or after the War he had seen Negroes so stunned it was a wonder they recalled or said anything. Who, like him, had hidden in caves and fought owls for food; who, like him, stole from pigs; who, like him, slept in trees in the day and walked by night; who, like him, had buried themselves in slop and jumped in wells to avoid regulators, raiders, paterollers, veterans, hill men, posses, and merrymakers.

Paul's POV is third person, yet some of his phrases are in the same words he would use in either speaking or in telling his story in first person: "beat all," "it was a wonder they recalled," "paterollers" for patrollers. In addition, the narrative at this point is inside his head; these are his memories of flight and his thoughts about the girl Beloved.

At the same time, close third person is not as claustrophobic as first person. It's easier for the narrative to pull back from the character and include sections of exposition about them, as with the opening of *Beloved*, which describes a house:

> 124 was spiteful. Full of a baby's venom. The women in the house knew it and so did the children. For years each put up with the spite in his own way, but by 1873 Sethe and her daughter Denver were its only victims.

This passage is clearly not in the close POV of Paul D., Sethe, Denver, or any other POV character in the book; it's exposition from the author. This sort of expository chunk feels much more natural in third person, even close third, than in first person, giving close third person more flexibility to include things the author wants included but the characters aren't necessarily thinking about.

Plus, of course, with any of the third-person points of view, you have the freedom to include more than one viewpoint character, thus including scenes at which a first-person narrator could not be present.

So why isn't third person the universal choice of writers? For much commercial fiction, it is. As I write this, there are ten novels on *The New York Times'* list of best-sellers, and nine of them are in third person. Nearly all romance novels, the fiction category with the most sales, are written in third person.

If you do choose close third, there are three things to keep in mind. First, its flexibility in distance isn't unlimited. If you jump back and forth from deep inside a character's head to a far-distant overview of the action, then back in close, then out again, the reader is going to get vertigo. The smoothness of your narrative will be compromised. One way around this is to start chapters with the more distant narrative you want to include, then move in closer into the character's mind and stay there. This duplicates the movement of a camera in film as it glides in from a set-up shot to a close-up. The opening of *Beloved* quoted above is such an establishing shot.

If you're going to include any outside views of your character, such as a description of his appearance, this establishing exposition at greater distance is the place to do it. Once you move in closer, you're subject to the same limits as first person. Except in special circumstances (for example, shopping for clothes), any attempt to have a person think about his own appearance in detail will probably feel artificial.

A second important aspect of close third person is that in order to keep it close, you should give us the character's thoughts as they occur to him, in his diction, and without distancing phrases like "he thought" or "he wondered." Consider these two passages:

> Sam spotted Sue across the room. He knew he wasn't good with girls. He thought about Sue: how pretty she was, how nice. He wished he had the nerve to ask her for a date.

> Sam spotted Sue across the room. God, she was pretty—and she was nice, too. How come he couldn't ask her out? How come he was always so spineless around girls? He was a dork.

Both versions convey the same information. But in the first, we are outside Sam, watching him "know" that he isn't good with girls, watching him "thinking" about Sue, watching him "wishing" he had the nerve to ask her out. In the second version, we aren't being *told* what Sam is thinking; we are privy to his actual thoughts, in his own words (including terms like "dork").

This, the essence of close third person, delivers maximum emotion and maximum reader identification with the character. It gives third person almost as much freedom to range over thought, memory, and emotion as you get in first person.

Finally, close third person carries the pitfall of confusion over which are the characters' thoughts and which are the author's exposition. This occurs because the POV is so close that we assume most passages occur in the character's head. If some are not, you need to make this clear. For instance:

> Brent carried the rifle—God, it was heavy—from the house to the barn, set it on the tripod, and aimed it at the barn door. He rigged the trip wire so that the gun would fire if anyone pushed on the door. That would show the trespassing bastards! The rifle had belonged to his father, and once, long ago, it had killed his older brother in a hunting accident in the woods.

Is Brent thinking about the rifle's history, or is the author giving us this information? Does Brent even know that this is the same gun that killed his brother? We can't tell. If this is authorial exposition, with information unknown to Brent, it belongs in another paragraph. If it is Brent's thoughts, it should be made clear through wording that includes Brent's reactions and feelings:

> Often he had seen the rifle in his father's hands, but never after Ben died. Don't think about Ben, about the crack of the rifle in those dark woods, about the sound Ben had made . . . don't think about it.

Use close third person when you want the intense, inside-the-skull focus of first person plus the free use of the character's natural diction, but with a bit more breathing room than first person.

DISTANT THIRD PERSON: I SAW HER ACROSS A CROWDED ROOM

At the other end of the third-person spectrum is distant third person. Since the author views the character from the outside, distant third person is a more formal and less personal POV.

Think of distant third as holding the camera on your protagonist from across the room. The camera then gets a wider view of setting, other people, and the protagonist himself. It's not only wider; it's a different view than if the camera were located inside the protagonist's head, as it is in close first person.

Here is the opening to Anita Brookner's *Latecomers*:

> Hartmann, a voluptuary, lowered a spoonful of brown sugar crystals into his coffee cup, then placed a square of bitter chocolate on his tongue, and, while it was dissolving, lit his first cigarette. The ensuing mélange of tastes and aromas pleased him profoundly, as did the blue tracery of smoke above the white table cloth, the spray of yellow carnations in the silver vase, and his manicured hand on which the wedding ring fitted loosely, without those deep indentations that afflict the man who has gained weight or age, a man to whom in any case his wedding might be presumed to be an affair of the irrelevant past.

We are clearly viewing Hartmann from the outside. We see his actions with sugar, chocolate, and cigarette. We are *told* that the results pleased him, rather than shown his pleasure as he experiences it. The last long sentence spirals away from Hartmann completely to mention things he is not (a man with indentations on his ring finger) and "presumptions" that Hartmann may or may not hold. This is very distant third person, almost a dispassionate spy camera observing a man without any direct contact. In fact, such dispassionate observation is Brookner's usual technique.

It works for her because she does not want us to identify with Hartmann. She wants us to observe him and draw our own conclusions about his behavior. Distant third person works very well for such stories.

Will it work for yours? Yes, if:

- Your character is unlikable, very complicated, or so different from most people that you need to include much exposition to make him clear and vivid.
- You prefer a standard, even formal, style to writing in the informal, often messy diction of thoughts inside characters' heads.
- You want the freedom to describe characters and scenes from the outside, without filtering all (or most) observations through characters' perceptions.
- Your prose is interesting enough to compensate for the greater distance from the characters. After all, it's always more vivid to be included in action than observe it from across the room. If we're going to do the latter, we need some other reward.

MIDDLE-DISTANCE THIRD PERSON: THE GOLDEN MEAN

It's important to emphasize that close, middle, and distant third-person viewpoints are not really separate and discreet categories. Rather, they're a continuum, just as a camera moving progressively farther away from a film subject would have no absolute point labeled "far." The terms are relative and flexible.

Somewhere in the ill-defined central territory of this flexible continuum lies middle-distance third person. It's the most flexible of all points of view. It means that, for the most part, you're viewing the action from a few feet away but with the freedom to slide in closer, into the character's head, or to back away, viewing him from the outside. Of course, this sliding in and backing away can't be constant or jarring, but certainly it's relatively easier to do both from a middle distance than from any other POV.

Martin Naparsteck effectively exploits the advantages of middle-distance third person in his story "Spinning." Here is the opening:

> Jeanie came from Mickey's right, stuck an envelope in his hand, and said "Here." She spoke flatly with a tinge of obligation; he saw that she didn't want to give him the envelope, she had to. He didn't open it because Dom, sitting on his left, and Trippi, on his right, were talking to each other, and he was certain if they saw him doing something with the envelope, particularly open it, they would insist on knowing what was in it. He had no idea what was in it except he was certain it was something that would hurt his feelings. For months, everything connected to girls hurt his feelings. It was the terrible new emotion that had arrived just after his 14th birthday.

From the first sentence we are inside Mickey's head, experiencing Jeanie approaching on his right. We are privy to his immediate thoughts about not opening the envelope and to his fear of being hurt. But none of this information is conveyed with the intimacy and individualized diction of close first person. If it were, Naparsteck might have written something like this:

> What was in the envelope? Mickey didn't know. Whatever it was, it was going to hurt. A girl had brought him the thing, and girls guaranteed hurt feelings. What could be in it? If Dom and Trippi would just go away, he'd find out.

Note that this closer version would not necessarily have been better or worse, but it *would* be a different story. And if he'd written the second version, Naparsteck would have lost the freedom to easily pull back for the last two sentences, which view Mickey from a farther distance. Those two sentences deliver information that is not on Mickey's mind at the moment but provides the greater context for what he is thinking about.

Middle-distance third person is also good for multiple-POV novels. Again using our camera analogy, it's more natural for the focus to swing from one person to another if the camera is positioned away from the characters rather than inside one of their heads. (More on multiple third person later).

MAINTAINING DISTANCE: HOW FAR CAN YOU JUMP?

Does an entire story have to be written with the same choice of close, middle, or distant third person? No, of course not. We've already seen that a single paragraph, such as that from "Spinning," can include more than one distance. Smooth transitions between distances are necessary. In general, there are three ways to do this.

First, you can move through middle distance to get from close to far (or vice versa) instead of jumping directly. Again, this is analogous to a long, gliding shot with a camera rather than a quick cut. Compare these two passages:

> Paul peered through the darkness—where was Jake? He'd told that screwup to meet him here at midnight! They had only a few minutes between dog patrols to climb the fence. They'd been planning this thing for weeks, and Paul needed Jake to pull it off. Actually, his whole life he'd needed Jake, and Jake had hardly ever come through, not even at the beginning. When Paul was born, Jake had been six, and Jake had tried to strangle him. The brothers were not close. No O'Riley had ever trusted any relative.

> Paul peered through the darkness—where was Jake? He'd told that screwup to meet him here at midnight! They had only a few minutes between dog patrols to climb the fence. They'd been planning this thing for weeks. But no O'Riley had ever trusted any relative.

The first version starts out inside Paul's head with such immediate, on-the-spot thoughts as "Where was Jake?" The first four sentences are in this close distance, concerned with what is happening that very minute in the story. The writing then pulls back to a middle distance for the next two sentences, which contain information that is not happening in story time but is certainly relevant to the current action and which might very well be on Paul's mind, given his annoyance with Jake. The last two sentences deliver a sweeping, Olympian pronouncement from outside the immediate situation, given at great distance.

In contrast, the second version, which omits all the middle distance, feels rough (despite that pathetic attempt at a transition, the single word "But"). The prose jumps right from close third to distant third, and the result is choppy. If the author did this consistently, the story would be very hard to read.

A second way to avoid such choppy jumps is to change paragraphs or even scenes. Read the second version again. If "No O'Riley had ever trusted any relative" might work as the lead sentence in a second paragraph, followed by reasons for the distrust that are also applied directly to Paul and Jake. This would still make more demands on the reader than the first version, but in the hands of a writer given to throwing challenges and jabs at his audience, it might work. Starting a new scene with the greater distance and then moving in closer, as discussed earlier, might work even better.

Finally, jumps in distance can be smoothed by rewriting the pieces that don't fit. Look at this version of the paragraph:

> Paul peered through the darkness—where was Jake? He'd told that screwup to meet him here at midnight! They had only a few minutes between dog patrols to climb the fence. They'd been planning this thing for weeks! Maybe Jake would be more reliable if he and Paul were closer . . . but maybe not. No O'Riley had ever trusted any relative, and Paul damned well wasn't going to start now.

Here the more detached sentences have been brought close into Paul's thoughts, eliminating the jump in distance entirely.

SOME BLUNT TALK: DOES DISTANCE REALLY MATTER?

This is a legitimate question. If you pick up many books that appear on the best-seller list, you will find distance jumps all over the place. They obviously have not interfered with the sales of these books. So why am I spending so much time (mine and yours) on the whole issue? Does knowing what distance you're working at, plus maintaining that distance well, really matter?

The answer is: It depends on how much control you want over your prose.

Many books that sell well are not, according to many critics, particularly well written. But—and this is an enormous caveat—they have something else that makes people eager to read them. That something may be an exciting story, sympathetic characters, breakneck pace, or fantasy-fulfilling situations. If any—or all of these—capture public interest in your book, the truth is that it doesn't matter if your prose is rough. This may be a disheartening truth, but truth it is. Grace Metalious, author of *Peyton Place*, put it with disarming bluntness: "I may be a bad writer, but a hell of a lot of people have bad taste."

However, a deft handling of such techniques as distance can do three things for your story:

- It can improve it, adding polish to whatever selling points the book may already possess.
- It can help convince that crucial first editor, the one who sees your book long before any indiscriminate public, that you can write well enough for him to read your entire manuscript.
- If you write literary fiction, in which more attention is paid to the prose (as opposed to the story) than in commercial fiction, your control of distance may make the difference between a salable or nonsalable manuscript.

MULTIPLE THIRD PERSON: A STORY FROM MANY ANGLES

Multiple third person is a very convenient POV. Done well, it has many advantages:

- It can cover a wide variety of scenes, not only those at which the protagonist is present.
- It provides a way for the writer to give to the reader information the protagonist does not have; another character can inhabit the scene in which the information is dramatized.
- It can develop a greater number of characters from the inside, letting us in on the thoughts and feelings that make fictional people seem real and complex.
- It can, in skillful hands, offer conflicting viewpoints on the same events. For instance, one character may see an action as moral, while another sees it as wrong. This can add up to a layered, ambiguous, rich view of life.

The list of classic novels written in multiple third person would be very long indeed, including Charles Dickens's *A Tale of Two Cities*, Leo Tolstoy's *Anna*

Karenina, Gustave Flaubert's *Madame Bovary*, Nathaniel Hawthorne's *The Scarlet Letter*, George Eliot's *Middlemarch*, William Makepeace Thackeray's *Vanity Fair*, Colette's *Chéri*, and John Galsworthy's *The Forsyte Saga*.

Nor is multiple third person any less popular in our own time. These examples demonstrate the wide variety of fiction in which multiple third person is successfully used: Jonathan Franzen's *The Corrections*, Anne Tyler's *Saint Maybe*, Charles Frazier's *Cold Mountain*, Toni Morrison's *Song of Solomon*, Connie Willis's *Passage*, Michael Ondaatje's *The English Patient*, Tom Wolfe's *Bonfire of the Vanities*, and Susan Isaacs's *Almost Paradise*.

There are, however, guidelines for successful use of multiple third person. They concern the POV characters' identities, continuity, introductions, and playing time.

CHOOSING THE POV CHARACTERS

We already discussed the importance of limiting POV characters to the smallest number that can effectively tell your story. A second criterion for choosing them is this: They should be interesting people in their own right.

We are going to be spending a lot of time with each POV character. In a four-hundred-page novel with five POV characters, we will spend roughly twenty thousand words with each one, part of that verbiage inside his head in the form of character thoughts. It better be an interesting head.

When you're planning your story, think about this: Which characters will provide both writer and reader with the most interesting internal dialogue? Who has original, complex, or rich interpretations of the action? Can those be your POV characters?

Conversely, are the characters you've selected as necessary viewpoints bland? If so, do they have to be? Sometimes, of course, the answer is "yes." The coming-of-age story demands an innocent protagonist, even though corruption is often more vivid than innocence (this was John Milton's problem in *Paradise Lost*; Satan is more interesting than Christ). If one or more of your POV characters is unavoidably mild, then at least give them a few minor quirks to make our time inside their heads more compelling.

CONTINUITY: ONE SCENE PER CUSTOMER

This is the most important consideration in multiple third person. As a general rule, you should not change points of view promiscuously. This means staying in a single POV for the length of at least one scene and changing viewpoints only when you change scenes, or even chapters.

The reason for this is the same as for avoiding abrupt shifts in distance; it disorients the reader. Indiscriminate jumps in POV are, however, more jarring than jumps in distance. With POV jumps, we are asked not only to move toward or away from inside the character's head—we are asked to enter an entirely different head. It's like having to cross national borders several times a day, readjusting ideas about language, local mores, and currency. It's tiring. It also weakens the idea that you story is "reality;" in real life, we don't jump from head to head.

Having said that, and said it so strongly, I'm nonetheless forced to admit that some types of commercial fiction sometimes ignore this rule. Here is a passage from Judith McNaught's romantic suspense novel *Night Whispers*:

> Sloan edged her way back to the corner of the ice cream stand, then began retracing her steps, staying close to the rear of the food stands so that she would emerge on the south end of the row of buildings. From there, she would be able to either watch him or follow him.
>
> Silently cursing the sand that filled his shoes, the man waited beside the dunes, expecting his prey to appear on the beach, beyond the snack stands. She'd been so unsuspecting, so easy to follow, and so predictable, that when she didn't appear where he expected to see her, it didn't occur to him to be alarmed.

The first paragraph is in Sloan's POV; the second in that of the man trailing her. In other places, McNaught changes POV within a paragraph. She gets away with it because her audience wants to read her stories and is unconcerned or unaware of any roughness in the way those stories are told.

For most fiction, however, you will do better to keep to one POV per scene. A corollary of this is that in a multiple-third-person novel, you must indicate at the very start of each scene whose POV we're in. It's disconcerting for a reader to read a page of character thoughts and reactions only to discover he's been attributing them to the wrong character.

INTRODUCING POV CHARACTERS: WE NEED YOU ON STAGE NOW

If you use more than one POV character, it's important that readers know this fairly early in the story. A book that goes for a hundred pages in Jane's

POV and then abruptly switches to Kenneth's POV will look like a mistake. The reader will think, "Kenneth? But Jane is telling this story!" The writer will look as if his story is out of control, and Kenneth has been introduced as a POV to hastily cover information Jane doesn't have.

The way to avoid this is:

- Be clear upfront about how many POV characters you're going to use and who they are.
- Write the opening in one of them.
- Switch in the second (or perhaps third) scene to another POV character, and write a section in his POV.
- Do the same for any other POV characters until you've rotated through the list.
- Go back and make sure each POV scene is necessary to the plot, interesting in itself, and capable of letting us see who this focus person is and how he behaves.

I can't overemphasize that the opening of a book is critical. Take time with these introductory scenes. Try them in a different order; experiment with various plot situations; try starting your story in a few different places in its sequence of events. Not only are the opening scenes critical to gain the attention of readers (and editors), they can also make writing the rest of the book much easier on *you*. Having all your POV characters well established early on is a tremendous boost to your confidence and your plotting.

PLAYING TIME: WHOSE PART IS BIGGER?

Not all the characters in your book will be equal, not even all the POV characters. The stars are the ones with the key actions, so they will naturally have more "playing time." This means that their POV sections are likely to be significantly longer than those of secondary POV characters. That's fine—within limits.

What's not fine is the POV character who has one or two scenes in the book, whereas the other POV characters have thirty or fifty. Again, this will look like sloppy construction. Try to give all your POV characters substantial actions to perform, consequences of those actions to deal with, and important reactions to others' actions. If you can't do that for a character, then perhaps he doesn't need to be a POV character after all.

Just as important as playing time is frequency of appearance. A POV character should not appear at the beginning of the novel, disappear for the next three-quarters of it, and then be the POV for the last three scenes. You don't need to follow a strict rotation, but you do need to keep reminding the reader that Jane is a POV character by actually *showing* Jane being one at fairly regular intervals.

Thus, the first few chapters of a book with three POV characters—Jane, Kenneth, and Detective Liu—might look like this:

CHAPTER ONE
Scene 1—Jane
Scene 2—Detective Liu
Scene 3—Kenneth
Scene 4—Detective Liu

CHAPTER TWO
Scene 1—Kenneth
Scene 2—Jane
Scene 3—Jane
Scene 4—Detective Liu

CHAPTER THREE
Scene 1—Kenneth
Scene 2—Kenneth
Scene 3—Detective Liu
Scene 4—Jane

Obviously, there are many other variations of this. The point is to be regular in featuring your POV cast, although you don't have to be completely uniform.

POV AT THE CLIMAX: A MAJOR DECISION

One of fiction's few inviolable rules (well, almost inviolable) is that the protagonist needs to be present at the story's climax. If the protagonist is a POV character, the climax is usually, although not inevitably, in his POV. In a multiple POV novel, however, there are many protagonists, and whose POV you choose for the climax affects the entire feel of the book. So choose carefully.

Suppose, for example, that you are writing a murder mystery with a ghost in it. Several people spending the summer at a remote Irish castle have "seen" this ghost. Each has a different idea of who it is and a different emotional reaction to it. The characters include a lonely vacationing schoolteacher who romanticizes the ghost; a rich financier with a shady past who disparages its reality; a mentally unstable teenage boy who is terrified of it; a young widow who is troubled by the thought it might be her husband; and an old caretaker who believes in ghosts and the spirit world. All are POV characters, and you have rotated carefully through them all several times.

Then another guest turns up dead. Is the "ghost" involved? Is there really a ghost at all? The climax of the story will answer these questions. Everyone will be present. In whose POV should this all-important scene be written?

That depends on the focus and meaning you want your book to ultimately deliver to the reader. If you give the climax to the teenager's POV, your book will focus on mental stability (or its lack), perhaps even on the consequences of madness. If you make the schoolteacher the POV, you could end up with either an offbeat, ghostly romance or an anti-romance in which, as in *Madame Bovary*, a terrible price is extracted for unrealistic yearnings. If you choose the widow, you could have a tale about transcending grief or one about being overwhelmed by it. If you choose the caretaker, the book becomes a spiritual quest about the afterlife.

All of these stories could succeed. In fact, all of them can be included in your novel—but whichever character gets the POV at the climax will predominate in the reader's mind. So ask yourself: What do *you* want your story to mean? What impression do you want to leave with readers? What, in your mind, is the heart of this tale? Give the climactic POV to the character who embodies it.

STRUCTURAL DESIGNS FOR MULTIPLE-THIRD-PERSON NOVELS

A structural design is a formal method of organizing a long multiple-third-person novel. You don't have to use such a design, but if you do, it can make it easier to include varying viewpoints. It can also make things easier for the reader; a formal design makes changes in viewpoint seem less fragmented. Three common structural designs are regularly recurring viewpoints, multi-viewpoint chronological sections, and parallel running scenes.

Regularly recurring viewpoints are just that: You rotate through each POV character's experiences in unvarying order. We already said that strict regularity in POV rotation is not necessary, but it does have its advantages. It lets the reader anticipate whose voice he will hear when, thus easing transitions and giving the whole a more coherent feel.

For example, Bradley Denton's novel *Buddy Holly Is Alive and Well on Ganymede* cycles regularly through six POV characters in each chapter. The characters don't have the same amount of playing time; Oliver Vale, the protagonist, has more playing time than the other five. But all six are there in each chapter, in unvarying order, and the regularity of Denton's structure goes far to compensate for the head-hopping he asks us to do.

You certainly don't need to include all your points of view in each chapter. You might assign one POV per chapter, especially if you have only two or three POV characters. This has the advantage of switching POV when the narrative reaches a natural pause anyway at the chapter's end.

The disadvantages of regularly recurring viewpoints are two. First, it can seem mechanical. Second, it can require distortions in your story to make events fit the predetermined pattern. If this happens, and you find yourself inventing peripheral events simply because it's a given character's turn to have the POV and you have to do *something* with him, abandon this structure. Its elegance is costing you too much in loss of tension and relevance.

Chronological sections means that you break the novel into clearly labeled, time-dictated chunks, and everything that happens during that time period is in that section, no matter whose eyes we view it through. You still must apportion points of view one per scene, but the whole gains some coherency from its clear time divisions. This helps the reader sort out complicated action; he may have to shift POV and place, but at least he knows when he is, and what each character is doing during that period.

Noah Gordon used this design in his best-selling *The Death Committee*. The novel features three viewpoint characters, all young doctors. To organize the shifting points of view, Gordon divides his novel into three sections: "Summer," "Fall and Winter," and "Spring and Summer, The Full Circle." Within this structure, the novel changes points of view from scene to scene, pretty much without pattern.

Although this design provides good flexibility and some plan to guide the reader, it's obviously weaker than regularly recurring viewpoints. This is because the structure resides in the design, not the actual content, and so doesn't give the reader the same sense of anticipation or inevitability. There isn't as much to count on.

In contrast, *parallel running scenes* provide a lot of rhythm and anticipation. In this design, two (or sometimes three) stories progress simultaneously, alternating with each other chapter after chapter until they come together somewhere far advanced in the novel. Some modern romances follow this pattern, telling us both hero's and heroine's stories until they meet. So does Thomas Perry's award-winning *The Butcher's Boy*, which alternates the story of a nameless criminal "hit man" with that of the FBI agent trying to catch him. The two never meet until the last few pages, when they're on the same international flight together—and never realize it.

Parallel running scenes have significant drawbacks. First, the novel may feel fragmented; readers are constantly being asked to shift POV. Second, the writer may have the same problem as with regularly recurring viewpoints: distorting the story to fit artificial requirements. Still, if you have equal amounts of compelling story for two protagonists (or, more rarely, three), plus enough inherent tension to compensate for constant switches from one "reality" to another, then parallel running scenes might work for you.

AND OH, THIS TOO: PROLOGUES, EPILOGUES, AND INTERIM CHAPTERS

Multiple-third-person novels can also gain organization through the use of a prologue, epilogue, or interim chapters. A prologue is most useful when you have a chunk of story that is separated from the rest. It might occur much earlier in time, as in Joan D. Vinge's *The Snow Queen*, whose epilogue narrates a crucial event twenty years before the main story.

Or a prologue might be told from the POV of someone who will not be a POV character throughout the novel but who is useful as the POV for setting the scene because he has information no one else possesses. Separating this one-shot POV into a prologue makes it feel not like a viewpoint lapse but a structural choice.

The final use of a prologue is as a teaser, much like a movie trailer. If your novel is going to start with a long, slow buildup of tension, it can be useful to pull out a very dramatic scene, put it into a prologue so the reader starts out with a bang, then cast that slow buildup as flashback, showing how things got to such an exciting pass. The prologue ensures that the reader wants to know the answer, thus becoming willing to read through the slower chapters that follow. This use of prologue, of course, is not limited to the multiple-third-person story; any viewpoint can use it.

Epilogues serve the same purpose. They let us know what happened to everybody after the story ends. But they also allow for a switch in POV to someone who heretofore has not been a viewpoint character. This may still feel a little jarring (employ with caution), but it will be less so if the rogue POV is set off in a clearly labeled epilogue. The label will lead readers to expect something different from the main narration.

Interim chapters can be a good solution when you just have too much story for even a multiple-third-person novel. There are things *none* of your POV characters know, but you really want the reader to know them. Inserting short—they must be short, or the book *will* end up too hard to follow— sections that are not in the numbered sequence of chapters alerts readers to change mental gears. Label these clearly "Interim" or something similar and put them in a different typeface. They should contain material much different from everything else in the book.

I did this in my novel *Stinger*, which concerns the introduction of a lethal, genetically altered form of malaria into the United States. The book has three POV characters, but I also wanted to show how various people were bitten by mosquitoes and contracted the disease. Since no one realizes at the time that this is happening to him, and since the victims all die, I needed a lot of additional, disposable viewpoints. I put one each into ten "Interims," each no more than a page and a half. These broadened the scope of the book, making the tragedy both more personal and more democratic; mosquitoes sting all social and economic classes.

Other writers have used interims to display FBI reports, newspaper articles, diary entries, polling results, phone conversations—almost any information or short scene not closely connected to the main story but still useful for enhancing it. You will, of course, pay for this in increased fragmentation, but the structure does provide a way to include points of view that otherwise just won't fit. And you may gain more than you lose. Only you can judge that for your particular tale.

CHOOSING YOUR DESIGN

So many choices—how do you decide which of these structures, if any, to employ? You have two choices. You can either choose one before you start writing it, use it, and see if you like it. Or you can write the book without any of these designs, then study your first draft and decide if you want to incorporate any of them in your rewrite.

Question:
What POV is most likely to win me the Nobel Prize?

Answer:
Seven American-born fiction writers have won the Nobel Prize in Literature, and they used a variety of points of view in their work.

Sinclair Lewis (winner 1930) favored omniscient POV in such works as *Main Street*, *Babbitt*, and *Arrowsmith* (his own favorite among his works).

Pearl S. Buck's (1938) best-known work, *The Good Earth*, is multiple third person.

William Faulkner (1949) is all over the map: *The Sound and the Fury* is multiple first person; *Absalom, Absalom!* is multiple third person; *As I Lay Dying* is first person.

Ernest Hemingway (1954) used first person in *A Farewell to Arms* and *The Sun Also Rises*; third person in *For Whom the Bell Tolls* and *The Old Man and the Sea*.

John Steinbeck (1962) favored limited, close third person in *Of Mice and Men*; multiple third person for *The Grapes of Wrath* and *East of Eden*.

Saul Bellow (1976) chose third person for *Herzog* and first person for *Humboldt's Gift* and *Seize the Day*.

Toni Morrison (1993) used multiple third person in her most acclaimed works: *Beloved*, *Song of Solomon*, and *Sula*.

Conclusion: Any POV can create a great novel. Choose the one best for your particular story.

Which you do probably depends on your overall working method. Some writers plan ahead, outline, and actually stick to the outline. They will want to choose a structural design ahead of time.

Other writers plunge in bravely and start swimming, thrashing around wildly until they somehow reach the other side of their novelistic sea. Then they take this chaotic first draft, tear it apart, and rewrite extensively. Such writers will probably incorporate a patterned structure in their second drafts.

Either way can work. Just keep in mind the purposes of a formal design:

to guide the reader through shifting points of view in a way that makes the various viewpoints seem more connected and natural.

Third person, limited or multiple, is a useful and flexible POV. It may be just what your material needs to bring out its strengths.

RECAP: THIRD-PERSON POV

Third-person POV can be limited (inside one character's head) or multiple (inside two or more heads). Either can take the form of very close third person, distant third person, or somewhere in between.

Close third person delivers almost as much immediacy as first person, plus strong character identification and the chance to use the character's distinctive diction. Distant third person works well when you don't want close identification with a character and/or when you want to make complex expository observations about him. It is less immediate than close third person and requires better prose. Middle-distant third person is the most flexible of all viewpoints. Distance changes should be written with smooth transitions to avoid choppy "camera jumps."

Multiple third person can cover diverse story lines, develop more characters from the inside than can limited third person, and offer interestingly conflicting slants on the same events. In a multiple-viewpoint book, you should introduce all POV characters early and at sufficient length for us to gain a sense of each as a person. After all points of view have been introduced, confine POV to one character per scene or (even better) one per chapter. Some commercial fiction, however, ignores this guideline.

Choose carefully the POV character for the climax; your choice will influence the story's meaning.

Multiple-POV novels can be organized through regularly recurring viewpoints, chronological sections, parallel running scenes, and/or the use of prologue, epilogue, and interim chapters.

EXERCISE 1

Pick something interesting outdoors: a tree, a building, a construction site. Stand fifty feet away from it and mentally compose a paragraph of description. Now move five feet away from the object. Are the things you notice different? What might your paragraph of description emphasize now? Repeat, standing five inches away.

EXERCISE 2

Choose a person you know well. Write a short physical description of him in close third person, from your personal POV. Now write another in distant third person. What different things are emphasized in each?

EXERCISE 3

Find a favorite multiple-third-person novel. Starting on page one, mark each POV shift. Do this for three or four chapters. In what order are the characters introduced? Can you guess why? How much "playing time" does each get? How regularly does the author cycle through his POV cast?

Do the same with one of your own stories.

EXERCISE 4

Search your library to identify three books with prologues. What function do you think each serves for that narration?

chapter 15

[OMNISCIENT POINT OF VIEW — PLAYING GOD]

Writers are gods. We get to create entire worlds, populate them, and even, as in some sort of novelistic *Götterdämmerung*, destroy them. Of course, writers can do this in any viewpoint, but omniscient point of view adds another layer to the process. In omniscient POV, the writer addresses the reader directly: the voice of the Creator commenting on his beings.

This direct address is one of the two hallmarks of the omniscient POV. The other is the freedom to violate all previously discussed strictures on POV and hop directly into and out of all characters' minds at will. ("Omniscient" literally means "all-knowing.") Why does the omniscient author get to do this? Why would he do this? What price does he pay, and what does he gain?

To answer these questions, we need to start by looking at what omniscient POV is—and isn't.

NINETEENTH-CENTURY OMNISCIENT

Omniscient POV was the choice of nineteenth-century writers, perhaps because the more tightly controlled third person limited was a later invention. The Victorians not only felt free to comment on the action they created; they practically considered it a duty. Here are random excerpts from Thomas Hardy's great *Tess of the d'Urbervilles*, in which Hardy explains whom he's going to focus on and how we should view the results. In the first sentence, he has just explained that a band of young women walking down the road includes the young, the middle-aged, and the elderly:

> In a true view, perhaps, there was more to be gathered and told of each anxious and experienced one, to whom the years were drawing nigh when she should say, "I have no pleasure in them," than of her juvenile comrades. But let the elder be passed over here for those under whose bodices the life throbbed quick and warm.

Tess Durbeyfield at this time of her life was a mere vessel of emotion untinctured by experience.

The President of the Immortals (in the Aeschylean phrase) had finished his sport with Tess.

None of these passages are dialogue or thoughts of any character. They are the author's opinions and interpretations, expressed directly to the reader. By the early twentieth century, this intrusive style of narrative presentation had faded from fashion, along with the head-hopping that usually accompanies it.

The latter was characterized by the author freely announcing what different characters thought, sometimes many characters inner thoughts being revealed in the same paragraph. All this was replaced with the tight POV control of writers who wished to make themselves invisible and let the characters act out their stories.

But pendulums inevitably swing. Omniscient POV reappeared, complete with blatant authorial presence. For example, in *The French Lieutenant's Woman*, author John Fowles is as present as his characters. Like Hardy, he comments on the action from a lofty perch ("One of the commonest symptoms of wealth today is destructive neurosis; in [Charles's] century it was tranquil boredom"). Fowles uses the nineteenth-century "I" to address the reader directly:

Charles detected, under the American accent, views very similar to his own; and he even glimpsed, though very dimly and only by virtue of a Darwinian analogy, that one day America might supersede the older species. I do not mean, of course, that he thought of emigrating there, though thousands of a poorer English class were doing that every year.

Fowles goes farther. He inserts himself into the novel, a bearded man staring at Charles on a train and wondering, "What will I do with you?" His decision is to include two separate endings to his novel, both plausible, and let the reader choose. In addition, he feels free to enter any character's mind without starting a new chapter section—or sometimes even a new paragraph.

STORIES ABOUT STORIES

Why does Fowles, or any author, choose to write in omniscient POV? Obviously, he loses reader suspension of disbelief. Omniscient POV destroys the reader's sense of entering a separate, self-contained world that, at least for the duration of the novel, becomes its own reality. Instead, the reader is offered intrusions from our world in the form of authorial opinions, reminders that this story is fictional, and fragmentation of viewpoint. Since fiction is always a matter of trade-offs, what does the author gain in return?

He gains exactly what he loses: a reminder that this story is fictional, not real. Some authors, and some stories, want that. Yes, it creates a greater distance between the reader and the characters, making identification more difficult. As the old saw says, "Three's a crowd," and there stands the author, a third wheel intruding between reader and protagonist. Omniscient POV deliberately increases reader distance to take in a larger panorama: reality itself. An author writing in omniscient POV is not after identification; he's after the kind of insight that comes from contemplating events rather than participating in them.

In a book like *The French Lieutenant's Woman*, this stance is taken to an extreme. Fowles is playing with ideas about reality, time, societal change, and the nature of stories themselves, and he wants us to play with him. This is metafiction, or fiction about fiction. Omniscient POV, which emphasizes the artificial nature of the story, is a natural for metafiction.

That is not, however, its only use. Omniscient POV also has the advantage of allowing more authorial steering of a story's meaning than do other viewpoints. This is largely a question of degree.

SECOND-DEGREE OMNISCIENT POV: HERE'S WHAT YOU SHOULD THINK

Not all omniscient-POV stories are as extreme in their authorial presence as *The French Lieutenant's Woman*. In fact, most are not, because they're not really metafiction. They're straightforward stories in which the author wants readers to suspend disbelief and accept this fictional world as temporarily real. However, he also wants to tell the reader how to interpret that world. Thus, the authorial presence does not take the form of "mind games" such as alternate endings or inserting himself as a character. It does take the form of freely editorializing on the action, in effect interpreting the story for the reader, as well as POV-hopping at will.

Here, for example, is Herman Wouk in *Youngblood Hawke*:

> No man can know what it is like to be a woman taking her firstborn in her arms
> for the first time, but a writer who holds a freshly printed copy of his first book
> must have a fair idea of what the woman feels. It lies rectangular and spotless

in his hands, with his name on the jacket. It is his pass to the company of the great. Fielding, Stendhal, Melville, Tolstoy wrote books. Now he has written one. . . . The exultation does not last. It cannot. It is too piercing. It has gone before he has drawn twenty breaths. But in that twenty breaths he has smelled the sweetest of all savors, the savor of total fulfillment. After that, no matter what success he may achieve, he is just another writer, with a writer's trials and pleasures. That joy never comes again in all its first purity.

These are not the thoughts of Wouk's protagonist, who has published only one book and has no idea what joys will or will not attend publication of another. These observations are Wouk's. He is steering readers' thoughts about this event, making sure we see its importance in the way he wants. Wouk does this throughout the novel, a definite authorial presence even though he also wants us to enter into his characters' lives as if they were real.

The advantages and disadvantages of this lesser-degree omniscient POV are the same as for Fowles's full-bore intrusiveness, although milder. To summarize, the advantages of omniscient POV are:

- ability to directly steer readers' interpretation of the action
- broad panoramic view of the story's context
- richness of author's POV added to, and sometimes contrasting with, the characters' views
- usefulness for metafiction, which comments on the nature of reality, fiction, and truth
- usefulness of entering any character's mind

The disadvantages of omniscient POV are that it:

- strains illusion that the fictional world feels real
- fragments the story
- distances reader from the characters even more than does distant third person
- demands a higher level of prose than straightforward fiction to compensate for the loss of simple POV continuity

DOING OMNISCIENT POV WELL

If you do choose to employ an omniscient POV, there are a few guidelines to keep in mind. First, decide on the degree of omniscient POV you want. Are you going to go all the way, calling attention to the artificiality of fiction by the sort of techniques Fowles employs in *The French Lieutenant's Woman*? Or are you merely going to be addressing the reader directly from time to time?

Next, set up the omniscient POV early—and I mean really early. The first paragraph is good; certainly within the first few pages. Don't do it by simply addressing one stray remark to the reader. Readers need to know beyond a doubt that the author will be visible in this narrative so they can adjust their expectations accordingly. The third paragraph of the Fowles novel describes the sea rampart at Lyme, England:

> Primitive yet complex, elephantine but delicate; as full of subtle curves and volumes as a Henry Moore or a Michelangelo; and pure, clean, salt, a paragon of mass. I exaggerate? Perhaps, but I can be put to the test, for the Cobb has changed very little since the year of which I write; though the town of Lyme has, and the test is not fair if you look back toward land.

In seventy-one words, Fowles has used "I" three times, has invoked "the year in which I write" (1969) even though the novel is set in 1867, and has referred to sculptures by Henry Moore, an artist not even born in 1867. Fowles is not concerned with inducing a reader to suspend disbelief and wholly enter his fictional 1867 world; instead, Fowles is doing everything he can to keep the reader's attention on himself as creator of the drama about to unfold. And, more important for the current point, he's doing it as soon as the book starts.

Similarly, you should also make clear that you, as author, are extending the prerogatives of Creator to dipping into the thoughts of any passing character you choose. Do this early and often enough so we expect it.

Finally, you must immediately convince us that it will be worthwhile to read such an author-infused story. Omniscient POV goes contrary to most contemporary fiction and may look startling to many readers (which is why, in this century, it tends to be confined to literary rather than commercial fiction). The usual practice is to convince us early on that this author will offer a viewpoint so interesting, amusing, or novel that it will compensate for his intrusive presence. Fowles does this in the usual way: by writing in prose rich in allusion, metaphor, history, and rhythm. If you cannot do this, if your writing is serviceable rather than interesting on a prose level, you might do better to choose multiple-third-person over omniscient POV.

COMMON ERRORS IN OMNISCIENT POV

These are the things you want to avoid in omniscient POV:

- Using it too sparsely. Once you've committed to omniscient POV, you must use it fully, for the entire length of the story. If you only add the occasional authorial comment every few chapters, they will look like mistakes rather than like a conscious POV choice.
- Dipping into characters' minds at will without also offering a strong authorial presence. This is not omniscient POV; it's just sloppy multiple third person.
- Not setting up omniscient POV early enough.
- Not having anything interesting for the authorial view to add to what the narrative already conveys. If the narrative is doing all the work, then *your* voice is unnecessary.

It's important to realize that all fiction involves the author's POV. It's the author who chooses what events to include, how to present them, and how characters react. An author shapes any work of fiction, and in that sense her presence is a given. The difference is that in other viewpoints, that presence is mostly invisible, working behind the stage set and off in the wings to create the story's effects. In omniscient POV, the author is on stage along with the characters, fully visible to the audience (the equivalent in drama is Thornton Wilder's Stage Manager in *Our Town*, a play that repays study by fiction writers as well as playwrights).

As such, omniscient POV is sophisticated and not suitable for every story or every author. But it can be a tremendously rewarding experience for the writer willing to give it a try.

RECAP: OMNISCIENT POV

Omniscient POV, a nineteenth-century convention, can also be used effectively in some contemporary fiction. The two hallmarks of omniscient POV are the freedom to dip into the thoughts of any character at any time—to "know all"—and a strong authorial presence, usually speaking directly to the reader. However, there are various degrees of authorial presence, from inserting the writer directly into the story as a character to merely steering reader interpretation through direct address to him.

The advantages of omniscient POV are emphasis on the author's interpretation of the story, broad context for its events, a richer presentation, and

Question:

What is the difference between omniscient POV and multiple third person with expository passages?

Answer:

There are strong similarities between omniscient POV and multiple third person when the multiple third person includes much exposition. This is because exposition is, after all, in the author's POV by default—none of the characters are thinking it or saying it. Exposition that is written in a distinctive style (playful, sarcastic, romantic) suggests even more strongly that a persona, not just information, is present, and that persona is, of course, the author's.

The answer is that omniscient POV and multiple third person are not discreet entities but exist on a continuum, one sliding into the other. However, if you write near the middle of the continuum, you get occasional dips into some characters' minds and the hint of an authorial presence, which looks a lot like either sloppy multiple third person or weak omniscient POV. Your best choice is to commit firmly to one or the other and then happily exploit all of its particular advantages. Decide what you want to do, and not only will you find it easier to avoid POV violations, but the discriminating reader (and editor) will have more confidence in your prose.

the ability to play with notions about reality. The disadvantages are fragmentation, greater distance between reader and characters, and the loss of the illusion that the fictional world is self-contained and "real."

To compensate for its drawbacks, omniscient POV usually requires a higher level of prose than do other viewpoints. In addition, to do omniscient POV well, you must set up this POV early, use it consistently and fully, and offer compensations to justify your intrusion into your creations' stories.

EXERCISE 1

Pretend that you are telepathic. Stand on a street corner, or some other public place, and notice the first three or four people passing. What do you imagine they're thinking? Write a few sentences describing the thoughts of each.

After you complete exercise one, read over your descriptions. Is there any pattern? Are most of the people (in your speculation) entertaining thoughts that are banal, amusing, frightened, or any other pattern? If so, what is *your* attitude toward this dominant impression? Do you find it sad, funny, boring, or indicative of the decline of civilization? (If there is no pattern, change your "overheard" thoughts until you get one. This is fiction, remember.)

EXERCISE 3

Try weaving the thoughts of the characters you created from exercise one into a paragraph with your authorial attitude toward them. This would set the stage for a story about one or more of them. It should also set the tone for the author's view of his created mini-universe.

EXERCISE 4

Read John Fowles's *The French Lieutenant's Woman*, John Cheever's short story "The Country Husband," or Thornton Wilder's play *Our Town*. Do you like this degree of authorial presence? Why or why not? (Note: If you don't like it, that's fine. Just understand why these authors employed it.)

EXERCISE 5

Take a scene from one of your own stories, preferably an opening scene, and rewrite it in omniscient POV. What decisions are you forced to make in order to do this? Do you like the results better than the original, or not?

chapter 16

[PUTTING IT ALL TOGETHER — THE FOURTH PERSONA]

You now have characters buzzing in your head (at least I *hope*, after fifteen chapters of suggestions, exhortations, and exercises, that you have characters buzzing in your head!). Those characters want things. They feel things. They have attitudes, hopes, dreams, and fears. They have viewpoints.

So what do you do with them now?

Sitting down to write a novel can be an extremely daunting prospect. A novel is so long. So much will happen in it. So many changes will occur to your characters. And, most of all, there is so much to keep in mind at once. How to do that? How to even begin?

WHAT IF IT ALL WON'T *GO* TOGETHER?

Perhaps the single greatest obstacle to writing fiction is self-consciousness. This can take several forms, all destructive:

- You feel you must produce wonderful prose or else what's the point? Even worse, you feel you must produce it on the first draft or you're not a "real writer."
- You feel you must hold in your head all the writing rules and guidelines (including the ones in this book) all at once in order to do the job well.
- You constantly measure your work, sentence by sentence, against the greats: Tolstoy, Austen, Hemingway, whoever are your particular literary gods.
- You wonder constantly if each paragraph is preparing the way adequately for the rest of the book.

Any of these problems can effectively paralyze your work. If you are afflicted with more than one of them, you may indeed be in the hell so graphically described by Joseph Conrad: "Sometimes it takes all my resolution and power of self-control to refrain from butting my head against the wall. I want to howl and foam at the mouth but I daren't." Anyway, howling and foaming seldom get words on paper.

There are even some research studies that confirm this desperate state of affairs. As early as 1908, Harvard researchers Robert M. Yerkes and John D. Dodson found that "both very low and very high levels of arousal interfere with performance" at tasks such as writing. This means that if you aren't aroused enough—you just aren't interested in writing your book—you won't write it (no surprise there). But it also means that if you are *too* interested, you may not write it, either. That "high level of arousal" affects hormones in the body, causing anxiety that can interfere with performance.

Add to that the fact that effective writing requires you to become the character *and* become the writer *and* become the reader, and it's not surprising that writing is so difficult for so many. However, there are techniques you can use to make it easier and more effective. One of them is to add a fourth persona to the trio: critic. Yes, you must become a critic—but *you must not become one too soon.*

TRUSTING YOUR INTUITION

To recap what we said at the beginning of the book: The first step, which will go far in easing writerly anxiety, is to forget about being a writer and become the character. Think, feel, see, and smell as he does. Get into his head.

Next, become a writer—but minus your own ego. You are only a channel through which your character passes on her way to the page. Write your first draft, striving to get the character's perceptions, speech, and actions down on paper. Depending on your individual makeup, "first draft" might refer to only that day's work, one scene, or the whole book.

If you have trouble writing this way, start with a short session, maybe twenty minutes. Trust your intuition and just write. Note: This is not the "automatic writing" of séances and journaling. You have actual characters in mind and you know roughly what they are going to be doing in this scene. The goal is to let them do it, without anxiety or criticism from you. Forget yourself. You can do that for twenty minutes. Later, as it becomes easier, writing sessions can be longer.

Third, become the reader. You are still going to forget about yourself, but now you are going to become the reader, not your character. Read the first sentence as if you'd never seen it before and have no idea what will come next. What images does it convey? Is that what you intended?

A specific example can make the process clearer. For instance, suppose this is your opening:

> The alarm bell sounded and Russ, startled awake, swung his legs off the bed, tangling them in the sheets. He sat blinking a moment and then leaped for his pants. "Terry! Terry!" he yelled. "Get up! Fire!"
>
> Across the room Terry was already moving. They both sprinted for the door.

What is your reader seeing so far? Not, I bet, what you are seeing. Are we in a home or a fire station? Is this the orderly action of professional firefighters springing into action or the frightened response of a husband and wife whose smoke alarm has gone off? Is Terry Russ's wife? Colleague? Is Terry male or female? Why does Russ sit bemused and sheet-tangled for a precious moment—because he's a civilian abruptly woken up? Because he's a professional new to the firehouse? Because he drank too much last night?

The writer knows the answer to all these questions. He can *see* the scene in far more detail than it's been rendered on the page. By becoming the reader, the writer can spot these discrepancies.

Read the passage again. Pretend you wrote it, and in your mind are all the details that would answer my questions. Now rewrite the opening to include them. Here is one possible result:

> The alarm bell sounded, filling the firehouse with clanging, insistent din. Russ, startled awake, swung his legs off the bed but then wasted a precious moment just sitting there, blinking. Where was he? Oh, God, his first day on this job . . . and *fire*! He leaped for his pants and tried to make up for his momentary confusion by yelling, "Terry! Terry! Get up! Fire!"
>
> Across the room, she was already moving. "Pipe down, kid, and get your pants on!" They both sprinted for the door, Terry—to Russ's annoyance—several lengths ahead.

Now we know where we are, who these people are, and even a little of their personalities. If the writer hadn't consciously decided to become the reader and see only what he sees, the writer might not have realized how skimpy the first version was.

This need for detail is, of course, greatest in openings, since at that point the reader has zero details about the scene and the characters. But even later on, it's valuable to look at your prose as if you knew only the information given on the page. You might, for instance, look at a sentence like this one: "Coming down the stairs, Megan glanced at Tom and Marla curled into one sleeping bag." To you, it looks fine. You can *see* the image. But are Tom and Marla asleep or awake in that bag? Is the sleeping bag in a room at the top of the stairs or a room at the bottom? Presumably Megan could see it in either location. Does the scene already make clear what time it is (dawn, noon) or how Marla feels about that shared sleeping bag? If not, is this the place to add those things? By becoming the reader, you find out.

ADDING A FOURTH PERSONA: BECOMING A CRITIC

The last part of your chameleon act as a writer is to become a critic. It's crucial that your inner critic not be added until now (which is why we haven't mentioned him until now!). You've written the book (or chapter or scene), and you've rewritten it as a "reader." Now, when there is something of substance to work with, is the time to call your critical self to the fore. If you do it before this point, you may paralyze your flow of words. If you never do it at all, your fiction will not be as good as it can be.

The critical self is exactly the one you've suppressed until this point—with modifications. It's beneficial to scrutinize your work for shortfalls. It's not beneficial to use Hemingway or Morrison as your standard for comparison. The goal is to improve your prose, not demolish your confidence.

Whole books can (and have) been written on how to rewrite. Briefly, here are the kinds of questions you should be asking yourself as you turn critic for a single scene:

- Does the scene have an interesting opening?
- Do we know where we are, when, and in whose point of view? Can you sharpen any details of setting?
- Is the POV consistent, without lapses?
- Does the scene have a good "shape"—that is, does it seem to progress and then finish up with something different from where you started? That "something different" might be that the character has learned new information, been given another choice, had her problem complicated, been introduced to a new person, discovered a conflict in her

values, moved further along a hopeless course of action, etc. But *something* should be different by the end of the scene or the scene itself is pointless.

- Will this scene contribute something significant to the book as a whole?
- Does the scene end in a way that makes us want to read more?
- Do the details of appearance, action, dialogue, and thoughts develop the character, bringing her into ever-sharper focus? Can you sharpen any details of character?
- Does the emotion in this scene seem honest and unforced? Is it complex enough to genuinely represent both the character and the way life really is?
- Does the dialogue sound natural, characteristic, and pertinent?
- On a sentence-by-sentence scrutiny, do you need to rewrite to eliminate clichés, awkward diction, dangling modifiers, redundant words or phrases, or outright grammatical errors?
- Do you like this scene? If not, can you articulate why? Is the problem something you can fix?

Many writers (again, I am one) find it difficult to switch back and forth from writer to critic many times during a book. It's easier for me to write the entire first draft and then become my own critic. Other writers find the opposite: They cannot build a story effectively until they have a well-written foundation. These writers critique themselves scene by scene. Try both and see which works best for you.

FRIENDLY HELP: THE OUTSIDE READER AND THE OUTSIDE CRITIC

There is another option for "becoming the reader" and "becoming the critic." That is to get someone else to do one or both.

A first reader for your work can be an immense help to a writer. Such a person can be given the raw first draft and be asked for reactions as a reader. Alternatively, he can be given the second draft, after you have "become the reader," and asked to function as a critic, including line editing. You can even use more than one person in this role. However, a caveat is necessary here. Your first reader must be the right person. The wrong one can give you bad advice, undermine your confidence, and end up making your fiction worse than it was before you enlisted his "help."

Who is the right person? That depends on what you want done. If you are asking for reactions "as a reader," then the qualifications are:

- Someone able to be objective without personal consequences. This often rules out spouses, best friends, parents, and others who may be too vested in encouragement rather than honesty.
- Someone who reads a lot in your particular genre (thrillers, mainstream literary, romance, science fiction, whatever) and likes it.
- Someone who is willing to be honest enough to write in the margin "I was bored here" or "I don't understand what's going on now" or "This is good!"
- Someone whose standards are neither too low ("I like anything at all set in the West") or too high ("The only decent romance writer ever was Georgette Heyer").

If you have such a first reader, treasure her. Take her to lunch. Dedicate books to her. Make sure she knows what a valuable service she's providing for you.

If you want a critic, the standards are tougher yet. All of the above qualifications still apply. In addition, you need someone who can not only spot deficiencies but also advise you how to correct them. This usually means another writer.

ORGANIZED HELP: THE WRITING CLASS OR WRITER'S GROUP

Writing classes, which are led by an instructor, and writing groups, which are self-help collections of peers, differ enormously in their effectiveness. The key factor is the makeup of any particular group. The criticism you receive can only be as competent and useful as the people giving it.

To find a good writing class, start with the instructor. I have a strong bias in favor of classes taught by published writers—preferably, by regularly published writers. After all, if this person can't or won't write publishable fiction himself, why should he be telling you how to do it?

To find a good instructor, take these steps:

- Call your local arts centers, college or university English departments, and high school adult-education programs. Find out what courses are offered in writing and ask for brochures or course catalogues to be mailed to you. Narrow your choices to the genres you're interested in.

- Read the instructors' bios or research them on the Internet. What have they written? How much? Can you get a sense of whether a given teacher likes your type of writing? This last is important. If you write romances and an instructor thinks of the entire genre as "popular trash," this class is not for you.
- Call the institution(s) again and ask the instructor(s) you're interested in to phone you because you'd like to ask some questions about the course. Institutions usually will not give out instructors' home phone numbers, but if you are politely persistent, the instructor will eventually contact you (this may take two or three tries).
- Ask the instructor how the course is structured. Will you get feedback on your work from everyone enrolled in the class or just from the teacher? Will the criticisms be written? Do you need to bring a whole, completed manuscript to the first session? Will she look at rewrites? Does she enjoy reading romance/science fiction/literary short stories/ whatever you're trying to write?

You should not expect even the perfect instructor to turn you into William Faulkner. The talent, hard work, and openness to learning must come from you. But competent criticism can help you make the most of your talent and work by suggesting changes that sharpen and focus your fiction.

You will also benefit from the feedback from the other class members. Most will function as readers, and some may also be good enough to function as critics. However, in a group as randomly varied as a class, there may also be people whose criticism is suspect because they have personal axes to grind or because they simply have not read very much and are poor judges of fiction. Your task is to listen to everyone with an open mind, weigh all criticism carefully, and then take what seems useful.

The same advice applies to writers' groups. Here there is no instructor, so groups can become even more uselessly approving ("I love everything all of us writes") or uselessly negative ("Become a plumber instead"). If you're not getting actual information about your stories that leads to actual productive rewriting, leave that group and find another.

SUCCESS AND ENJOYMENT

You don't have to enjoy writing to write well; many writers hate the process. (Fran Lebowitz said, "I hate writing. I will do anything to avoid it. The only

Warming Up: Whatever Works

Famous writers have prepared themselves for the task of writing in a variety of ways, some healthy and some not. A sampling:

- Agatha Christie claimed that washing dishes stimulated the flow of plot ideas.
- Graham Greene relied on the right tools, claiming that a typewriter "never connected with my brain." He needed "my hand on a pen . . . A fountain pen, of course. Ballpoint pens are only good for filling out forms on a plane."
- Norman Mailer used alcohol: "I usually need a can of beer to prime me."
- Honoré de Balzac preferred coffee; when he was up to more than fifty cups per day, he died of caffeine poisoning.
- Ernest Hemingway sharpened a dozen pencils and then assumed an odd position: He wrote standing up.
- Mark Twain wrote lying down.
- Ray Bradbury found himself "sparked" by a line in a poem or a strong sentence by another writer.
- Thomas Wolfe took a long walk.
- Willa Cather read a passage from the Bible.
- Tom Robbins recommends cloud watching ("The reason for this is that most of the great philosophical ideas of humankind have come from the sky. . . . It's just very good discipline, philosophically and poetically, to look at the sky").
- Miguel de Cervantes and Sir Walter Raleigh found being in prison a stimulus to composition—but this is *not* recommended.

way I could write less was if I was dead"). However, if you do enjoy writing, you're more likely to sit down and actually do it.

So what makes the process more enjoyable? There are some simple things and one non-simple, very important one. The easy things first:

- Figure out the warmup activity that puts you in the right frame of mind: going for a run, drinking a cup of coffee, doing the crossword puzzle, reading a writer you admire. Take twenty minutes and do it before you begin writing.

- Work with your natural biological clock. If you're a morning person, try getting up an hour earlier to write. If you're a night owl, do it after your housemates are asleep.
- Write a small amount every day, or nearly every day, rather than binge writing for ten hours on Saturday. This takes some pressure off you. Producing one page looks less daunting than producing seven.
- Reward yourself after you write.

The most important thing, however, is your attitude toward your characters. Writing is far more likely to be enjoyable if you are so interested in them that they take on lives of their own. Entering fully into their stories, rather than staying preoccupied with yourself ("How am I doing? Is this any good? Where can I market it?") makes the entire writing process feel lighter, more interesting, and more rewarding.

Characters. Emotion. Viewpoint. But *theirs*—not yours.

And if you can capture theirs, you will end up with a story all of us out here want to read.

RECAP: PUTTING IT ALL TOGETHER

Some writers enjoy writing and some don't. Performance anxiety is often what destroys enjoyment as well as preventing many people from even getting started.

You can reduce anxiety by breaking writing into four steps: becoming the character, becoming a writer, becoming your reader, and only *lastly* becoming a critic. Outside help with the last two steps is available in the form of first readers, writing classes, and writers groups.

Choose your writing class very carefully. The right one can greatly benefit your work by providing you with valuable feedback, but the wrong one can harm it.

Writing can be made more enjoyable through warmup activities, pacing, and small rewards. However, the single largest aid you can give yourself as a writer is to regard your fiction as your characters' story, not yours.

EXERCISE 1

Take a story or even just a scene that you wrote at least three months ago. Try to read the piece, sentence by sentence, as if you'd never seen it before. How would it strike you? Can you add details that would make this a more vivid reading experience?

Ask someone else to read the same piece you read for exercise one and have him jot down his reactions in the margin, two or three per page. Are they the same as yours? Can you account for any differences?

EXERCISE 3

Now engage your critical self. Go over the same story or scene from exercise one and answer all the questions in the section of this chapter called "ADDING A FOURTH PERSONA: BECOMING A CRITIC." Are there changes you need to make in the manuscript?

EXERCISE 4

For a month, keep a log of your writing. Note how many pages you write every day, when you write them, where, and how productive you felt the session was. At the end of the month, scrutinize your log. Under what circumstances do you seem to write the most? The most easily? The best? What can you do to create those circumstances on a regular basis?

EXERCISE 5

For several hours, pretend you are one of your characters. Engage in your usual activities (job, lunch, laundry, etc.) but carry them out as if you were this other person, not yourself. What do you do differently? Feel differently? Can you enter into this character fully when away from your desk? If so, do the same thing when you sit down to write. (Note: If this exercise is going to endanger yourself or others because your character is a psychopathic murderer, don't do it!)

EXERCISE 6

Call up local arts centers and colleges to see if they offer writing classes. Even if you don't choose to enroll just now, the information will lie dormant in your mind in case you wish to act on it later.

EXERCISE 7

Write one page a day, every day, for two weeks, *no matter what*. You can do it. Yes, you can.

appendix

[CHECKLIST — CRITICAL POINTS]

CHARACTERS

- You have four sources from which to draw characters: yourself, people you know, strangers you hear or read about, and pure imagination. For the first three sources, characters are usually more effective when they are modified from their real-life models.

- Once you have a list of potential characters for your story, the next step is to choose a protagonist. The others will then become featured players. Any character can be chosen as your star. Different choices will result in much different stories.

- Before you start writing, try to examine your assembled cast from the viewpoint of your potential reader. Are they interesting? Sufficiently diverse? Plausibly connected to each other and the situation you want to write about? Are you excited about writing them?

- Different kinds of books include different amounts of backstory; however, no matter how much backstory is included, you should always have a strong sense of your characters' pasts.

- Your character's motivations should grow out of his backstory. The more unusual that motivation is, the more backstory we need to see. Backstory creates personality/character, which in turn creates motivation, which creates emotion.

- Interesting characters often hold two conflicting values and/or desires. Which they choose helps readers to know their personalities and beliefs. Small choices should be consistent with, and sometimes foreshadow, larger choices the characters make later in the story.

- Characters may or may not change their basic beliefs and reactions over the course of your story. They also may or may not change motivation, progressing to a new goal when the old one is fulfilled or thwarted. All changes must come about as plausible consequences of story events.

- A character who genuinely changes needs a *validation scene*, usually at the end of the story, to dramatize that the change is permanent.
- Genre fiction requires the same attention to characterization as mainstream fiction, but it also presents additional requirements. Since these vary with subgenre, the first step for writers is to be very familiar with the subgenre they wish to write.
- The basic techniques for creating humorous characters are exaggeration, ridicule, and reversal of expectations. Any of them may be employed in mild, medium, or outrageous form, depending on the degree of plausibility desired.

EMOTION

- Emotion should be dramatized through action, dialogue, character's thoughts, and bodily responses. Don't talk about emotion; *show* it.
- The key to juggling emotion, motivation, and character changes is to write in scenes. Before writing, decide all the things the scene should accomplish.
- "Breaking points" are an effective way to dramatize emotion. Exploiting a character's breaking point requires dramatizing both the pressures on her and her previous self-control.
- Frustration, in addition to driving plot, is one of your best chances to build characterization. How your character responds to frustration, plus his ability to modify those responses, should be in keeping with the rest of the personality you've given him so far.
- The main expression of your character's frustration should be action that moves the story forward.
- Fictional dialogue, even in moments of high emotion, differs from "real-life" dialogue by being shaped through compression, understatement, or emphasis.
- Metaphors, implied comparisons in which a word or phrase primarily used for one thing is applied to another, can build emotion in fiction.
- The most important thing to remember about love, sex, fight, and death scenes is that the character should perform them in keeping with the personality you've given her so far.

POINT OF VIEW

- Point of view means through whose eyes and mind we experience your story. The usual choices are first-person, third-person-limited or third-person-multiple, and omniscient point of view. Rarer points of view include second person, epistolary, and first- or third-person plural.

- Your protagonist and point of view character(s) may or may not be identical. Any story can be told from the point of view of any of the characters. Imagine your story from different points of view before you commit to one.

- First-person point of view has the advantages of immediacy, individual language, and internal range, but the disadvantages of limited flexibility, claustrophobia, and greater difficulty for the writer in being objective.

- First-person point of view is inherently an artificial point of view because no one recounts long, completed, perfectly edited stories, with full dialogue, as if the narrator does not know what will happen next. You can choose to ignore the artificiality of first person (as most readers accept this convention) or you can use a double-aged narrator, young and old, to account for it.

- Third-person point of view has the advantages of greater flexibility, external range, and objectivity, but may be less immediate and individualistic than first person. In third person, use as few point-of-view characters as you can get away with and still tell the story you want to tell.

- Third-person point of view can be written as very close third person, distant third person, or somewhere in between.

- Multiple-third-person point of view can cover diverse story lines, develop more characters from the inside, and offer interesting, conflicting slants on the same events.

- Omniscient point of view has the advantages of emphasis on the author's interpretation of the story, broad context for its events, a richer presentation, and the ability to play with notions about reality. Disadvantages are fragmentation, greater distance between the reader and characters, and the loss of the illusion that the fictional world is self-contained and "real."

- There are degrees of authorial presence, from inserting the writer directly into the story as a character to merely steering reader interpretation through direct address to him.

WRITING

- Some writers enjoy writing and some don't. Performance anxiety is often what destroys enjoyment.
- Reduce anxiety by breaking writing into four steps: becoming the character, becoming the writer, becoming the reader, and only lastly becoming the critic.
- The single largest aid you can give yourself as a writer is to regard your fiction as your characters' story, not yours.

index

The Best Books on Writing Instruction Come From Writer's Digest Books!

Dictionary of Disagreeable English—You don't have to be a curmudgeon to enjoy the use of correct grammar! Let Robert Hartwell Fiske, a.k.a. the Grumbling Grammarian, help you identify and correct tricky grammar and usage problems. This is the perfect-sized, indispensable reference for every writer on the go!
ISBN-13: 978-1-58297-313-5, paperback, 352 pages, $12.99, #10949
ISBN-10: 1-58297-313-X, paperback, 352 pages, $12.99, #10949

Page After Page—Learn to write with confidence and passion! In the same vein as *Bird by Bird* by Anne Lamott, this brilliantly written, highly original book will help you achieve your writing goals and establish a productive, satisfying writing life.
ISBN-13: 978-1-58297-312-8, hardcover, 240 pages, $19.99 #10948
ISBN-10: 1-58297-312-1, hardcover, 240 pages, $19.99 #10948

Some Writers Deserve to Starve—This practical book will acquaint you with the brutally hard truths of getting published and understanding how the industry works. Written to better your odds for writing success, the advice found here—delivered with a dash of wit—will help you get an agent, pitch your work, and get it into print.
ISBN-13: 978-1-58297-354-8, paperback, 240 pages, $14.99 #10985
ISBN-10: 1-58297-354-7, paperback, 240 pages, $14.99 #10985

Write Great Fiction: Dialogue—Write snappy sentences, clever quips, and realistic conversations for your characters. Innovative exercises, clear instruction, and excerpts from today's most popular novels will help you create dialogue sure to grab your reader's attention.
ISBN-13: 978-1-58297-289-3, paperback, 240 pages, $16.99 #10936
ISBN-10: 1-58297-289-3, paperback, 240 pages, $16.99 #10936

Write Great Fiction: Plot & Structure—Create a story your readers can't resist! Strong plots with solid structure can be yours by following the techniques, exercises, plot examples, and comprehensive checklists found in James Scott Bell's detailed instruction.
ISBN-13: 978-1-58297-297-8, paperback, 240 pages, $16.99, #10942
ISBN-10: 1-58297-297-X, paperback, 240 pages, $16.99, #10942

These books and other fine Writer's Digest titles are available from your local bookstore or online supplier, or by calling 1-800-448-0915.